I0752996

THE READEPTION OF COLONEL BRERETON

Scapegoat of the Bristol Reform Riots 1831

JOHN BRERETON

Grosvenor House
Publishing Limited

This book is published by
Grosvenor House Publishing Ltd
Link House
140 The Broadway, Tolworth, Surrey, KT6 7HT.
www.grosvenorhousepublishing.co.uk

A CIP record for this book
is available from the British Library

ISBN 978-1-78623-185-7

Lt Colonel Thomas Brereton
1782–1832

Contents

List of Maps and Illustrations

Chronology of Lt Colonel Thomas Brereton 1782–1832

1782 4 May, born at Ashgrove, Lusmagh, Kings County (Offaly) Ireland. Son of William Brereton, Attorney of Banagher and Miss Coghlan daughter of James Coghlan, of Cloghan (not Coghlan) House, Kings County.

1797 Left with his uncle Captain Andrew Coghlan for the West Indies as a Gentleman Volunteer.

1798 25 June, received Commission as Ensign in the 8th West Indian regiment (but not in Army List).

1800 29 March, exchange Ensign-to-Ensign (*London Gazette*). 21 July promoted Lieutenant in 8th W.I.R. Published 7 October (*London Gazette*).

1802 Placed on Half Pay after 8th West Indian Regiment disbanded after mutiny.

1803 14 April, appointed Lieutenant in the 2nd West Indian Regiment.

1804 20 April, promoted to Captain in the Royal African Corps.

1805 March, promoted Brigade Major for his relative Major-General Robert Brereton, Governor of St Lucia.

1806 25 October, the R.A.C. serving in West Indies changed name to Royal West Indian Rangers by Royal decree.

1809 Fought at the Battle of Martinique.

1810 Appointed Brigade Major to General Sir C. Wale 3 February and fought at the Capture of Guadalupe. 15 March promoted to Major in West India Rangers.

1811 Placed on the left wing and preceded with it to the colony of Surinam.

1813 Injured in a Hurricane that devastated the garrison of Mount Bruce Dominique and sent home to England to recover.

1815 20 July, promoted Lt Colonel of the Royal Africa Corps and Lt Governor of Senegal and Goree West Africa.

31 August, a son Thomas, baptised at St Georges, Hanover Square, London. Mother Catherine Bowe.

1816 Officers paid up to the 24 December and returned to England after returning the Colony to the French who arrived during the Medusa Tragedy. Thomas in ill health, due to the climate.

1817 Around January/February 1817 in London, Thomas made the acquaintance of a young lady called Mary Harriet Pellett.

Nevertheless, later in the year he also met an old acquaintance the widowed Mrs Whitmore the daughter of John Allen Olton a rich plantation owner from Barbados and Marylebone London. However, on 28 October Mary Harriet Pellett gives birth to a son and he is named William Pellett Brereton.

1818 1 January 1818, Thomas Brereton marries by licence, Margaret Anne Olton the widow of Major W. Whitmore of the Royal West Indian Rangers.

Appointed Commander of the Frontier Colony Grahamstown South Africa .

12 June in St Marylebone Westminster, William Pellett Brereton baptised

8 September, Margaret Brereton dies overlooking Swellendam South Africa.

5 December, Brereton leads his troops to confront Ndlambe during the 5th Frontier war in what was to be called the "Brereton Raids".

1819 14 March, Lt Colonel Brereton was presented with a handsome engraved sword by the officers and men of the Royal Africa Corps.

16 April, Colonel Brereton received permission from Sir Charles, to return to England after the sudden death of his wife

12 August, transferred to the 53rd or Shropshire Regiment of Foot.

1820 24 February, transferred to half pay of the Royal York Rangers.

1821 Returned to full pay in the 49th Regiment (or Princess Charlotte of Wales's, or the Hertfordshire) Regiment of Foot, which was then stationed in Ireland but left for Cape Town in November.

1822 Promoted to Commander of the Cape Town Garrison until December when he was granted leave.

1823 14 February, leave extended by the Commander-in-Chief, Frederick, Duke of York.

19 June, resigned from the 49th.

15 July, Married the 19-year-old Olivia Ross in St Marylebone London.

23 July, their daughter Catherine Leticia Brereton is baptised while they are living at Seymour Place Camden Street, Old St Pancras London.

That same month Appointed Inspecting Field Officer of the Bristol Recruiting District.

1826 Catherine Letitia Brereton born (first child of this name having died). Baptised 10 June St Augustine the Less, Bristol.

1828 2 October, Mary Sarah Coghlan Brereton born.

1829 14th January Wife Olivia dies at Hambrook Court, Bristol

1831 Saturday 29 October, placed in Command of the troops during the Bristol Riots.

Thursday 17 November. Court of Inquiry is convened.

1832 9 January, Court Martial convenes at the Merchants' Hall Bristol.

Friday 13th January, shot himself through the heart at his house Redfield Lodge, Lawrence Hill, Bristol.

Thursday 19 January, burial takes place at St Andrew's Church, Clifton

Special thanks to Angela Mohun for all her help, encouragement and advice and also for putting up with me virtually living in the 19th century for far too many years.

(Taken in September 1939 on his way to war in France aged 20 years)

I dedicate this book to my father Percy Edgar John (Jack) Brereton who first planted the seed of family history into my consciousness and unknowingly started me on my long journey of family discovery. My father just like his predecessor and the subject of this book was also a proud army man who also fought for King and Country, but alas, also like his predecessor died tragically young.

Introduction

When I was a young boy around 13 years old, my father told me a story about a gentleman coming to my grandfather Percy Edgar Brereton's house in Chiswick, West London; telling him that he was tracing the descendents of a family from Ireland. This gentleman told my grandfather that he had traced the line down to his family and wanted to know of any family details or other information he could recollect that would further his research. He also said he found it fascinating tracing the family and one of the facts he discovered was of an ancestor who was executed on the orders of King Henry VIII due to allegations concerning Queen Anne Boleyn. In fact, he said the story he had uncovered was so interesting that he intended writing a book about it, and if he did, he would send my grandfather a copy. He never did though and I often wondered who this mysterious gentleman was.

My family had no idea we had any relatives in Ireland let alone any connection with Henry VIII. This story fascinated me as a young boy and what my father told me planted a seed in my imagination that started me on a lifetime journey of searching for my ancestors.

I soon found some basic history of the Brereton family and the links to Henry VIII and Anne Boleyn. Later tracing back from my grandfather, I also found the subject of this book, Lt Col Thomas Brereton. In order to find out more about him, I researched his Army records and amassed a lot of information, so much so, that to make it more accessible I arranged it into chronological order. It then dawned on me that I had the makings of a biography of the Colonel. Later when I read books about the 1831 Bristol Reform riots I realised that the person described seemed at odds with the character that came to life from the records and letters of his service, so I contemplated writing his full biography. This was not only because he had a very interesting life in the time of conflict, wars and empire building, but also because most of what had been written about him before was inaccurate.

Later while researching at the Society of Genealogist in London, I encountered the name Patrick Montague-Smith. I later found out that he had been a fellow of the Society, and was widely regarded as one of the leading genealogists of his time. The reason our paths had crossed was that he had done a lot of research on the Irish line of the Brereton's. His maternal grandmother was also a Brereton and like my family descended from this line. I also found out that in the late 1940s and 50s he had written quite extensively in British newspapers at home and throughout the Empire trying to find descendants of Lord Brereton of Leighlin whose title had become extinct unnecessarily, as he believed that there were in fact qualifying descendants. I also found a letter he had received in the late 50s from one of Col Brereton's relatives in South Africa. So it now dawned on me that it was indeed Patrick Montague-Smith who had spoken to my grandfather all those years ago, just as he had to other relatives of the Colonel. He was in fact, the Brereton family historian and had also been the head of Debrett's *Peerage* dying unknown to me in 1986, while I was engaged in my own research. Imagine if I had gone to the society earlier and actually met the man who had spoken to my grandfather all those years ago. Alas, this was not to happen as I started fairly inept at genealogy and had to learn as I proceeded and by the time I realised who he was, he had passed on.

Colonel Brereton was born in Ireland, which made it more difficult to find any official information there about his family, as nearly all the public records were destroyed by fire in 1922 after a massive IRA explosion at the Four Courts in Dublin during the Irish Civil War.

Nevertheless, Thomas Brereton's personal story was much better documented after 1797 because he had joined the British Army, whose extensive records are stored in the National Archives in London. Also, because in his later life he had become infamous throughout the Empire after the devastation of the Bristol riots. Therefore, his personal disaster had in effect left a treasure trove of information for me searching his past. Much as William

Brereton of Malpas' personal tragedy had done in the Tudor period. The more research I did the deeper into the life of the Colonel I descended, and it is true to say I became a little obsessed with him and the heartless hounding of him that resulted in his tragic premature death. So much so, that I often found it hard to sleep at night as I mulled over the facts and the cruel lies and deception that marked him out as the scapegoat of the Bristol riots. His innocence was well known by many at the time of his death, though for political reasons their voices were ignored and only the opinions of his detractors were heard. In addition, these same detractors had a vested interest in the Colonel getting all the blame, as it was only by his conviction that they would escape justice themselves.

This resulted in his tragic death and leaving his former home empty for many years while tales of an unquiet spirit roaming through its halls seeking redress soon spread around the district. Yet still no one told his tale or researched the truth, even two books published in the 20th century toed the official line as fact as this became the accepted "truth". However, as his contemporary and erstwhile adversary Napoleon Bonaparte said; *"History is a set of lies agreed upon"*.

But even so, some lies are so heinous that like their victim, they will not go quietly to their eternal rest and so need to find a voice amongst the living to at last record the truth;

For when I lay my head to sleep
Ancestral voices whispered unto me
And told me tales of perfidy
And so it was, and so I found it to be,
But as the dust of time was slowly blown away
Truth rose like a phoenix and was revealed to me
So now dear reader, take time and read this tome of woe
To realise at last, it was cruel deceit and lies that made his story so
So judge him not upon the erstwhile story set
But on the truth revealed within this text.

The Rise and Fall of the House of Brereton

The Brereton Coat of Arms
Motto, With Gods Help

(From *Ormerod's History of Cheshire*.
Cheshire Archives and Local Studies)

This chapter confirms what Patrick Montague-Smith told my grandfather about our ancient ancestors was indeed true and verifiable. It also goes into greater detail than I believe has been available in one publication before, particularly as regards the Irish branch, which on the death of Francis Brereton of Brereton Hall, the fifth and last Baron Brereton in 1722, became the representatives of the elder line. This was 60 years before Thomas was born and marked a major step in the decline of the Brereton family in all the principle English lines who not only lost the baronetage, but the peerage, lands and manors that went with them after all the major lines apparently descended to females. Though according to the research of the Rev E.W. Brereton, a Yorkshire vicar and a descendent of Lord William Brereton second Baron Brereton, this was not in fact the case as there were indeed qualifying male descendants.

In later chapters, it also shows for the first time how my own family descends from Thomas Brereton himself, which is unique to my research. For to understand whom Colonel Thomas Brereton was, it helps to go back in time and see the family he came from, and how this would influence his life. For though my family had lost all knowledge of our ancient family history, Thomas would have been fully aware of it.

The Brereton family originated in Cheshire, England. And are descended from a family that fought at the battle of Hastings in 1066 with William Duke of Normandy. The patriarch of the family was a man called Venables, from a place of that name in Normandy and is recorded on the role of honour at Battle Abbey near Hastings Sussex. The Normans or *Northmen* were of Viking decent and Duke William had previously been known as *William the Bastard*, due to his illegitimacy. For people at this time did not have fixed surnames as we do today, just a descriptive personal or Christian name. The Normans themselves introduced surnames for taxation purposes, sur actually means over or in addition. The Normans also practised primogeniture meaning that the first-born male had precedent over later born sons and would inherit all the fathers wealth and property and the name that went with it, as in Giselbert De Venables, meaning Giselbert Of Venables. Any younger sons had to find their own way and so could all adopt various different surnames to their father depending on what estate they acquired. Just as Giselbert was previously a nameless younger son from the house of Blois and had to make his own way and fortune. Therefore, in 1055 after the death of Mauger de Venables he was offered the modest Fiefdom of Venables by his uncle Roger de Blois, the Bishop and Count of Beavais. Later when William Duke of Normandy was raising an army, Giselbert De Venables was conscripted to fight for his lord in England and so was to spend little time in Venables itself. After the battle of Hastings, many other battles had to be won before the Saxons were finally defeated and one of the last regions to fall was Mercia controlled by the Saxon Edwin, Earl of Mercia who in 1068 with his brother Morcar, Earl of Northumberland attempted to raise a rebellion, but later submitted to William. Edwin died in 1071, while attempting yet another rebellion during which he was betrayed to the Normans and killed.

After this final defeat and because Cheshire had put up such stiff opposition to the Normans it was laid to waste by William as punishment during the genocidal *Harrowing of the North*.

After which, Hugh Lupus *the wolf, was* installed as Earl of Chester in what would be a Palatine or separate kingdom where the Earl would hold full powers to govern autonomously and independently of England. This was to become one of the most powerful in the country. Within this Palatine was the Barony of Kinderton, which was granted to Giselbert de Venables, the Manor of Brereton was one of the dependencies of Kinderton, which he in turn granted to one of his sons. Brereton is an Anglo Saxon word and means a briar enclosure, so one could imagine an early settlement surrounded by briars for protection. As has been explained, in those days a name was not fixed as it is today and a man could have six sons who all could adopt different surnames. Therefore, it was at this time that this nameless Venables adopted the name of his new estate just as his father had done at Venables in Normandy.

The first known record of such is Ralf de Brereton, who was a witness to a charter for his elder brother Gilbert de Venables some time in the reign of William II 1087–1100. Therefore, it is here, about 21 years after the battle of Hastings that the Brereton pedigree begins. So it now becomes easier in one respect because the surname is now kept by all sons and all generations of the family. However, it becomes more complicated as time went on because of this custom of naming their eldest son with the same first name as their father and so it can be difficult so far back, to define which generation you are dealing with. In the Brereton family, William was a favourite name almost from the start, and one imagines it was in honour of their illustrious forebear William the Conqueror. So William as a Brereton first name, is confusingly used by generation after generation, right up to modern times. Even the father of Thomas, the subject of this book was named William and Thomas would also name his second son William no doubt in honour of his father. Over the centuries, the Brereton's consolidated their power base in Cheshire, as younger sons started other branches of the family spreading throughout the county but now all keeping Brereton as their surname.

In October 1415 William de Brereton died at the siege of Hafleur during the Hundred Years' War with France, on route to the famous battle of Agincourt. He was the elder son of Sir William de Brereton who had fought at the famous battle of Crecy and his second wife Anyll de Venables, who had married in 1386. Because of their close family ties with the Venables the Brereton's were required to obtain a dispensation before any intermarriage. Sir Williams younger son Randal, who no longer used the prefix "de", married Alice de Ipstones and started the Malpas Hall and Shocklach branch of the family and his descendent Sir Randal Brereton was to further cement the Brereton's power in Cheshire and North Wales.

(Details obtained from: *Observations upon the History of one of the Old Cheshire families*. By Sir Fortunatus Dwarris, BA., FRS., FSA.)

On 28 January 1457 Henry Tudor was born in Pembroke Castle in West Wales, he was the son of Edmund Tudor and the 13 year old Margaret Beaufort, Countess of Richmond and Derby. Henry assumed the crown after he defeated King Richard III at Bosworth with soldiers supplied from Cheshire and his native North Wales.

After Bosworth, Henry Tudor now King Henry VII, rewarded local Cheshire men like Sir John Savage who had commanded the left wing at Bosworth. Sir John was himself a descendent of King Edward I, known as Longshanks, one of the greatest Plantagenet Kings. Sir John married Dorothy Vernon and together they had seven children, the youngest of which Alice around the year 1505 was to marry the 22-year-old Sir William Brereton of Brereton who was born circa 1483.

King Henry VII appointed many other local men to his court in London, as a reward for their loyal services, including Sir William's kinsman, the aforementioned Sir Randall Brereton of Malpas who had also fought with Henry in the last battle of the War of the Roses, *The Battle of Stoke* in 1487. This was a much larger battle than the more famous battle of Bosworth two years before, where King Richard III was killed and there were much greater casualties, including many of the remaining Yorkist leaders. Sir Randal was created knight bannerette and Knight of the body to King Henry VII on the battlefield and later in 1504 rose to become Chamberlain of Chester. After the death of Henry VII in 1509, Sir Randal continued to serve his son and successor King Henry VIII.

Sir Randal Brereton's sister Eleanor, the widow of Philip Egerton was later to marry Sir William Brereton of Brereton around the year 1510 and their daughter Katherine would also marry her cousin, Sir Roger Brereton who was the sixth son of Sir Randal and joint High Sherriff of Flintshire Wales, with his younger brother William. Sir William's aforementioned first wife Alice Savage had died in 1506 after the birth of their only son and heir also called William. Therefore, through these marriages, these two branches were reunited and in 1521, Sir Randal's seventh son William was appointed groom of the chamber to King Henry VIII, and in 1524 he was made groom of the privy chamber as was his brother Urian. This put him in close contact with King Henry VIII and led to him receiving many honours and privileges and grants of land. This made him very powerful in Cheshire and North Wales holding many titles there, including on the death of his father in 1530 at *Champagne France the office of Chamberlain of Chester. (1) (*Incidentally the seat of his ancestors the Compte De Blois).

(1) (*Cheshire and the Tudor State*. Page 150.)

William in turn appointed his older brother Randal as Deputy Chamberlain. This position as Chamberlain was a very important role in Cheshire, the holder was the guardian of the palatine seal of the earldom and issued judicial writs, and intervene in the judicial process, as well as cases linked to finance since 1520, the exchequer had also acted as an equity court. In March 1530 through his contacts, he was able to arrange a substantial loan for his uncle Sir William Brereton of Brereton with Richard and William Greasham, merchants and financiers of London. (2)

(2) (*Letters and Accounts of William Brereton.* Edit, Ives. Page 55)

Throughout this chapter, I shall use the terms, "William", for William Brereton of Malpas, and "Sir William", for Sir William Brereton of Brereton when referring to these two related individuals, though in many books you will see William of Malpas referred to as "Sir", but he was never Knighted and so was not in fact a "Sir". (3)

(3) (*William Brereton and the Pork Barrel.* Professor Ives. Page 4)

In addition, and just to confuse matters further, though he was from Malpas Hall, Sir William Brereton of Brereton, also had lands at Malpas ([4]) and was Baron of Malpas Castle. ([5])

([4]) (*Letters and Accounts of William Brereton.* Edit, Ives. Pages 255 and 264.)

([5]) (*Observations upon the History of one of the Old Cheshire families.* By Sir Fortunatus Dwarris. Page 73)

William of Malpas married in 1530 Elizabeth, the daughter of Charles the Earl of Worcester, King Henry's cousin, which of course further cemented Williams place at court. Elizabeth was also the widow of Sir John Savage, who died in 1528 and who was the grandson of Sir John of Bosworth fame. After this marriage William acquired control of the Savage estates and fortune, dated until 1547, which according to the research of Professor Eric Ives accounted for more than half his income.

This Sir John Savage was the grandson of the Sir John Savage who had fought with Henry's father at Bosworth, but he and his father who died the year before him in 1527 had handled the estate badly, resulting in debt and the temporary forfeiture of their lands to the crown. Brereton gained the leases, and after marrying Elizabeth in 1530 he also gained the wardship of John Savage 1506–97 until his majority. It was this John Savage who later built the Savage mansion called Rocksavage and his daughter Margaret Savage 1550–1631, married the later Sir William Brereton of Brereton 1550–1631 who became the First Baron Brereton of Leighlin in the Kingdom of Ireland. It was this Sir William Brereton, who built Brereton Hall at Brereton, and where he was buried aged around 80 years old. Brereton Hall was modelled on Rocksavage, the house of his father in law Sir John Savage and still stands today.

BRERETON HALL, CHESHIRE

(From an engraving in *Ormerod's History of Cheshire.* Cheshire Archives and Local Studies)

Meanwhile as William Brereton of Malpas gained more privileges, wealth and power, he also gained enemies both in Cheshire and at court, one was none other than Henry's chief minister Thomas Cromwell. Therefore, in 1536 when King Henry was growing tired of his new wife Anne Boleyn, Cromwell cooked up a plan to get rid of her and later added William in the charges. This was despite the fact that earlier William had been so trusted by King Henry that in 1530 he had toured the country gathering signatures on a large parchment petition to present to the Pope in support of the Kings annulment of his marriage to Mary so that the King could marry Anne. Though this annulment never came to pass the velvet box that Henry paid William £40 to procure is still in the Vatican archives complete with the enclosed parchment scroll hanging with the ribbons and seals of the great and the good.

William was not only closely associated with the King but was also a friend of Anne's who would often go hunting with his brother Urian. Anne even named her pet dog Urian in his honour. William was also Steward of the Lordship of Henry FitzRoy, First Duke of Richmond, King Henry's natural son, who was also the son-in-law of the Duke of Norfolk, Anne Boleyn's uncle, and also Brereton's patron and yet another of Cromwell's rivals.

Therefore, Brereton was now at the heart of the faction now under scrutiny and was belatedly included in the charges and was put on trial at Westminster Hall 12 May 1536. He pleaded innocent of all charges from the start, but like all those charged, was predictably found guilty and condemned to be hung drawn and quartered, a very gruesome and painful death.

This was the standard punishment for treason but they all later had this sentence commuted to beheading. After the trial William was taken to the Tower of London and on 17 May he was lead to Tower Hill and beheaded along with the others, all except Mark Smeaton who as a commoner was hanged.

Looking at the evidence against Brereton it is hard to come to the conclusion that he was guilty of this particular crime either. It seems much more probable that Anne's downfall came because she had not produced the heir Henry desired. Also as Henry grew tired of her his attention had been diverted by a Catholic faction at court to Jane Seymour a devout Catholic. This was part of a clandestine plot to restore the Catholic religion and came just at the time when Brereton himself was becoming a problem as well as an obstacle to reform in Cheshire and the Welsh Marches. Therefore, it was very convenient to include him in those accused and getting rid of him at the same time as Anne. In fact, Brereton seems to have realised this himself for he confided in an old friend George Constantine. The two men had been born only four miles apart, and had gone to the same grammar school. George recounted that before his execution Brereton had said four or five times;

"I haue deserved to dye a if it were a thousands deethes, But the cause wherefore I dye judge not: But yf ye judge, judge the best"

(*Memorial from George Constantine.* Page 65.)

In other words, William Brereton admitted that though he had committed many crimes that would be punishable by death, he had not committed this one. But though he pleaded from the start he was innocent he couldn't say that the King was wrong or he might end up having his sentence reverted back to the very painful and gruesome norm, and also his family and friends might also have to pay the price.

After all, he left a wife and two sons Henry and Thomas, his wife must have believed in his innocence though because nine years later she gave his last treasured gift to her eldest son;

"one bracelet of gold, the which was the last token his father sent me."

(*The Fall of Anne Boleyn Reconsidered.* By Professor E.W. Ives. The English historical review 1992. Page 652.)

Therefore, William Brereton of Malpas despite all his earthly power and prestige was no more.

Born the seventh son of Sir Randal Brereton of Malpas who due to primogeniture inherited very little from his father except £3. 4 shillings and 1 penny* (the value of that income today is about £1,557.55) which works out at around £4 per day. Imagine trying to live today on such a small amount. It was just enough to stop him starving to death if he was careful. But by the time he died he was earning £12,000* per annum and the value of that income today is a whopping £3,865,200.00 Yes that's nearly four million per annum.

*These original figures are from Professor Eric Ives.

(The modern calculations are from the National Archive historic currency converter)

After William Brereton's execution, his offices in Cheshire were divided up, and never again was one man to hold so many offices and power in Cheshire again. The *Act of Union* between England and Wales meant that the whole area would now be controlled by central government. Nevertheless, other members of the Brereton family were not penalised as one might suspect. In fact William's brother Urian continued at court and was awarded some of his brother's grants and even used his position there to help his late brother's widow.

In addition, Sir William Brereton of Brereton who had been fighting a successful campaign in Ireland for his King during all of 1535 defeating a rebellion by *Silken Thomas* the Tenth Earl of Kildare, arrived home in early 1536 only to see his nephew executed for treason against the very same King. He later found himself appointed Chamberlain of Chester and granted the offices in Broomfield and Yale all previously under his nephew. However, other grants of the late William Brereton relating to the Delamere forest were distributed to the Brereton's greatest adversary, Sir Piers Dutton. Williams widow Elizabeth; later married Sir Edward Nevill who now wanted to sell the office during John Savages minority but Dutton alleged Sir William Brereton was preventing it. After the fall of William the feuds between the Dutton's and Brereton's escalated during *the Pilgrimage of Grace* in the autumn of 1536. This was mainly a catholic rising in protest against Henry VIII's break with the Roman Catholic Church and the Dissolution of the Monasteries. Dutton reported he had dispersed the rebels and arrested the Abbott and three of the Cannons and taken them to Hatton Castle. Dutton claimed Sir William had been reluctant to act against the Abbott.

Nevertheless, in October 1536, Sir William's services again were called upon, and he was engaged in recruiting 250 Cheshire archers to travel to Ireland.

In a letter to The Lord Privy Seal Thomas Cromwell, Brereton asks to be permitted to take his own sons with him to command the troops under him. This operation in Ireland was again a success and he returned to Cheshire in June 1537 but was later accused in a letter by Bishop Rowland Lee to Cromwell dated 16 March 1538 of taking the lead after the death of his nephew William Brereton, in the factional struggle against Dutton. This had been festering for 30 years and Bishop Lee claimed Sir William was destroying all order in Cheshire.

On 2 October 1539, Sir William was again called into service in Ireland after the O'Neal rebellion and a week late on the ninth, he expressed his concerns in a letter to Cromwell that Sir Piers Dutton might use the occasion to make mischief in his absence by abusing his adherents and associates. This was given some credence when later in Star Chamber Sir William Brereton's absence was cited as reason the plaintiff could not get justice there.

(Cheshire & the Tudor State. Page 230.)

All this dissention and infighting by the powerful families in Cheshire and Wales only went to reinforce the King and his minister Cromwell's determination to centralise the power at court, and it was probably this very reason that lead to the execution of William Brereton in the first place as he was seen as an obstacle to these moves. In addition, some of the Marcher Lords were supporters of the Pope and Henry was worried that the Catholic monarchs in France and Spain might try to gain supporters in his other rebellious realm *Ireland*, and then invade by landing on the sparsely defended coasts of Wales.

One William Brereton had been seen as an obstacle to reform in Cheshire and Wales, but yet another Sir William Brereton was going to be instrumental in achieving the Kings reforms in Ireland.

So despite his concerns and difficulties, Sir William left England in late 1539 and sailed with his sons across the Irish Sea to fight yet again against the King's enemies and begin yet another chapter in the story of the Brereton's, this time in Ireland.

After his successful campaign, Sir William Brereton was appointed Chief Justice and Lord High Marshal of Ireland, dying there in 1541, he is buried at Kilkenny, Leinster. This left his descendants well placed at this early stage to take advantage of the opportunity available there, just as they had in England 500 years earlier. This included his younger son John, who was with him when he died and continued his father's quest and was granted the office of Seneshal of Wexford from 1546. Also during this period from the 1540s–50s his grandsons Andrew, Arthur and Edward all settled permanently in various counties within the province of Leinster, forming the Irish branch of the Brereton's.

"*The province of Lenister containeth all that portion of land which was first conquered by our nation, including all that ground southward from Dublin to the river of Suyre and the City of* Waterford, *which parteth it from Muster. The river of Shannon in MacCoghlan country devideth the west part from Connaught and Meath; northward it endeth with the barony of Balrothry and the river Boyne, and on the east side is bounded with the sea. It is divided into seven shires. The county of Dublin, Kildare, Carlow ,Wexford, Kilkenny, Kings county and Queens county. They have gone about of late to add to other shires of the county, Wicklow and Fernes.*"

(Tracts relating to Ireland, Irish Archaeological society 1841 Vol 2. Page 12.)

By Thomas Kitchin for the *London Magazine* 1760

A New Map of the Kingdom of Ireland, Divided into its Provinces and Counties (Leinster is bordered in yellow.)

In 1549 Andrew, like his grandfather and his uncle John before him went into battle to quell yet another rebellion when 200 Scottish islanders arrived as reinforcements to the rebels, which he met in the north with only 35 horsemen, but despite this, still defeated them with much slaughter.

(*Cox's History of Ireland*. Vol. I. Page 289.)

As a reward he was made Governor of Ulster that same year, and he later married Catherine FitzSimon of Dublin and together they had one son William and five daughters. Andrew also had a natural son also called Andrew who married Catherine Lynch from County Meath.

Andrew, Governor of Ulster's younger brother Edward of Loughtioge Castle Queens County and Provost Marshal of Connaught, 1530–99, married Edith Birch of Lancashire and had six children, his first son also named Edward died young but his second son Henry married Margery Bowen and his son Edward, the High Sheriff of Queens County married in 1665 Helen Bowen. Edwards younger brother Roger of Dublin and MP for old Leighlin would marry Miss Bulkely and would father William the founder of the Carrigslaney line. Later these two branches would forge further links when Edwards's son Bowen Brereton married as his first wife, Eleanor Brereton of Carrigslaney his second cousin. She was the daughter of William Brereton of Moyle Abbey and Carrigslaney, who died around 1690. He had five children, his grandson also called William 1696–1777, is credited with succeeding his Kinsman Lord Brereton in 1722 as the representative of the elder line, when the Brereton's of Brereton Cheshire were claimed to have had no male heirs. His son Major William Brereton 1723–1813 had fought at the Battle of Culloden in Scotland, the final conflict of the Jacobite rising of 1745. It was probably there that he met his first wife Marion Edmonston first cousin to Flora MacDonald, who as a 24-year-old helped Bonnie Prince Charlie escape in June 1746 from the island of Benbecula in the Outer Hebrides.

Major William Brereton of Bath
1723–1813

Image credited to *Bath in Time*.

Reproduction by kind permission Art at the Heart.
Royal United Hospitals NHSFT. Bath

Marion gave Major William two sons, Major General Robert Brereton, (1747–1816) Governor of St Lucia, and William (1751–87 an actor of Drury lane and two daughters Janetta and Julia. Patrick Montague-Smith had speculated that either Major William or his son Robert, Patrick's great great maternal grandfather could be the father of Thomas.

Personally, I was doubtful that Robert could be the father of Thomas though he did have an illegitimate son also named Robert who was born at Roseau Dominica in 1788. Indeed, at the time of Thomas's death it was stated in *The Times* and many other

Newspaper reports that Roberts brother William the actor was the father of Thomas.

This is even currently stated in the *Oxford Dictionary of National Biography.*

However, after the death of Thomas this was disputed in the Bristol papers, but without any source and only saying instead he was descended from; *"an ancient and respectable family"*. Indeed, Thomas was certainly not the son of actor William with his wife Priscilla Hopkins as stated, as Thomas's mother was a Coghlan. However, it still seemed possible he could have been an illegitimate child of either William junior or as Patrick wondered, his father Major William. Major William's later son from his second wife was to become the very distinguished; Lt.-General Sir William Brereton 1789–1864, who fought in both the Peninsular Wars, and the Battle of Waterloo where he was badly wounded. He received the Knight, Hanoverian Order and Companion, (K.H.) and Order of the Bath (CB.).

He lived with his widowed half sister, Julia, the younger daughter of Major William by his first wife, at 36 upper Berkeley Street St Marylebone London W1; which was only a 10-minute walk from Duke Street where Colonel Brereton had lived when in London. Moreover, it was also very close to St Marylebone church where Colonel Brereton would marry for the second time and where his son William Pellet Brereton was baptised. This is also all in the same area that both sons would live together at little Stanhope street Mayfair, again all in W1.

Another curious coincidence is that Julia was to die in November 1832, only 10months after the Colonels suicide. So was the Colonel's death a contributing factor to hers?

Julia's death also left Sir William in need of new accommodation, so he purchased an apartment at the former home of Prince Frederick, Duke of York and Albany, which had been converted into a prestigious block of bachelor apartments, called The Albany. This was even closer to Mayfair and only 10 mins walk from where Thomas and William junior lived later in 1838.

Also in 1838, only six years after the death of Colonel Thomas Brereton he was appointed the Inspector-General of the Irish Constabulary. In the announcement reported in the Irish papers he was revealed as being; *"a relative of the late lamented Colonel Brereton"* this time there was no mention of Thomas being the son of his half brother William and this time there were no denials.

During my own research, I discovered that Thomas's father William had two other children by two different women *after* the death of William the actor so it could not be the same man. I also discovered that Thomas's father was actually an attorney who lived in Banagher in Kings County Ireland. However, I could not discover where *he* was born or who *his* father was. For someone of such high social standing it is strange that he left no trace at all in any family records, unless of course this was deliberate.

The revelation of Thomas's father William the attorney who was born around 1760 eliminated both Lt General Robert and his brother William completely as they would have been far too young at 13 and 9 respectively.

However, that still left their father Major William Brereton who would have been 37 yrs old when William the attorney was born. It is also interesting to point out that Major William and his wife Marion had their two sons in Ireland in 1747 and 1751 and their two daughters in 1752 and 1753 but would never have any more children together despite her still being only 28 when her last child was born.

William was born around 1760 and shortly after Major William and his young family all left Ireland forever, is this all just coincidence or was there another reason?

Later around 1764, they settled in Somerset, south west England, in the fashionable Spa town of Bath. Where Major William took to visiting the popular Lower Assembly rooms where he became Vice President and was described as "*tall manly and elegant*". A few years later in 1769 the position of Master of Ceremonies became vacant and he was felt by some to be "*the certain successor to the vacant throne*". However, not every one agreed and a rival candidate a Mr

Plomer from the nearby Hot Wells in Bristol was invited as a challenger, this caused rioting between the two opposing parties that became know as "The *Contest of Bath*"

In an attempt to restore order, a Captain Wade was appointed and William was offered an annual Ball as compensation, but nine years later, the Captain resigned over an affair of gallantry. William finally assumed the role of Master of Ceremonies in 1777. However, only three years later in 1780 he too was forced to resign after his nephew George Brereton who was also married to his daughter Janetta angrily entered the assembling rooms brandishing a sword. George a famous duellist was looking for a Captain Spooner who owed him a gambling debt; this outraged the assembled nobility who felt Major William should have acted more robustly. George finally caught up with Captain Spooner and fought a duel with him at Prior Park gravely wounding him. The outrage this caused led not only to Major William having to resign but also George selling his house in Queens Parade and returning to Ireland where he was finally killed in yet another duel in 1781. A year later Thomas Brereton was born in Ireland the same year the Majors wife Marion died. Though we can speculate as to the reasons for the couple's barren years of marriage, he soon proved it was not down to a lack of virility on his part. For after taking young Harriet Hooley as his new wife and despite no longer being a young man himself, age didn't stop him having two more children aged 66years old, a son the afore mentioned Lt General Sir William and later a daughter Harriet. He remained in Bath another 23 yrs until his death in 1813 aged 89 and was buried at Holt Wiltshire only a few miles from Bath.

However, Major William was not the only family related to Thomas resident in Bath, as his mother's family the Coghlans including his Uncle Andrew and wife Sarah and his aunt (Margaret) Mary Coghlan also lived there. Thomas would later name his second daughter in their honour, Mary Sarah Coghlan Brereton.

Mary Coghlan, c1761-1821, married three times;

1st George LeStrange and lived at Moystown Cloghan Kings County not far from her parents house at Cloghan or indeed Banagher where Thomas was born.

2nd she married Col Arthur Blennerhassett and lived at 8 Russell Street, Bath where he died in 1810

3rd marriage in 1816 Valentine Richard Quin 1st Earl of Dunraven becoming *Viscountess Mount-Earl* and moving to 24 Circus Bath where she also died in 1821.

This is of course is just where Major William was living and it is recorded that the Coghlans also had a long association with Bath. For the famous painter Gainsborough had painted one of the Coghlan sisters in 1772 entitled, *Miss Coghlan of Bath.*

Therefore, it looks more and more likely that Patrick Montague–Smith was indeed right in his assumption but perhaps not quite in the way that he thought.

For it seems Major William was not the fathers of Colonel Thomas Brereton but his grandfather through his natural son William the attorney.

Thomas's maternal line was through his father first wife Miss Coghlan whose father was James Coghlan of Cloghan House (not Coghlan), Kings County. James Coghlan had five sons, Edmund, John, Andrew, Charles, James and four daughters, Margaret Mary, Bridget, Clarinda and Catherine and possibly another. Andrew Coghlan 1771–1837 would fight in many of the battles of the 18th and 19th centuries many of which were with France. He served under Wellington and become a Colonel as would his older Brother Edmund 1761–1828, who was a classical scholar speaking fluently in French, Italian, German, Spanish and Portuguese, and who would rise to the position of Governor of Chester. This was of course the very place where the Brereton's originated and where William Brereton had been constable of Chester castle during 1528–30.

(*Roscommon Journal,* 3 January 1829)

It was their older sister who married William Brereton and together were the parents of Thomas, born at Ashgrove, Kings County on 4 May 1782. William would later go on to have other children including Benjamin Bowen Brereton 1806–77 who married Jane Drew of Mocollop Castle, County Waterford, they later immigrated to the USA. Jane's brother Francis Drew Esq was later one of the witnesses to the will of Lt Colonel Brereton in Bristol dated 12 January 1832. In addition, the Colonels daughter Mary Sarah Coghlan Brereton (named after her two aunts in Bath) would marry her cousin Charles Hunter Hodgson in South Africa and his brother would in turn be named in his honour, as Francis Drew Hodgson. Catherine Dix Brereton the Colonels sister, 1826–1916, married John Brereton 1810–88 the nephew of Dr Joshua Brereton a Dublin Surgeon. Together with their five children they later emigrated to North America first to Canada and then later the USA, probably after the Irish potato famine of 1845. This was caused by a disease called late blight, that ironically had arrived from North America, which destroys both the leaves and the edible tubers and caused the most devastating famine of the 19th century where one million died in Ireland alone and a further one million emigrated abroad.

However, these must have been half siblings to Thomas, as his mother would have been around 44 years old when Benjamin was born and 64 when Catherine was, so it would be impossible for her to have gone on and have two more children.

It was the custom at the time to include the mother's maiden name in the name of the child just as others in the Brereton family were to do. Therefore, we can speculate that William married twice again to a Miss Bowen and later a Miss Dix However again, because of the destruction of many of the official records at the Dublin record office at the start of the Irish Civil war in 1922; it is very difficult to trace with complete certainty much beyond 1800. Nevertheless, I also believe that his younger brother Benjamin Bowen Brereton was related through his mother to the Dublin Alderman, Benjamin Bowen, who died in 1756. Well-to-do families often married in to each other's, generation after generation and would incorporate the surname of their forbears into their own and the Bowens were a constant presence in this branch for generations, in fact right back to Margery Bowen of Queens county who had married Henry Brereton in the 16th century.

Ashgrove where Thomas was born is on the western border of Kings County and the Shannon River separates it from counties Galway and Tipperary. The Shannon is the longest river in the British Isles (though for political reasons it is no longer referred to as such) at some 240 miles long, rising from its source in the Cuilcagh Mountains until in runs finally into the Atlantic Ocean at Limerick. In its long journey to the sea, it passes through 11 counties and separates a portion of the east from the west of the country. One of the counties it passed on its route to the sea is Kings County named after the Catholic King Philip of Spain the husband of Queen (Bloody) Mary (now again called Offaly), which contains the Barony of Garrycastle and the little town of Banagher on its eastern bank where the water is dyed black by the rich peat soil. One and a half miles outside Banagher on the Birr road is Garrycastle the ancestral home of the Coghlan's and from which the Barony gets its name. When Thomas was born Thomas Mac Coghlan who was chief of his Sept and MP for Banagher still lived there. Described as the oldest hereditary tenures passed through male decent anywhere in Europe, perhaps young Thomas Brereton was named after him.

Through the centuries, the fordable crossing at Banagher has been an important crossing point of the Shannon and so to facilitate this there had been a bridge since the 11th century. So by necessity it was also the site of many defensive fortifications, one of the earlier being a MacCoghlan castle, which was later, built over with an English fort when they settled the area during the reign of King Henry VIII.

The Coghlan's who once ruled *DevlinEathra* the ancient barony of Garrycastle, were to take advantage of *Surrender and Regrant* to protect their own land and property. The ruins of several castles show how powerful they were in ancient times, one of these is Clonony Castle, which was also ceded to King Henry VIII by John Óg MacCoghlan and is where Queen Elizabeth I cousins are buried. They were the daughters of Thomas Boleyn and so here we have yet another link between the Brereton's, and Boleyn's, this time through the Coghlan's.

Therefore, it is somehow fitting that the representatives of these ancient families should join together in matrimony. There paths had crossed before however as Sir William Brereton had been created Baron of Leighlin in County Carlow in 1624 and Roger had been MP for old Leighlin in 1639 and in 1647 Charles Coghlan was the Vicar General of the diocese there. Later Captain Terence Coghan sat as the parliamentary representative for Banagher as did his son also called Terence.

The road that follows the Shannon south for two miles from Banagher leads to Lusmargh, which means "Plain of Healing Herbs" and where Cloghan Castle is situated, built in 1140 and claimed to be the oldest inhabited Castle in Europe and is also where Ashgrove is situated and where Thomas was born.

The reason for King Henry taking full control of Ireland was a continuation of his wishes to centralise power as he had in England and Wales. Although Ireland would cost the exchequer more to run than it received in taxes it was of lasting tactical importance, as the Catholic world would try to use it to launch attack after attack upon his Kingdom long after his death when the conflict turned from religion to revolution and the building of Empires.

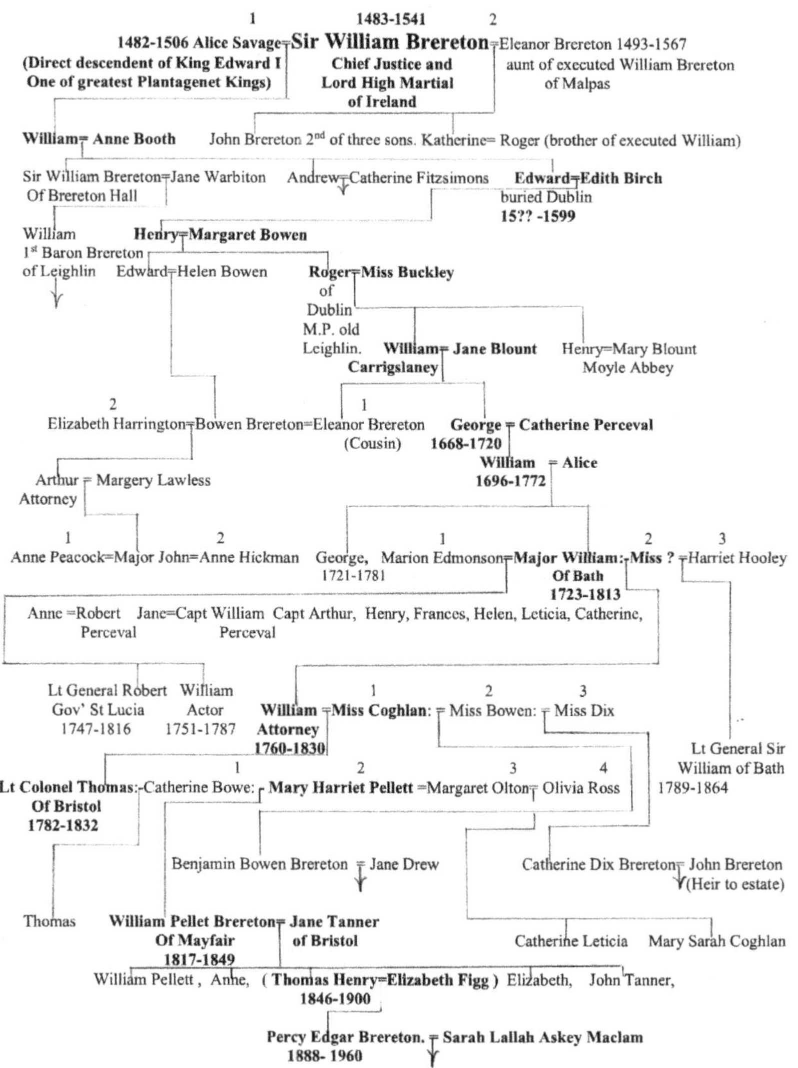

1 1483-1541 2
1482-1506 Alice Savage = Sir William Brereton = Eleanor Brereton 1493-1567
(Direct descendent of King Edward I One of greatest Plantagenet Kings)
Chief Justice and Lord High Martial of Ireland
aunt of executed William Brereton of Malpas
William = Anne Booth
John Brereton 2nd of three sons.
Katherine= Roger (brother of executed William)
Sir William Brereton=Jane Warbiton Of Brereton Hall
Andrew=Catherine Fitzsimons
Edward=Edith Birch buried Dublin 15?? -1599
William 1st Baron Brereton of Leighlin
Henry=Margaret Bowen
Edward=Helen Bowen
Roger=Miss Buckley of Dublin M.P. old Leighlin.
William= Jane Blount Carrigslaney
Henry=Mary Blount Moyle Abbey
2 Elizabeth Harrington=Bowen Brereton=Eleanor Brereton (Cousin) 1
George = Catherine Perceval 1668-1720
William = Alice 1696-1772
Arthur = Margery Lawless Attorney
1 Anne Peacock=Major John=Anne Hickman 2
George, 1721-1781
1 Marion Edmonson=Major William:-Miss ? 2 =Harriet Hooley 3
Of Bath 1723-1813
Anne =Robert Perceval
Jane=Capt William Perceval
Capt Arthur, Henry, Frances, Helen, Leticia, Catherine,
Lt General Robert Gov' St Lucia 1747-1816
William Actor 1751-1787
William Attorney 1760-1830
1 =Miss Coghlan: 2 = Miss Bowen: 3 = Miss Dix
Lt General Sir William of Bath 1789-1864
Lt Colonel Thomas: Of Bristol 1782-1832
1 -Catherine Bowe: 2 - Mary Harriet Pellett 3 =Margaret Olton 4 = Olivia Ross
Benjamin Bowen Brereton = Jane Drew
Catherine Dix Brereton= John Brereton (Heir to estate)
Thomas
William Pellet Brereton= Jane Tanner
Of Mayfair 1817-1849
of Bristol
Catherine Leticia
Mary Sarah Coghlan
William Pellett, Anne, (Thomas Henry=Elizabeth Figg) Elizabeth, John Tanner,
1846-1900
Percy Edgar Brereton. = Sarah Lallah Askey Maclam
1888- 1960

A Gentleman Volunteer

When Thomas Brereton was born on 4 May 1782 the world was in turmoil. Great Britain had just lost their thirteen North American colonies after the American Revolutionary War and this defeat escalated political tensions at home. During this war when British regular troops were engaged in fighting abroad, Irish men were encouraged to join local militias to protect Ireland from invasion by France who were fighting alongside the American colonists. However, these fighting men later became a worry to the British government who conceded to their demands and agreed to the Irish Constitution Act of 1782, which granted legislative independence to Ireland. This did not stop further demands however and when the French Revolution started in 1789, the prospect of further reform inspired a group of Protestants in Belfast, mostly Presbyterians and Methodists and even some Catholics, to join together in the *Society of United Irishmen* in 1791.

After the French Revolutionaries executed King Louis XVI in 1793, Britain was now once again at war with France. This now forced the *Society of United Irishmen* underground as they now sought French assistance and even joined forces with another Catholic group called the *Defenders*. However, the Roman Catholic Church itself was firmly on the side of the Crown, particularly after the French had captured Rome.

In 1796, the French responded to the rebels' request by sending General Hoche and 14,000 troops to Cork, but due to bad weather the troops could not land and returned to France. There followed widespread public disorder and so the British government imposed martial law while the Irish revolutionaries raided homes for weapons and planned an uprising in May 1798. Government intelligence alerted them to the plans and Loyalists throughout the country rallied in response and a large military force was assembled, but this did not stop the uprising, which quickly spread around the country, resulting in rumours of atrocities on both sides. Nevertheless, the rebels were slowly pushed back after their defeat at *Vinegar Hill* in June before the remnants were defeated in July. But two months later the French returned to the affray when General Humbert landed with 1,000 troops in County Mayo and he was soon joined by 5,000 Irish rebels, after a few minor battles they were again defeated in County Longford in September. However, in October a larger French Force of some 3,000 men tried to land but were intercepted by the Royal navy and after a battle that lasted three hours they too were defeated, which left the remaining rebel forces on land to fight a guerrilla war.

This was the turmoil that Thomas Brereton was born into, and it would greatly influence his life and even his death. We know little else about his childhood, but with all this war and turmoil all around him, he would have been militarised from an early age. Particularly as the Brereton family had been loyalist soldiers for centuries and came to Ireland in the first place as such, so it comes as no surprise to find that as Thomas grew into a young man he was also to choose the Army as a career.

As a young boy, Thomas had also become close to his young uncle, Captain Andrew Coghlan 1771–1837 of the 1st West Indian Regiment. Captain Coghlan no doubt regaled the younger Thomas with stories of his daring deeds in the Revolutionary Wars with France and so at the tender age of only 15 years old Thomas decided to go with him to the West Indies as a volunteer in 1797.

Imperial Federation map of the world showing the extent of the of the British Empire in 1886 from a supplement to The Graffic *with inset map, showing the extent of the British Territories in 1786.*

The West Indies are a group of islands set in an arch between North and South America covering some 2,400 miles. They contained some of the wealthiest colonies in the world at the time as well as being of great strategic importance. Control would allow the dominant power to exercise its will over the whole region from North to South America and the important Atlantic trade routes.

Therefore, Britain invested a lot of effort and resources here, which lead to it being by far the country's largest overseas capital investment. However, in return, it provided £31.5 million net revenue to the treasury plus much indirect tax income. The French possessions in the area were even more lucrative contributing almost half of all her overseas trade and necessitating a large maritime presence, which the British eyed with both envy and alarm. So to counteract this, a large British naval and military force was needed to protect and expand their enterprise. Therefore, it is no surprise to learn that 52 of the 105 regiments serving abroad were either in, or in transit to the region. The voyage to the West Indies itself would have introduced the young volunteer into the rigours of army life as the ships made there way through the gales and tempestuous seas. It was a long and arduous journey that took well over six weeks if weather and winds were kind and up to fourteen if they were not. However, many never reached their destination due to shipwreck or were condemned to die on the way as they were tossed and buffeted in the unsanitary conditions below decks.

War had been declared between Britain and the recently created French Republic only four years earlier in 1793 and by 1795 the Batavian Republic had been formed by the French in Holland, and by 1796 Spain had also declared war on Britain. So Britain was now at war with nearly all the Great European powers, France, Holland, and Spain and this created great turmoil, not only in Europe but also around the world. Included these strategically important West Indies, extending across the whole region, from Surinam in South America, to Belize in Central America and their former colonies in North America. This widespread conflict needed the constant supply of fresh troops from Britain and though many of the battles were extremely hard fought, it was not just war causalities that were depleting the numbers, it was the actually conditions that they were fighting in too. For unlike British troops fighting in Europe in temperate familiar conditions, the troops here in the tropics had another invisible enemy to contend with, tropical diseases! This unseen enemy killed more than the conventional foes combined, the 96th Regiment was to bear testament to this when they were almost entirely wiped out in 1795.

(*Public Record Office* -*WO* 17/1987)

Six hundred men of the 23rd regiment and twelve officers also succumbed in less than a year. In the very year that Thomas was making his way across the sea in 1797, 800 men of the 31st regiment and 22 officers were laid to rest as a result of disease.

A Young Lieutenant, Thomas Phipps Howard of the York Hussars wrote in his journal how the heat in August was unimaginable and soldiers in their thick woollen uniforms were fainting in the streets in Port Au Prince, When 2,000 men were marched in these conditions 50 died on route with some reduced to drinking their own urine.

If they had survived the journey there and then the heat, it wasn't long before they were struck down with yellow fever or malaria. The symptoms of these diseases were truly dreadful, blood would pour from the men's noses and the corner of their eyes and a foul fetid puss would ooze from their gums, they would also become incontinent and in the summer heat the stench was unbearable. These two were the main killers and men such afflicted would be placed into the primitive hospitals like the one at Port au Prince in Saint Domingue where Dr Hector Maclean a Captain in the 84th Regiment of foot wrote;

"their low, muttering, grim melancholy, which is lost in meditating wrath without an attempt to move. The eye has an expression," he said, "of anguish unspeakable, and a languor in its movement, an inclination to shut out all objects." As death approached, the patient would throw up large quantities of digested blood, the fearful "black vomit".

(Captain Hector MacLean journal and orderly book)

During the six-year period from 1793–98, 100,000 were killed or made ill from the disease with fatality rates among British troops in the West Indies (including Saint-Domingue) as high as 70%.

(*The 1802 Saint-Domingue Yellow Fever Epidemic and the Louisiana Purchase*. by Dr John S. Marr, MD.; John T. Cathey, MS. Page 77.)

These rates of deaths were so great that the men were buried five to a grave, the digging of which keep thirty black slaves busy daily from dawn until dusk. In Parliament, it was claimed that not a family in England could say that they had not lost someone and new recruits were fearful that they might be sent to the West Indies "*The soldiers grave yard*" and certain death. Indeed such was the notoriety of a West Indian posting that new recruits in Newcastle and Essex refused to sign the muster book when they learned of their destination, and troops in Cork rioted. However, regular more experienced soldiers took a more stoical attitude to their posting and in typical military fashion went where they were sent without complaint, even if they harboured misgivings about such a hazardous destination. Such was the fate of one Arthur Wellesley in 1796, Arthur Wellesley was of course the future Duke of Wellington, his regiment the 33rd Foot was due to go, only for a last minute change sent them to India instead, though his brother-in-law Edward Packenham wasn't so lucky, there was no reprieve for him. He was later to serve and survive alongside Thomas Brereton in battle at Martinique and earlier with Thomas's relative Robert Brereton at St Lucia only for his luck to run out when he was killed at the Battle of New Orleans in January 1815 while serving as commander of British forces there. Unfortunately, he died just months before Wellington won the last battle against Napoleon's French at Waterloo.

The decimation of troop numbers was causing a problem for British commanders, but it had been noted that the black soldiers, more used to the local conditions faired much better than their British counterparts did. This was not only due to their resistance to diseases, but their lifestyles were also more in tune with the conditions that they had to operate under. The British soldiers were still fed salt pork and beef the same as in Europe and their thick woollen uniforms were not suited to such a hot climate. The Black soldiers would often trade their meat rations for fresh local produce, which would be much healthier, while the British soldiers after eating them in the heat would be driven to quench the ensuing thirst often by drinking their ration of rum, which again only acerbated the condition and further reduced their capabilities.

In recognition of this, Lieutenant-General Vaughn the commander of forces in the West Indies wrote to the home secretary with the view to form a Corps of black soldiers, and so by October 1794 their were over three thousand black irregulars available, and were used in a similar way to the Carolina Corps in the American

War of Independence. They were lightly dressed, which again was advantages in the searing heat and were perfectly suited to skirmishes instead of the close rank fighting used by the regular British soldier. However, as the death rate increased in the regular troops and regiment after regiment was devastated, Lieutenant General Vaughn sought permission to enlist more black soldiers to replace them as regular troops. Nevertheless, this did not go down well with the powerful West Indian planters who were alarmed at the thought of arming and training a large force of black men. They of course, employed large groups as slave labour to work their plantations.

In Britain at the time, the election process was very corrupt by the use of Rotten Boroughs, many controlled by the West Indian planters who had bought up the votes and controlled a large number of politicians who they brought to bear on the Government and so permission was refused.

The West Indian planters and the rotten boroughs in England, along with the effects of the climate on his health, would all play a part, and have a major influence on Thomas Brereton later on, with disastrous consequences, as will be revealed later.

This set back however was overtaken by circumstances for an uprising had broken out in St Vincent and Granada by French planters and the local Caribs against British rule, so the refusal was quickly overturned and permission was finally granted and 5,000 men over eight companies were formed into numbered West Indian Regiments. The total number of troops in the West Indies varied throughout the period from 17,000 to 22,000, though it dipped to 15,000 during the Peninsular War when troops were redeployed there. So in effect these new West Indian Regiments made up from a third to a quarter of British military personnel in the region.

These troops needed officers of course and to become an officer you had to be over 16 years old, a gentleman, a protestant, educated, and with independent wealth. If you qualified in these respects you then needed to obtain the Kings Commission, which was a document signed by the King giving you authority to command his troops. At this time it was possible to buy a commission, the first step as an officer in the infantry was as a ensign, which would cost around £460, around £14,798.20* at today's value.

*(Source – National Archives historical currency converter.)

This system of purchasing a rank may seem strange to us today but it was thought at the time in a rigid class structured society that an educated propertied person would fight harder in order to maintain his position, and wealth, than a person who had none of these advantages. The gaining of a commission would also set the seal on a gentleman's social standing.

Thomas's first priority was to find a regiment, and because the West Indian regiments had been decimated by disease there were plenty of openings for those brave enough to chance it. In 1795 Thomas was only 15 years old, so he was too young to become an officer straight away so he went as a Gentlemen Volunteer or *Gentleman Ranker,* starting at the very bottom as a gentleman soldier in the ranks. So together with a copy of *The Principles of Military Movement* by Colonel David Dundas, first published in 1788, he would be well versed in military procedures. This book of Infantry drill and tactics was the most influential British military book of the 18th Century and by 1792 had with small alterations became the regulation manual for the army. However, this manual was based on the Prussian School of Frederick the Great, advocating a formalised, densely packed, three-line method. Though well suited to European warfare and defeating cavalry charges, it was less suitable to West Indian conditions where cavalry was fairly useless. Nevertheless, as a Gentleman Volunteer he would also learn in the ranks by training with the soldiers who were now learning the American School of Light Infantry practised by such as Sir Charles "no flint" Grey, named as such because of his preference for the bayonet over firearms during skirmishes and particularly nocturnal attacks. Grey had learnt these tactics in North America during the 1770s where his troops were renowned for steely charging the enemy without firing. This method also utilised a lighter packed, less formalised two-line formation and so was more flexible and suited to the dense jungle and mountainous terrain of the West Indies. This varied training would prove invaluable to Thomas Brereton not only here in the West Indies but also later in South Africa. However, though training with the common soldiers, at meal times young Thomas would mess with the officers of his own class. This routine would continue until he became fully competent in his military duties and after a position became available and he had hopefully made an impression he would be offered a commission.

Captain Thomas Brotherton, of the 14th Light Dragoons who served in the Peninsular, During the Napoleonic War recalled the type of men that formed these volunteers:

"... always recklessly exposed themselves in order to make themselves conspicuous, as their object was to get commissions given to them without purchase. The largest proportion of these volunteers were killed, but those who escaped were well rewarded for their adventurous spirit."

(*A Hawk at War.* The reminiscences of General Sir Thomas Brotherton whilst a Captain in the 14th Light Dragoons in the Peninsular War.)

Therefore, although young Thomas was only 15 years old by joining these ranks he was already showing the fearless spirit and qualities needed to gain the advancement he wanted.

The year after Thomas arrived, four more black regiments were formed which opened up an opportunity for Thomas to take his first step in promotion as an Officer. For on 25 June of that year, 1798, a month after his qualifying 16th birthday he received his first commission as an Ensign in one of them, the Eighth West India Regiment (WIR). The Eighth West India Regiment was first raised in 1795 as Skerrett's Foot but disbanded the next year only to be re raised in 1798 with drafts from the loyal Dominica Rangers providing the young Thomas with this opportunity.

(The journal of Lieutenant Thomas Howard of the York Hussars. *Yellow fever in the 1790s.* The British Army in occupied Saint Domingue 1979)

The Army imposed its rigorous daily routine wherever it served. The common soldier would rise before the break of day around 5.30am to the sound of bugle and drum; this would be the start of a monotonous day of drill, broken by breakfast between seven and eight after which they would return to their barracks to escape the burning rays of the rising sun, though not its heat. In this airless heat, they would maintain their weapons and kit before the monotony was finally broken by dinnertime at 12.30, still the main meal of the day just as it was in England. However, under the boiling sun of the West Indies, this was not the best time to eat, but the money for this food was deducted from their meagre wages so they had better make the most of it. After dinner it was back to barracks for more kit maintenance before the bugle call at 5pm and back to the parade ground for more drill and kit inspection followed by general orders and by sundown they were back in their barracks for lights-out at 10.30pm.

Typical daily rations would consist of;

1lb. of bread per man, 1lb. beef or 9oz pork,

half a pint of rice or half a pint of oatmeal,

a half pint of brandy, 1lb. sugar per week

and candles issued when they can be procured.

(*Historic records of the Royal African Corps*
by Major J.J. Crocks. Page 14.)

For Thomas, life now as an officer was a little easier, but there was no escaping the harsh conditions and many officers died in horrible circumstances just as the soldiers in the ranks did, disease took no account of a man's rank. However, there were compensations to be had to alleviate the bleak reality of life in the West Indies. Many officers would have a native "housekeeper" who some would treat just like a wife. Also as always, near soldiers' barracks there were brothels. But though Thomas was only 16 years old it's fair to think that he would have been no different to the other officers, and availed himself of these worldly pleasures to alleviate the many harsh realities of life in these parts. Also in these times, life was not only harsh but also short, so a soldier would grow up quickly.

Thomas though, still busy making himself noticed was again rewarded after the untimely death of Lieutenant Miller in 1800 which enabled Thomas an opportunity to move up to take over the unfortunate fellows vacant rank. So just two month after his eighteenth birthday in July he was appointed Lieutenant Thomas Brereton.

Lieutenant-General Thomas Trigge had taken over as Commander-in-Chief soon after the taking of Trinidad in 1801 and was now ordered to seize the Danish and Swedish settlements (Now known as the US Virgin Isles). Thomas landed with the Eighth WIR on the Swedish Island of St Bartholomew on 20 March, the tiny garrison surrendered without firing a shot and three hundred men from the third regiment took over the garrison and their commanding officer Lieutenant-Colonel Wilson became governor. A few days later after the arrival of the Second WIR they together with the remaining Eighth WIR including Thomas left for the French/Dutch Island of St Martin, which was on route to the Danish Virgin isles.

1780 West Indies Map by Rigobert Bonne and Guillaume Raynal's *Map of the Lesser Antilles, West Indies.*

(St Bartholomew is in the centre of this map at the top coloured in yellow and St Martin lies just above it in red.)

Brigadier-General Frederick Maitland landed at Cole Bay with a force of 1,500 men in the early hours of 24 March on the Dutch side of the Island. Lieutenant Colonel Packenham with the 64th Foot, and Thomas with the 8th WIR proceeded to the main town Philipsburg to attack Fort Amsterdam. The Dutch troops seeing the British approach sent out 300 men and two field pieces to repel them but after fierce fighting and losing around 50 casualties they were driven back into the fort abandoning the two guns. Fierce fighting continued all day until the town of Philipsburg was mostly in the possession of the British. Meanwhile on the French side of the island, a large British force of the first1st and 11th regiments together with the 2nd WIR had surrounded the town of Marigot where the French surrendered. While back at the Dutch side they were still fighting and holding out in the Fort. General Maitland called on the Governor to surrender and when he heard that the French had already done so, he agreed to the terms, and the whole island was taken into British possession. Thomas, together with the four companies of the 8th WIR and the 1st first regiment of foot were left to garrison the island. While on 26 March, Lieutenant-General Thomas Trigge sailed west to continue the operation in taking the remaining three Danish possessions of St John, St Thomas and St Croix, who all surrendered to the British force without firing a shot.

A few months later in October 1801 peace was declared between France and Britain and the terms of this peace were ratified in March 1802 at the *"Treaty of Amiens"*. However, unfortunately under the terms of this treaty all the islands taken were returned to their previous owners, all except Trinidad and Belize, which was kept by the British, both former Spanish colonies. Every other possession was returned, so the fighting over the previous nine years had all been for nothing.

1802 Dominica

Map of the Island of Dominica for the *History of the West Indies* by Bryan Edwards, Esq. (Copper engraving by J. Cooke, 1794.)

At the end of the year Thomas and the 8th WIR were stationed back in Dominica at Fort Shirley, on a peninsular at Prince Rupert Bluff in the north of the island guarding Prince Rupert Bay. The fort was separated from the mainland by extensive and unhealthy swamps so it was decided to drain these areas to make it healthier for the soldiers and more accessible for the fort, and so orders were delivered to the Colonel of the Regiment Andrew James Cochrane-Johnstone who was also the islands Governor, to make the necessary arrangements.

Johnstone had adopted this last name after marrying the daughter of James Johnstone the Earl of Hopetoun after which he added the name to his own. He was the youngest son of the Scottish Earl of Dundonald, and unlike Thomas who earned all of his promotions by merit alone; Johnstone's father had bought all his commissions from age 16 onwards until he reached the rank of Lieutenant Colonel. Therefore, after being promoted to a full Colonel in 1797, this was the first rank in his military career that no money had to change hands to achieve.

Colonel Johnstone was just the sort of self-serving officer that the Army could do without. For this sort of officer was also one of the reasons that Prince Frederick, the Duke of York and Commander-in-Chief of the British Army would strive to stamp out the purchase system in the British Army altogether. He was also instrumental in establishing the Royal Military Academy at Sandhurst in 1801, to train officers in the military arts, and show how to be effective leaders of men, as well as in army discipline, and the latest tactical methods.

What was about to take place in Dominica under the grasping hands of Colonel Johstone would only help to speed up this process and make it even more desirable.

In the British Army black soldiers were treated exactly the same as their white counterparts, they were paid the same, and provided with the same rations, clothing, and arms. When Johstone received orders to clear, and drain the marshland, he was given explicit instructions that if black soldiers were employed they should be paid an extra nine pence per day just as their white counterparts would. Johnstone however always on the look out for self-enrichment ordered the 8th WIR to clear the land, but when the soldiers complained about not being paid they were told they would be paid on completion. Worse than this however was the fact that Johnstone had not been paying the soldiers their regular wages for some time, paying them irregularly and in arrears, so the soldiers were already discontented.

Generally the black soldiers serving in the British army were very proud of their position, even though conditions were harsh, they were fed, paid and clothed, which give them a certain prestige just as it did their white counterparts. In fact they looked down on the common field slave and all the time they were treated fairly, and paid for their duties they were both proud and happy to serve. In fact the 8th WIR were fine soldiers as General Trigge had reported after their recent expedition;

"I have particular satisfaction in being enabled to add that the 8th West Indian Regiment, formed within the last three years, and composed almost entirely of new negroes, who had never before seen an enemy, engaged with a degree of gallantry, and behaved in a manner, that would do honour to any troops."

However, clear communication could sometimes be a problem as these soldiers didn't all speak the same language and there grasp of English was also rudimentary. These misunderstandings were further compounded after three weeks of working from dawn until dusk clearing the swamp with neither their regular, nor extra pay being paid to them. It was during this time that they came into contact with black slave plantation workers, working nearby. No doubt jealous of these free and proud soldiers and anxious to pull them down a peg or two. They started a rumour that the soldiers along with their regiment were to be disbanded, and that they were there to be trained as field workers before being sold as slaves. Further rumours in the local market place at Portsmouth only reinforced their fears, causing panic and confusion, which quickly spread through the already discontented ranks. These rumours were not true of course but due to misunderstandings and the way the soldiers were being treated it did seem plausible, especially to the newest recruits who were truly terrified of being sold into slavery. Around March 1802 two warships, *Excellent*, and *Magnificent,* were seen to arrive in Prince Rupert Bay and it wasn't long before rumours started to circulate that these ships were there to transport them into slavery. Back at the barracks during the night of Friday 9 April discontent and mistrust reached fever pitch and fearing the worst, the terrified troops mutinied and after a couple of hours took complete control of the fort from their startled officers. Five officers were killed in this action including Captain Cameron, Lieutenant McKay, Lieutenant Wastneys, Barrack Master Sergeant McKay and the Clerk of the Check Barron and the remaining three were taken prisoner along with a few women. Major John Gordon and two others managed to escape in the darkness and make their way to the main town Roseau where the next day, Saturday the tenth, Johnstone was informed of what had taken place, whereby he immediately ordered a state of Martial Law.

By the evening Johnstone was in Prince Rupert Bay with the 68th Regiment and the local Militia, and found that marines from *Excellent* had already been landed to surround the fort. The other ship *HMS Magnificent* was sent to Iles des Saintes just off the coast of Guadalupe for reinforcements returning on 12 April. However, before the plan to storm the Fort with the 1,300 men available, the mutineers agreed to surrender unconditionally. In response at 5pm Johnstone at the head of the troops, which must have included Thomas together with artillery entered the fort as had been agreed. The mutineers were lined up in ranks with the captured officers restored to their companies. This was now a very difficult situation that needed to be handled sensitively; unfortunately Johnstone was not the man to act thus. Sitting on his horse, he arrogantly started ranting and admonishing them for their disloyalty, but most of what he said could not be heard or understood. Therefore, the confused and nervous mutineers started to get agitated as to what was happening. Johnstone rode to the line of mutineers and ordered them to shoulder and ground their arms and then he rode to the rear of the line, where he then ordered them to advance three paces in front. At which point, Sergeant Church called out, "No, General – no". But Johnstone replied if they did not obey his orders instantly he would order the troops to open fire. It is highly probable that the mutineers who were made up of African born soldiers and some English and French speaking Creoles could not understand all what was being said.

Therefore, to add to the already tense situation we now had confusion, and in this confusion only a few understood and obeyed, while other shouted out that; "Governor Johnstone would cheat them". Shortly afterwards as the tension mounted the British troops opened fire. Seventy of the mutineers were killed or wounded, but the three former imprisoned officers managed to escape despite being at the front of their mutineering troops. In panic most of the mutineers tried to escape, only a few shots were returned killing a number of soldiers. In the melee that ensued the mutineers made their escape from the fort, running out onto the bluff where they jumped in panic into the sea. Some were killed in this desperate escape but most swam to the shore where they were arrested by the waiting troops. Others ran into the very swamps that Johnstone had been ordered to clear, and tried to hide there, but eventually all were captured with about 50 killed, with twenty British troops killed or wounded. The body of Lieutenant Wastney was found tied to a tree, stripped naked, and mutilated by bayonets in such a way as to prolong his agony. Another casualty who also received particular barbaric treatment was their first victim Lieutenant McKay who was dragged, "about the post in a manner to horrid to relate".

Several of those held responsible were Court Martialled and sentenced to death, which took place on 27 April in front of the whole regiment on the Island of Martinique.

At the end of the month in Port Royal, a Court of Inquiry was convened so as to ascertain the reasons for the Mutiny. During this inquiry, Major Gordon and the other officers were questioned along with some of the men, where it finally came to light that most of them had not be paid for several months and that none had received the extra nine pence due to them.

So another Court of Inquiry was formed on 24 May to investigate the regimental accounts, which as well as identifying irregularities in pay, also discovered shortcoming in their rations. Therefore, by June, a Court Martial was convened and 24 soldiers were found guilty and executed. The rest of the regiment was disbanded with those who it was deemed had played an active part in the mutiny, which numbered 284, were reduced to prisoners to serve various white regiments. The remaining 100 or so who had not played a part in the mutiny were redistributed amongst the other West Indian regiments.

Lurid tales appeared in the local press and Pierre Franc McCallum wrote a *Series of Letters, Addressed to a Member of Parliament of Great Britain*;

"The Negro troops already trained, are ready when an opportunity offers, to plunge their bayonets into the bowels of the whites, and will aid the endeavours of their colour in the work of emancipation. The black barbarians of the 8th West Indian Regiment have their prototypes in all the other West Indian Corps, who are only waiting for a proper opportunity to wreak their vengeance on all whites, like Lt Wastney."

(*Travels in Trinidad during the months of February, March, and April, 1803,* in a series of letters, addressed to a member of the imperial Parliament of Great Britain. page 118. Illustrated with a map of the island. (1805 By Pierre Franc McCollum.)

As a direct result of this, the Administrations intentions of discharging the black soldiers into West Indian society as a result of the Amiens Treaty had to be reluctantly scrapped. So, did the architect of all this misery receive any just punishment himself?

Well Johnstone was dismissed from his post as Governor of Dominica in disgrace; he also lost his appointment as Brigadier and reduced back to a Colonel and retired on half pay. After returning to England he had Major Gordon, who had also been sent home on half pay, arrested and Court Martialled in February 1804 but even with Johnstone acting as prosecutor, he was reluctantly found not guilty by the jury, but was retired permanently on half pay.

Johnstone himself was Court Martialled later in 1805 due to some of the evidence brought up in Major Gordon's trial but he was strangely acquitted on several charges. It always helped if you were rich, well connected, titled, and from a family of the ruling classes of course. He was however passed over for promotion and so resigned his commission to pursue another career in which he was eminently qualified... *Fraud*! For after being behind a plot to defraud the London Stock Exchange he escaped to the West Indies and returned to Dominica only to find his estate had been confiscated. He later died in Paris in 1833 after again being charged with fraud, this time against the French Government.

Though the "Peace of Amiens" had been signed less than fourteen months ago, by Thomas's 21st birthday in May1803, a new conflict erupted when Great Britain declared war on Napoleon's France, which would come to be known as "The Napoleonic Wars", and so the conflict between France and Britain resumed.

Therefore, when the West India regiment was disbanded and all those responsible were punished Thomas who was innocent of any impropriety was put on half pay. Then on 14 April 1803, he was promoted to the rank of Lieutenant in the 2nd West India Regiment. He is then sent to Jersey from the spring of 1803–04 serving under the command of Lieutenant General Purdon and Colonel Forbes, as Adjutant to the 1st East Indian battalion which was raised to protect the island from the threat of French invasion.

Later, on 20 April 1804, he is promoted again to Captain in the Royal Africa Corps, this was a very difficult regiment indeed, made up of deserters and prisoners who had agreed to serve for life rather than be imprisoned. Therefore, the Royal Africa Corp was in fact a penal regiment, composed of criminals and military miscreants from all the other regiments who had received a pardon on the condition that they served with the Royal Africans for life. However, once the reality of their existence became all too evident, it was now even more forlorn than many had imagined, with no exit. For far away for ever from their country, families and friends, the lonely desperation which, drove many to try and obliterate this and find comfort in excessive drinking and often declaring;

"a short life but a merry one"

The problems with the Royal African Corps was well known, even in 1794 an old General had said that when he was promoted to a Lt Colonelcy in the regiment that;

"They were the sweeping of every parade ground in England, for when a man was sentenced to be flogged, he was offered the alternative of volunteering for the Royal Africans. They were not a bad set of fellows when there was something to be done, but with nothing to do they were the devils incarnate."

(*Notes and Queries* third series, VIII.134)[1]

On 1 July 1804, Captain Brereton is now on Alderney one of the other Channel Islands, together with six other companies of the Royal Africa Corp. So I expect he along with the other officers, were glad that later on 9 October the six companies embarked from Alderney for England and there onto the West Indies, the effective rank and file being 558.[2]

[1] *The United Service Journal* 1832 part 1. Page 286

[2] Major J.J. Crooks; *"Historical records of the Royal Africa Corps"*. Page 95.

St Lucia 1805

English Map of St Lucia made in 1775 by Thomas Jeffreys, Geographer to the King

Captain Thomas Brereton arrived in St Lucia in early 1805; the Governor of the Colony was his relative, Lieutenant-General Robert Brereton.

Lt General Robert Brereton, Governor of St Lucia 1747-1816
(Pastel on board from the author's collection)

Robert Brereton was a well seasoned officer who had entered military academy at 14 years old and had spent most of his life on active service including the American War of Independence as well as the occupation of Toulon in Corsica and the battle of Egmont in Holland to name but a few. He had been involved in the conquest of St Lucia in June 1803 when he along with George Provost defeated the French to retake control of St Lucia with amongst others, troops of the 68th regiment who had helped to put down the mutineering troops of Thomas Brereton's 8th West Indian regiment only the year before. During the battle at Morne Fortune, St Lucia, on the 22nd, Robert Brereton had saved the life of the injured brother of General Nogues the French Governor, when he rescued him from the wrath of the advancing British soldiers. It was after this successful conquest that Brereton was later appointed Governor of St Lucia that same year.

St Lucia is located northwest of Barbados and south of Martinique and northeast of the island of Saint Vincent. It covers a land area of 238.23 square miles and had a population of which 1,533 were white, 4,053 free people of colour and 1,330 slaves. Its capital Castries was built on reclaimed land next to a sheltered harbour on the west coast. The heavy stone built Fort Charlotte, lies up a winding and steep road from the capital to the summit at Morne Fortune which forms a spacious flat table-like summit of 80 acres and stands at an altitude of around 1,200 ft. There are also two others hills above Castries, Morne Chabot, and Morne Duchazeaut, which is even higher and it was from here in 1796 that Sir Ralph Abercromby bombarded the French at Fort Morne Fortune into submission. It must have been a truly herculean effort to manhandle the heavy cannon and armaments up the steep overgrown slopes of Morne Duchazeaut to achieve this, let alone storming the heavy stone walled fort at Morne Fortune with its works in two tiers and a triangular ravelin fortification in front. It must have been a very similar effort when General Brereton was tasked to repeat this action just seven years later.

To protect this new possession General Brereton arranged his armaments in strategic areas around the island, like the imposing Fort Charlotte (named after Queen Charlotte). The fort looks down protectively upon the rooftops of the capital beneath and its principal avenue right down to its harbour at Carenage that lies close by. Behind the fort and inland, lies a wooded country of steep hills and black ravines and valleys that lead far off into the mist covered distance. To the north of the island on the east coast another fortification was built at Pigeon Island where the batteries of Fort Rodney were constructed mounting three 24 pounders and two 11½ inch mortars and commands the anchorage of Gros Islet which is situated seven miles north east of Carenage.

On 12 January 1805, information was received by Governor Brereton, from a Captain Corbett of *HMS Seahorse* that an enemy fleet of 18 ships of the line had been seen by the Frigate *HMS*

Sirius off the coast of Portugal heading towards the West Indies. Captain Corbett cruised off Cape St Vincent long enough to confirm that the ships were neither heading towards Cadiz or to the Mediterranean which confirmed his suspicions. So the resourceful Captain, took it upon himself to push ahead to warn the colonies. As he approached the windward of Barbados he fell in with a sloop of war the *Flereaux* which took his intelligence to the head-quarters of the island and then northward to Antigua to inform them. Captain Corbett then sailed on to Martinique to see if the ships were anchored there and then onto Jamaica. Martinique had been returned to France after the treaty of Amiens in 1802.

On 22 January a large fleet was observed near the coast off Roseau Dominica where Captain Thomas Brereton had recently been stationed and as the light increased it was observed that they were flying British colours. However, suspicions were raised when these ships came in too close to Fort Young, so the Governor, Major General Prevost ordered that they should be fired upon and shortly after, 19 landing barges were seen to appear from the leeward of the ships as the British colours were struck and the French flag raised. They then attempted a landing to Prevost's left flank between the town of Roseau and the post of Cachecrow. The 1st West Indian regiment went down to support Captain Senat and the Militia, quickly followed by the Grenadiers of the 46th regiment who all fought valiantly throughout the day. Meanwhile the *Majestueaux* using her 120 guns constantly broadsided Fort Young and the town, followed closely by the other French ships. This fire was returned by Lt Colonel Broughton the commanding officer and the British soldiers who were supported by several merchant captains and their sailors in a constant uninterrupted fire. Major Nunn of the 1st West Indians was mortally wounded and as Captain O'Connell took over the command he too was hit, but he carried on and despite being constantly attacked resisted all, forcing the French to leave their advance position and causing them great slaughter. Meanwhile the French landed a large force of 2,000 men near Morne Daniel with only a small British force of 200 to defend it and so despite a spirited defence they were eventually overrun. The town of Roseau was now in flames after the constant bombardment by the French ships and was forced to capitulate after the French landed some 4,000 men, leaving Prevost's wife and children marooned there at the mercy of the French commander. The French Commander General Le Grange however treated them with respect though he did ask the council for £20,000 to be paid within 24 hours or they would be taken to Guadalupe as prisoners. Prevost himself and his remaining troops marched for 24 hours through the jungle, helped and assisted by the local inhabitants and the native Carib's to reach Prince Rupert's garrison at the other end of the island on the 23rd He was joined four days later by the wounded Captain O'Connell and the remains of the 46 regiment and the 1st West Indian light company together with their wounded. Meanwhile after some renegotiation General le Grange accepted a payment of just £7,000 before leaving with his troops and the Kings stores together with some British ships he had captured full of there valuable cargoes and some 20 square rigged vessels that were taken on route back to Guadeloupe. On the journey the whole fleet stood off Prince Rupert's and were there joined by General Ernouf with reinforcements from Guadeloupe. The General offered to lead the attack on the garrison, but the Admiral was reluctant to risk his ships and valuable plunder, so after cruising up and down for all of the 27th, to the great relief of the British, they finally sailed on to Guadeloupe.

Nevertheless, although the French had taken Roseau and received a bounty and some valuable plunder they had fought very hard to achieve it, losing some 500 men and several officers of rank. The British losses were much fewer with 19 killed, 24 wounded and eight taken prisoners, who were no doubt returned after the ransom had been paid. *

* (Based on Brigadier General Prevost, report to Sir W. Myers after the attack. 1 March, Headquarters Prince Rupert's Dominica 1805, *Annual Register* page 31.)

On 3 March the French fleet had anchored off the British colony of St Kitts at Base Terre were they landed 500 men who greatly outnumbered the small detachment and soon took over the town and demanded £40,000 or they would burn the town to the ground. After some difficulty, the inhabitants managed to raise £18,000, which the French took along with six valuable ships, which they set fire to before leaving them to drift in the open sea. Major James Forster of the 11th regiment felt that they were not prepared to attack where any great opposition was offered, but rather to plunder the inhabitants and burn the shipping if there was none.

After receiving intelligence, General Brereton in St Lucia sent word to his field quarters to be in readiness in case of attack and as part of this reorganisation; Captain Thomas Brereton was appointed Brigade-Major. And soon after in May the enemy fleet was sighted, comprising of 11 French battleships of the line, seven frigates one armed-en-flute and three brigs and also five Spanish ships of the line, one frigate and *The Cyane* a captured British ship. Therefore, plans were laid out to defend the island from attack and lookouts were mounted on the top of the hills so as to warn the colony of any further sightings, but due to a heavy mist for several days very little could be seen which only had the effect of raising the tension further. A boat was sent to Fort Royal, Martinique, on the 24th to make contact with *HMS Diamond* on route. *HMS Diamond* was not as one would suspect one of his majesty's ships of war, but a large rocky island situated at the entrance to Fort-de-France Bay Martinique, which lies only 50 miles north of St Lucia. The British had occupied the Diamond since the year before to harass French ships as they tried to get in and out of the large Fort-de-France Bay, which lies on the western side of the island. It was commanded by Captain Maurice and manned by 100 British sailors and was regarded as a sloop of the Royal Navy with its own officers and crew. The French Commander of Martinique, Louis Thomas Villaret de Joyeuse had tried to dislodge the British by building a road opposite the Diamond and established a battery there to bombard them. However, the British were forewarned by the black population of the island, who were largely sympathetic to them after the French had brutally put down a rebellion the year before. Now after the arrival of the combined French/Spanish fleet the balance of power was starting to change. Back at St Lucia without knowing when the British convoy would be sailing to confront this threat, tensions were running high. Governor Brereton however, was pleased with his new increase in troops of the Royal African Corps, which had swelled the strength of the garrison. He was now very confident he could repel any attack on the capital Castries, or the shipping in the bay at Carsenage, which was protected by a battery at Pigeon Island and Vigie and an additional battery of two heavy guns mounted at Rat Island. In the event of a full invasion, Governor Brereton felt that they were now well placed to halt any advance until further reinforcements arrived from England, whom he advised to land in Esperance Bay on shallow draft vessels should they be needed. In an effort to get further intelligence a canoe was sent out by Captain Maurice from *HMS Diamond* and reported seeing two large frigates leaving Fort-de-France Bay under full sail and as they hadn't been seen since they were suspected of cruising off the reach of Barbados. Captain Maurice further stated that the combined fleet was due to leave Fort Royal harbour Martinique after being supplied with provisions on the morning of the 27th to attack St Lucia and Trinidad. On 2 June, with visibility now restored, a fleet was observed from the heights of St Lucia steering down the windward of St Vincent's, General Brereton fearing them to be the enemy immediately dispatched a ship to Barbados with the intelligence. At the same time General Prevost had also sent a neutral vessel from Prince Rupert's Dominica to Barbados with dispatches but had asked him to sail past Fort Royal harbour and report what he had seen. Both ships reached Barbados at the same time and though the Captain reported, he had seen the fleet anchored in Fort Royal harbour, the report from General Brereton, which also seemed to confirm Captain Maurice's intelligence seemed to be the correct one to act upon.

On 4 June, Admiral Horatio Nelson who had been informed of the French fleet's position also arrived in Barbados with his own small fleet and was informed of the latest intelligence that the French/Spanish fleet had been spotted from St Lucia and were thought to be heading towards Trinidad and Tobago.

However, Nelson was not convinced that this was the case, and replied;

"If your intelligence proves false you lose me the French fleet."

(From Robert Southey's, *Life of Nelson.* Vol 2. Page 216.)

However, in his despatch of 11th June to William Marsden at the Admiralty Nelson states that; *"having no reason to doubt the information from St Lucia, as sent from General Brereton,"* referenced in an earlier dispatch on 4 June.

He in fact knew General Brereton referring to him in another letter *as "an old acquaintance"*. The two men had served together at the sieges of Bastia and Calvi.

(From, *The Dispatches and Letters of Vice Admiral Lord Viscount Nelson.* Page 451.)

So perhaps he trusted the Generals account because he knew him to be a trustworthy person and so the next morning he set sail and later as the fleet hove into sight at Tobago a worried merchant sent out a schooner to check whether this fleet was friend or foe. It was at this point that fate took a hand, for the Captain of the schooner used by pure coincidence the very signal chosen to indicate the enemy fleet was indeed in Trinidad and it was so late in the day there was no opportunity to realise the mistake. To make matter worst an American brig was encountered at around the same time and with a national inclination for foiling the British and helping the French, the Captain falsely confirmed this misunderstanding, by claiming that he had been boarded off Trinidad by a French ship only a few days before. Therefore, Nelsons doubts were now reduced and before dawn, the decks were cleared and the fleet readied for action. By the 7th Nelson and his fleet entered the Bay of Paria expecting to encounter the enemy fleet, and in doing so making the mouths of the Orinoco as famous as that of the Nile. Alas though, it wasn't long before their mistake was realised and Nelson ordered the ships "about turn", and headed for Granada. On route, intelligence was received that the combined enemy fleet had blockaded *HMS Diamond* from 16 – 29 May and after three days fighting had captured her on the 2nd and also confirmed that they were anchored there at Martinique on the 4th and had been due to leave that night to attack Grenada. Nelson now knew his original instinct had been correct, so he headed towards Granada, which he reached on the 9th, only to learn that they had passed by the day before without incident after hearing of his arrival. For even though his fleet was half their size they were intimidated by his reputation and decided that caution was the better part of valour, and made their way back to Europe without delay. Therefore, if Nelson had not received the contradictory intelligence and he had gone straight to Granada he would have been waiting when the enemy fleet arrived. At the time however, it is easy to see why the authorities would take more notice of two pieces of intelligence that seemed to confirm each other rather than just the one. Nevertheless, Nelson seemed particularly annoyed with General Brereton's information. He remarked in one letter that his lookout must have been blind, before excusing himself in a letter of the 18th June to Major Generals Villettes, explaining how; *"Unwell and out of humour I am by my disappointment," before saying; "I am sure you will regret, with me, our old acquaintance Brereton's wrong information"*.

(From, *The Dispatches and letters of Vice Admiral Lord Viscount Nelson*. Page 459.)

However it wasn't just Brereton's information that was wrong and it seems they did not know that the intelligence from *HMS Diamond* was out of date or that they were under siege at the time, so there was no chance of it being updated. History is littered with "what ifs" but fate had worked against Nelson on this occasion; and so he would have to wait a little longer for his date with destiny.

(Details from, Robert Southey's, *Life of Nelson*, Vol 2. Page 216 and the Correspondence of Major General Brereton)

Public Record Office CO253/3

At 11am on the morning of 15 September, a fire broke out in the capital of St Lucia, just as it had in 1795 under French control, when it had burnt to the ground during the slave's revolt. However, just as they were then, all the houses were still built of wood and with the fire fanned by the strong coastal breeze it wasn't long before it took hold. As soon as it was discovered, Brigade-Major Thomas Brereton was involved in organising the response in fighting the blaze, including the additional support of all effective off-duty troops. However, it was not until 3.30 pm that it was brought under control and by then 200 houses were completely destroyed as well the colonies stores. A rough calculation at the time put the damage at £150,000 (over £9million in to day's money) several affluent people were ruined, losing not only their houses but also their businesses. The loss was alleviated somewhat by a voluntary subscription of 150 barrels of flour and 50 barrels of salt beef and pork which had been sent from the legislature of St Vincent and several other nearby British colonies. In order to facilitate this, the port of Castries was opened for three months due to the calamity. This had also been agreed with Major General George Beckwith Governor of St Vincent's (from 29 March until 31 December) and who was also commanding officer of the troops

On 24 October, the barracks went into official mourning after hearing of the death of his Royal Highness the Duke of Gloucester and later on 20 November, a letter from His majesty King George prohibited the introduction of any slaves into the colony. This was no doubt influenced by the slave's revolt under the French 10yrs earlier and also the rising tide of anti slavery feeling back home in Great Britain. Around this time the Colony was to hear of the magnificent defeat of the combined French and Spanish navies at the battle of Trafalgar on the 28th October 1805. Nevertheless, this great victory was tinged by the tragic death of the nation's hero, Lord Nelson, who was killed during the battle. This victory would make the Royal Navy masters of the world's oceans that would last for a hundred years. Therefore, when Great Britain abolished the slave trade in 1807 the Royal Navy's mastery would play a large part in enforcing Britain's will, in trying to bring this vile trade to its end.

In an Official communiqué from His Majesty the Commander in Chief from Horse Guards dated 31 October 1806 the following was stated;

"His Majesty's pleasure is that from the 25th instance the Royal African Corps who under particular circumstances had been augmented to 12 companies, six of which were now stationed in the West Indies and so should now be separated into two distinct Corps of eight companies.

Eight companies of rank and file each;

1 Colonel,
1 Lieutenant Colonel,
2 Majors,
8 Captains,
16 Lieutenants,
8 Ensigns,
1 Paymaster,
1 Adjutant,
1 Quartermaster,
1 Surgeon,
2 Assistant Surgeons,
44 Sergeants including Staff Sergeants,
16 Drummers,
40 Corporals,
760 Privates,
Total 902 men of all classes.

Common soldiers comprised of the same description of men as before given to the R.A.C. i.e.; Deserters and persons on board hulks who will be pardoned if they serve his Majesty.

In 1807 the detachment of the Royal African Corps now stationed in the West Indies shall now be known as 'Royal West India Rangers' and be commanded by Brigadier-General William Wynyard from the Coldstream Guards leaving Colonel Fraser to remain in Command of the Royal African Corps stationed in Africa."

It was during this time that Thomas Brereton met up with a fellow officer in Barbados, a certain Captain W. Whitmore and the woman who would later become his wife, Margaret Olton. However I believe that Thomas was already acquainted with the Whitmore family as his uncle Andrew left money to John Whitmore of the London Auction market in his will of 1837 and this John and Edward Whitmore perhaps his brother, made a counter claim* to the will of John Allen Olton (Margaret Whitemore's Father) in London in 1809.

*(*Parliamentary Papers* p. 326. Barbados 2959A & B (Harrow)

In 1807, Brigadier-General Robert Brereton became ill and was obliged to return to Great Britain to recuperate. It was during this time that he purchased New Abbey the former home of his sister Janetta, who had married their cousin George Brereton the heir apparent to Carrigslaney and a Bombardier in the Royal Horse Artillery at Bath in 1771. Janetta wanted to sell New Abbey after the sudden death of George during a duel at a coffee house in Browns Street, Cork. New Abbey was a large house on the banks of the river Liffey in County Kildare Ireland.

1809 The Battle for Martinique

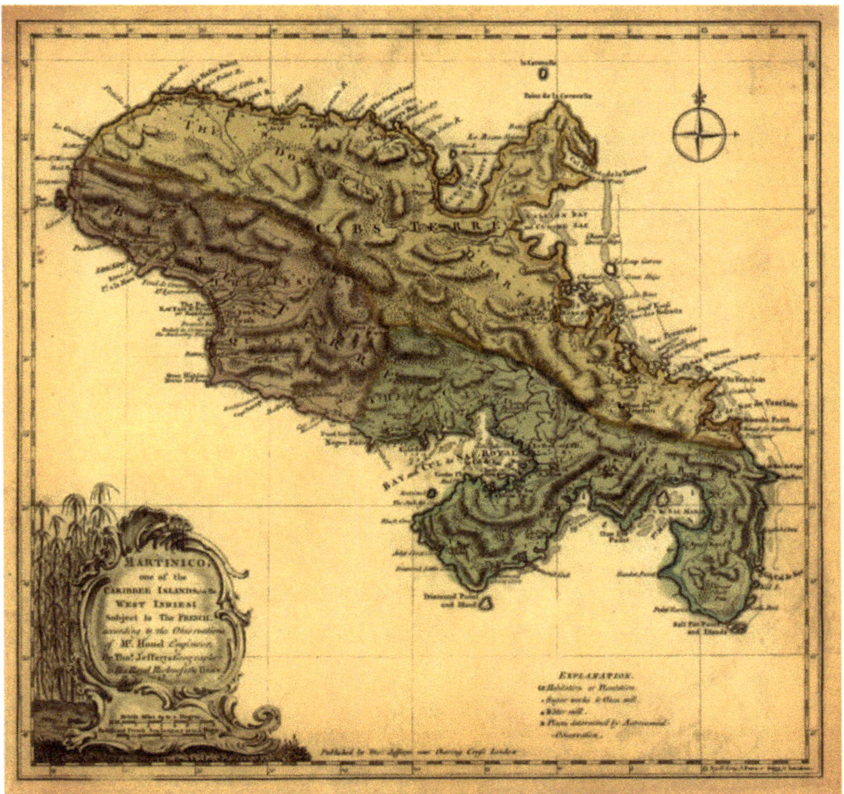

Map of Martinique Island published in 1775 by Thomas Jefferys, Charing Cross London. Geographer to his Majesty the King

The French Fleet, that only in 1804 had been at Martinique, was completely devastated at the battle of Trafalgar in October 1805, and what ships they had left were confined to French ports due to the British blockade, making communication and supply with their colonies very difficult.

By the summer of 1808, only three ships remained at Martinique and the lack of supplies were starting to have an effect. The Governor, Vice Admiral Villaret de Joyeuse sent frantic messages back to France, but these were intercepted by the Royal Navy. Moreover, when the British realised the dire straights they were in, it was decided during the winter of 1808 to mount an invasion from Barbados. Sir Charles Beckwith was amassing a battalion of 10,000 troops, together with 29 Royal Navy ships under the command of Sir Alexander Cochrane and General Ware, to whom Thomas, after the return of General Brereton would now be serving as Brigade-Major.

Also amongst these troops were the 23rd Regiment or Welsh Fusiliers with a certain Major Thomas Pearson freshly arrived from Canada. While they waited, the soldiers would entertain themselves at the notorious taverns of Nancy Clarke, or her rival Susan Austin in the capital Bridgetown. Before arriving, the troops had many warnings of deadly diseases that awaited them, and that the local churchyards were full of their former compatriots. However, as young men will, they ignored them. Consequentially, only a week later a young lieutenant was suddenly struck down with yellow fever and by nightfall he was dead, he was the first of many. This had a sobering affect on their remaining conduct as they waited for orders. It makes you wonder if Thomas Brereton and Thomas Pearson met each other during these days either militarily or at the establishments of Madam Clarke or Austin. They would certainly meet again years later in much less desirable circumstances, particularly for Thomas Brereton, as you will see.

The French tried to send supplies and reinforcements to Martinique, but the Royal naval patrols in the Atlantic stopped all but one ship getting through, and this was insufficient to make much of a difference.

The British Fleet under the command of Vice Admiral Sir Alexander Cochrane who was the older brother of Thomas's former commanding officer the now disgraced Colonel Andrew James Cochran -Johnstone, (former Governor of Dominica) sailed from Carlisle Bay Barbados on 28 January 1809. The troops were to land on the south and east of the island and be supported by 30 ships of the Royal Navy. The island was well defended, and the capital Fort Royal, was overlooked by the imposing Fort Desaix, situated on the rugged hills above and armed with many cannons placed to protect the capital and the important Fort Royal Bay. The plan was for Maitland to land at St Luce, and march overland to Cape Solomon and seize the two batteries protecting Fort de France Bay. This would allow the Royal Navy to enter Fort Royal Bay and unload the tons of equipment needed to mount the attack on the formidable Fort Desaix, before marching on to the capital Fort de France. At the same time as Provost and the first division would march 12 miles across the island to attack the rear of Fort Desaix, the main fort overlooking the town.

Landing on the 30th, the first division under the orders of Lieutenant-General Sir George Prevost, and consisting of up to 7,000 men on board *HMS Forester* and *HMS Acasta* landed at Malgre Tout in Bay Robert on the windward coast. They marched seven miles through the night through difficult country and appalling weather, dragging two six pounder, but by the 31st they held a position on the banks of the Grande Lizarde river. His first task was to capture Morne Bruneau, a pass that would allow them through the mountains that ran down the centre of the island. So on 1 February, an advance party of the 7th Royal Fusiliers under Lieutenant-Colonel Packenham, set out supported by the light infantry battalion of the Royal West India Rangers under the command of Major Campbell, with the Royal Welsh Fusiliers in reserve. They soon encountered the enemy for the first time in a battle that would last several hours. Their first assault drove the enemy from Morne Bruno before being counter attacked by a determined French force and ground was won and lost but despite their efforts the French were finally driven back to the heights of Desfourneaux and Surirey above a mountain torrent where the enemy had mounted their artillery to make a divisive stand. Provost ordered the flanking companies of the 7th to attack the right while the 23rd (RWF) attacked the left leaving the remaining 7th together with the Royal West India Rangers to attack the centre across the rushing stream under heavy fire. However, the enemy had a commanding position and superior numbers but the ferocity of the attack drove them from their position and they were forced to retreat.

Provost was later to praise; *"the innumerable proofs of the valour and judgement of the honourable* Colonel Packenham *and of the spirited and judicious exertions of Lieutenant-*Colonel *Ellis, and Major Pearson and Ostely of the 23rd, or Royal Welsh Fusiliers, also of the bravery of* Major *Campbell and the light infantry battalion; all of which have enabled me to retain this valuable position without artillery, within 300 yards of the enemy's intrenched (sic) camp, covered with guns"*[1]

[1](Lieutenant George Prevost dispatch from the heights of Surirey 2 February 1809)

(So Major Pearson gets a particular mention in this dispatch but though Captain Thomas Brereton doesn't, Major Campbell and the light infantry do, and of course Thomas Brereton was in this with the Royal West India Rangers.)

As the second brigade joined them, they continued their advance only to encounter another French attempt to halt them. But the French were forced to retreat again and seek shelter under the cannon of Fort Desaix in two redoubts. These were protected by fallen trees and three 12-pound cannons, where they made another attempt to halt the British advance. After two days of fierce fighting two attempts to over run the redoubts were repulsed with heavy loses before darkness brought an end to hostilities, and during the night the French abandoned their positions and retreated into Fort Desaix.

Meanwhile the second division of 3,000 men under Major-General Frederick Maitland had also landed on the 30th on the opposite side of the island and lower down near St Luce and point Solomon. The French troops panicked at the sight of the British and escaped to a small island, which the British commenced to bombard them until on 4 February they surrendered. Fort de France Bay was secured by a third force of 600 men of the Royal York Rangers, under Major Henderson.

Now with control of the bay three Royal navy ships sailed in, panicking the French into setting light to their own ships and by 10 February the British had control of most of the island with the only French resistance at Fort Desaix. The Royal Navy now in control of Fort of France Bay began to unload their cannons, ammunition and supplies and then began the arduous task of dragging them along the sodden tracks in torrential rain and over the steep rocky hills to Fort Dasaix, where the Army was digging in and setting up their guns and preparing their positions. This all took weeks of hard graft to complete but by 19 February all was ready and the Royal Artillery opened fire at half past four in the afternoon, with 14 heavy cannon, 28 mortars and howitzers, from six separate points. This deafening assault continued day and night for four days until the morning of 23 February when a trumpeter with a white flag was seen coming out of the fort. However, the French terms of surrender were that the French troops be sent to France, which would allow them to rejoin the war. This of course was not acceptable to General Beckwith, and so the bombardment was resumed until the next morning at 9 o'clock, when three white flags were seen flying in the fortress, after which Villaret de Joyesuse finally surrendered unconditionally. Over 2,000 French troops marched out of the fort, no doubt relieved to be still alive, unlike the many corpses of their fallen comrades found inside as the British entered to take charge. The French also surrendered their regimental eagles the first such trophies to be won by the British in the Napoleonic wars. These were sent to Britain with Beckwith's despatch, detailing his victory and enclosing the articles of capitulation. These along with the captured Eagles were sent with Captain Preedy of the 90th regiment, one of Beckwith's Aides-de-camp; *"to be laid at the Kings feet"*.

So now after 25 days of fighting Martinique was no longer a base for French ships to strike at British interests but British losses had been heavy with over 97 dead and around 350 injured, but the French loses were much worse, with over 900 casualties.

A grateful British Government sent the following:

Sir, *House of Commons, 15th of April, 1809*

"In obedience to the commands of the House of Commons, I have the honour of transmitting to you their unanimous vote of thanks, for your able and gallant conduct in effecting , with such signal rapidity, the entire conquest of the important island of Martinique; together with the like vote of thanks to lieutenant-General Sir George Prevost, Baronet; Major-General Frederick

Maitland; Brigadier-General Hoghton; Brigadier-General Sir Charles Shipley; Brigadier-General Stehelin; and to the several officers of the army under your command, for their gallant and meritorious exertions in effecting that conquest......."

"Lieutenant-General George Beckwith &c &c &c

(Signed) Charles Abbot, Speaker.

But before this letter had even been written, word had reached Beckwith from Admiral Cochrane that five French warships had been seen and that they had taken refuge amongst a small group of islands called Ile des Saintes close to Guadeloupe, the largest remaining French possession in the area. Maitland left on the 12th with less than 3,000 men and landed two days later on one of the islands Terre-de-Haut and drove the five French ships out into the arms of the waiting Royal Navy. Maitland then set about taking the islands from the French who were very well placed to defend it. Nevertheless, by 16 April the British had established themselves on a ridge overlooking the two French forts. The next morning their position was attacked by troops from both forts, but the British held their nerve, and resisted the attack. Later in the day the French capitulated, and 800 men were taken prisoner and the islands were placed under the control of Admiral Cochrane, who took over their administration, leaving Maitland and his force to return to Martinique. Where on 1 March, Captain Thomas Brereton was promoted to the rank of Major of the Royal West Indian Rangers, probably as a result of his efforts in the taking of Martinique the month before, he was 27 years old.

Prevost's force was to remain in Martinique before returning to Halifax in Canada on 15 March, Major Pearson amongst them. The only Island now remaining in French possession was the nearby Guadeloupe, and it took until 2 December before Beckwith received permission from London to mount an assault. Not only was the Army reduced by the return of Prevost and his units to Canada, but also by the losses incurred in the fighting, and that ever present, but unseen foe, Yellow fever! Therefore, it was over a month later before numbers were increased and Beckwith could commence this new mission.

1810 Guadalupe

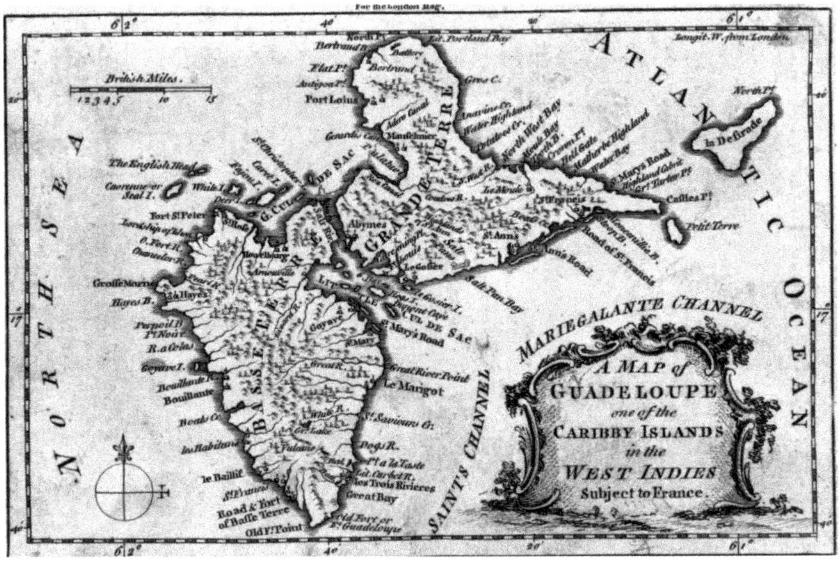

Map of Guadeloupe printed for the London Magazine 1759

Guadeloupe is comprised of two main islands Basse Terre and Grande Terre which are separated by a narrow channel called the River Salee or salt river. Confusingly the capital of Basse Terre, is also called Basse Terre, and is situated at the southern extremity of the western coast not far from the islands of Iles des Saints that were recently captured. This, like the year before, would be a joint Military and Naval operation, so Lieutenant-General Beckwith made the necessary arrangements with Admiral Sir Alexander Cochrane and sailed from Martinique on 22 January 1810, arriving at Prince Rupert's Dominica to rendezvous with the 6,700 troops assembled for the mission. As before the troops were divided into two divisions, the first division under the command of Major-General Hislop and the second under Major-General Harcourt. Each division was composed of two brigades with a fifth brigade under the command of Brigadier-General Wale in reserve and on his staff was Brigade-Major Thomas Brereton of the Royal West India Rangers. On the morning of the 26th, the second division sailed from Dominica and anchored at the newly acquired Iles des Saintes islands, close to the south of Basse Terre. With the first division and reserve, sailing in the afternoon and arriving at Isle Gosier Grand Terre on the south of the island on the 27th under the command of Beckwith, with Major General Thomas Hislop, second in command. Early the next morning the 28th, the troops were moved across the bay on the smaller warships, and other available low draft boats landing without opposition at St Mary's in Capesterre. Later in the afternoon Major-General Hislop and the first division moved forward, dividing into their two brigades, with the third brigade to Capesterre and the forth Brigade to Grand Rivere, leaving Brigadier-General Wale and Brigade-Major Thomas Brereton and the reserve to guard the landing of supplies. By the 29th the reserve with two days provisions reached Grand Rivere by nightfall to set up a supply post with two days provisions for the first division who had now moved to Bannaniers River.

Meanwhile Brigadier-General Harcourt and the second division had also crossed from the Iles de Saites and had harassed the enemy from the other side of Three Rivers facilitating the advance of the rest of the army. After landing at Du Plessis to the enemies right and rear, the French decided to consolidate their position beyond the Bridge of Noziere, with the river in front and the Mountains to their left, in a more easily defendable position. But before abandoning their defences at Three Rivers at Palmiste and Morne Houel, they spiking the guns and destroyed the ammunition as they left. By the 30th the British first division had moved unopposed through the Trou au Chien pass with the head of the column reaching Three Rivers about 11o'clock and encountering the enemy for the first time in small detachments in skirmishes which were soon forced to retreat before them. Brigadier General Wale and Brigade-Major Brereton with the reserve had also marched earlier that morning and reached Three Rivers by sunset. They remained there at Three Rivers until 2 February While the Navy busied themselves with resupplying them with a further five days provision. After this was completed, they marched in two columns, the reserve forming the right, and advancing by the mountains and took possession of Palmiste. While the first division marched by the heights of D'Olet, which had been fortified with field artillery, but abandoned by the enemy leaving the ordinance behind. When they reached the great road to Basse Terre the first division divided into two at the foot of the heights with the fourth brigade ascending at the centre and the third lower down. While the Reserve reached, the post at Langlais to find it also abandoned and again the guns had been spiked. Beckwith's next objective was the important Morue Houel so Wale and the Reserve was sent to seize it at 4 o'clock in the afternoon and by 8 o'clock this had been achieved without any resistance from the enemy and here as before, they found the guns spiked and the ammunition destroyed.

The next morning 3 February the first division crossed the river Gallion while the fourth brigade was posted a mile from the bridge of Noziere, on the river Noire. While the third brigade occupied the house of Mr Peltier, where the enemy had abandoned their provisions.

The French Governor, General Jean August Ernouf took up his position at Beaupere-Ste Louis ridge three miles from the sea in the highlands that overlooked the approach to Basse-Terre at 2,000 feet. A formidable place to defend it from, with the natural barriers of the river and mountains leaving Beckwith with little choice but to choose a route of attack across the river Noir and then through the mountains, which was heavily defended.

Brigadier-General Wale and the reserve were therefore instructed to carry out a demanding exercise during the night of the 3rd and attack the enemy from the rear. Beckwith gave Wale the orders and the route to take to achieve this end, but the wily Wale received intelligence of a shorter route and took it upon himself to take this route instead and without having time to inform Beckwith of the change. This new route was half the distance of the intended one but would have to be taken during daylight, due to its difficulty. Nevertheless, Wale undaunted decided on the spot to abandon the former plan and adopt this new revised one, and attack immediately. He had also noticed that the enemy was already engaged with Major General Thomas Hislop, who had brought his division of the army around to challenge Ernouf from the opposite direction, and so resolved to take advantage of this to accomplish his task. So by 4 o'clock, Major Henderson at the head of the Royal York Rangers, and Major Edden, with the Grenadier Battalion, were instructed to create a diversion and force the bridge, while the artillery were urged to take advantage of any opportunity that might appear. Wale and his staff, including Brereton, accompanied the Royal York Rangers as they proceeded to the banks of the river, meeting little resistance apart from a few random shots and shells. The pass of the River de la Pere was by nature very difficult but to add to this natural difficulty was the fact that the French had placed every possible obstruction in the way and erected Abbatis lined with snipers as they had on Martinique only the year before. These Abbatis were probably of the most rudimentary kind, comprising of trees half cut through and pushed over to impede the progress of the troops especially the movement of artillery while at the same time offering cover. On this occasion, the Royal York's forced their passage under musket fire, and crossed the river before dividing into two after 100 yards, with three companies leading the way, and holding their fire, while the remaining companies fired on the enemy from behind to give them cover. The further they climbed the steeper and more difficult the route became and to add to these difficulties 500 of the enemies best troops rained down hot lead upon them. Major Henderson, with three companies of the Royal Yorks, was first to ascend the heights, and found the enemy secured behind Abbatis and stockaded redoubts. These French Abbatis, with stockaded redoubts, were much more sophisticated than the earlier ones, and were usually composed of stakes driven into the ground, with a sharpened end facing skywards, and a trench dug out, and the earth piled high behind them where the soldiers could hide in the redoubt and fire down at the attacking troops with impunity. Major Henderson was however undeterred by this almost insurmountable obstacle, and the hazards involved and bravely lead his troops against these positions head on and without firing until within 25 yards and such was his audacity that the French were shocked and so taken by surprise that they were completely overrun. However, in doing so Major Henderson received a shot in the chest, which put him out of action. Nevertheless, his brave and decisive action was to earn him the approbation of his senior officers and a particular mention in dispatches urging for his promotion before the King, as Beckwith felt his merits were beyond mere praise. With the battle, now raging Brigadier-General Wale was also disabled, and both men were carried off the battle site to safety during the night. Captain Darling and Captain Stark, who would have rightly taken over command but they too were both also wounded in the ferocity of the mêlée. But this didn't dampen the Royals metal and they continued to engage the enemy, Brigade Major Brereton of Wale's Staff was noticed for his conspicuous meritorious conduct on this occasion, as being constantly involved at the front of the attack and was also to receive particular mention later in despatches. This brave and audacious attack upon the French was not without costs which including the aforementioned but also included four lieutenants killed, one field officer and four Captains wounded, and over 80 men killed and wounded. However, through this act of courageous daring, that completely took the French by surprise, it won the day. For while Hislop's men were attacking the front Harcourt's men came ashore to the north of Basse-Terre also outmanoevering the French at Trois Revieres, forcing them to fall back to Basse-Terre, which the Royal Navy gun battalions were now starting to bombard.

On 3 February as Governor, General Jean August Ernouf marched his men onto the plain of Matabar to drive the British back, only to realise that his flank was turned by General Wales's audacious attack and having been completely outmanoeuvred was left with no other option than to retreat. Beckwith was as surprised as Ernouf, as he was not expecting the rearguard action until nightfall but was fulsome in his praise. For the Reserve force had won the day, and had fought against insurmountable odds and against a well trained determined and a well dug in enemy with the added benefit of artillery. But due to their valiant and relentless pursuit of their goal, completely routed a superior enemy of 3,500, without a single piece of artillery at their disposal, and so it was, that this single action decided the campaign in Britain's favour, and would later result in a decisive British victory. Such victories however don't come cheap and the Royal York rangers suffered 120 casualties During the fighting. Wale himself was also seriously wounded, and suffered 40 casualties amongst his men though it is not recorded whether Thomas suffered any injuries. And while Ernouf was retreating, Fahie attacked and captured the capital Basse-Terre, cutting off Ernouf's retreat. And so on 4 February with his troops in disarray and surrounded, Ernouf asked for a truce to bury his dead and the next day the 5th, he surrendered.

The British dead numbered 52 with 250 injured while the French faired much worse with around 600 casualties and over 3,500 captured with all their armaments and their Regimental Imperial Eagle in British hands, the second one to be captured in the Napoleonic war and both by Lieutenant-General Beckwith's Troops in the West Indies. Unfortunately, the Brave and valiant Major Henderson who was instrumental in the success of this mission, succumbed to his wounds and died on 28 August 1810.

Captain Wilby, one of Beckwith's Aides-de-camp was entrusted with the captured eagles of the French 66th Regiment, along with the despatches.

Brigadier General Wales despatch contained a particular reference to the valour of Thomas Brereton;

"To the Staff of my brigade I feel much indebted: Brigade-Major Brereton was amongst the foremost in the attack, and continued with them all night;"

(Brigadier General Wales Despatch,
Morne Houel, February 5th 1810)

Back in Britain both Houses of Parliament pledged their thanks to the officers and men who fought so decisively in the conflict.

Beckwith was Knighted and Hislop and Cochrane promoted, Wale was made Governor of Martinique in recognition of his valiant service, and was later also Knighted. While Thomas, along with the others who served were later awarded the medal, the Battle Honour of Guadalupe 1810.

The fall of Guadalupe marked the end of French influence in the region and with it a boom in trade with the islands of the Caribbean, who saw a surge in there economies, although it had of course the reverse affect in France itself.

It was also the final nail in the coffin for the slave trade in the region, which had been banned by the British since 1807, and vigorously enforced by the Royal Navy.

1811 The Garrison at Surinam

In 1811 Major Thomas Brereton was placed in command of the left wing of the West Indian Rangers and preceded together with the new Governor of Surinam, Lt General Pinson Bonham to the colony. After arriving in the colony, the troops returned to humdrum garrison duties which is not an ideal occupation for troops who when idle became *"devils incarnate"*.

Surinam is on the north-eastern Atlantic coast of South America and was first colonised in 1630 by the British when Captain Marshall set about cultivating tobacco crops near the Surinam river at a place still called Marshall's creek. Later in 1651 the Governor of Barbados Lord Willoughby, supplied three ships with goods to build a fort (Fort Willoughby) and defences to defend the newly built plantation.

However, in 1667 the Dutch invaded with seven ships, and after three hours of fighting the Dutch took Fort Willoughby renaming it Fort Zeelandia. That same year the Dutch signed a treaty with the British where they exchanged their colony in North America – New Amsterdam – to the British, which the British renamed New York, after the ancient walled town of York the county town of Yorkshire. After this exchange, the British relinquished their claim on Surinam.

New Amsterdam had been the main Dutch slave trading colony in North America since 1624 when they started to import them to work on the Hudson Valley farms and so by 1655 it is estimated that 2,500 slaves were traded there annually.

As a slave-trading nation, the Dutch were comparatively minor players, having been responsible for trading an estimated 550,000-600,000 slaves. However, what they lacked in numbers they made up for with brutality. For Suriname under Dutch control gained a notorious reputation, which induced many slaves to escape and live with the native Indians in the surrounding forest, raiding the colony from time to time for supplies.

During the Napoleonic wars in 1799 when Holland was swallowed up and became part of the French inspired and later controlled Batavian republic, Surinam returned to British rule with a brief interruption in 1803 but after the battle of Surinam on 5 May 1804, it was again under British control.

Now in 1811 when Lt General Pinson Bonham became Governor and Commander in Chief, replacing the deceased Charles Bentinck, Earl of Bentinck. After his arrival Bonham was quoted as saying;

"I have stayed 21 years in the West Indies and in each colony I have heard a very heavy penalty it was to be sold into a plantation in Surinam, I think now that this is true. I have never been to a colony where slaves have been so badly treated, such bad food and such sober clothing and where they are forced to work so hard beyond their endurance."

(From a letter 8 June 1813 to Henry Bathurst 3rd Earl Bathurst, Secretary of State for War and the Colonies.)

An eyewitness account of life in Suriname can also be gained by reading the harrowing recollections of Captain John Gabriel Stedman of the Dutch Army. Born to a Scottish father and a Dutch mother he wrote of his arrival in Surinam 40 years earlier and relates about his senses being assailed by the sweet perfumed air as he gazed at the beautiful landscape, but contrasts this with the violence and cruelty he found there. He describes seeing a near naked slave woman, chained to a heavy iron weight, which she was forced to carry for a whole month after receiving 200 lashes. This was her punishment because she was unable to fulfil a task that had been demanded of her.

In his diaries, Stedman tells of many sexual encounters with slave girls, but in particular, a beautiful 15-year-old half-cast girl named Johanna the daughter of a respectable gentleman named Kruythoff and a slave woman.

When he later becomes ill, Johanna nurses him through his sickness showing him great kindness and devotion. Soon he falls deeply in love with her and later they have a son who they name Johnny who like his mother is born into slavery. Therefore,

Stedman tries to see if he can purchase their freedom and is offered them both for 2,000 florins, which equated to around £200. Later his unit is ordered back to Holland but Johanna, still only 19 years old refuses to return with him, saying she will only bring him shame back in western society. Johanna does not fare so well back in Surinam where she dies of suspected poisoning by jealous neighbours. Her freed brother Henry also suffers the same fate. Johnny now on his own sails to Holland to be with his father, but is not welcomed by his father's new Dutch wife and children, and so is sent to boarding school. On the completion of his education, he joins the Royal Navy where he served with distinction as a midshipman but dies off the coast of Jamaica aged just 17.

Details from; *Narrative of a five year expedition against the revolted negroes of Surinam*

In this book, he tells of many brutalities to the slaves in Surinam, the book is illustrated by William Blake who becomes a close friend and it is used to further the calls to abolish slavery. Stedman however, strangely approves of slavery throughout his writings, saying that though some slave master treat their slaves abominably, others treat them with great kindness, and that the English treat their slaves better than other nationalities.

In his 20th century critical biography of Stedman, Wayne Glausser claimed Stedman's favourable opinion of the English is due to him being;

"impressionistic and suspiciously patriotic".

Nevertheless, Stedman is not himself English, he is half Scottish and half Dutch and grew up in Holland and served as a Captain in the Dutch Army so I'm not sure how he can be accused of being patriotic to the English?

(Wayne Glausser, *Locke and Blake: A Conversation Across the Eighteenth Century.* Gainesville, FL: University Press of Florida. 1998. Page 77.)

This criticism of Stedman's account of life in Surinam however was even attempted at the time it was published. But its content was confirmed by many other accounts including another Dutchman, Marten Douwes Teenstra, who witnessed the same atrocities himself and wrote a book in 1835 entitled *Agriculture in the colony of Suriname* and *The Negro slaves in the colony Suriname,*1842.

I am sure we can find cases were the English and indeed the British in general badly treated their slaves but these were brutal times when everyone was treated in ways we would today find completely unacceptable. However, both Pinson Bonham and Stedman lived during slavery and so their accounts reflect what they thought, even at a time of widespread brutality.

Into this brutal and toxic environment, Major Brereton and the troublesome soldiers under him, now returned to garrison duties in contrast to the recent ardour and excitement of warfare

However, young troublesome men whose fighting prowess had so recently been honed in the white heat of battle now had more than just disease and the enemy to threaten their existence. For in this testosterone charged atmosphere these penal soldiers returned to type and any slight to a fellow soldier could end in violence or a challenge to a duel, as it did on 15 January for Captain Bordman of the Second Battalion 60th Regiment. When due to a trifling quarrel with a member of Major Thomas Brereton's Royal West Indian Rangers, Ensign De-Betton was tragically shot through the heart at the first firing, he died instantly. Captain Bordman did not wait around to see how he would be disciplined, deciding instead to desert and escape from the scene altogether before he was discovered.

(*Duelling in Great Britain and Ireland.*
14 March 1811. Page 204.)

Nevertheless, when virile young men are not fighting they turn their attention to their other preoccupation of course, Women!

Although many soldiers enjoyed the company of prostitutes, who were never very far away from a soldiers barracks, those of a more romantic disposition, who preferred to indulge in a more permanent relationship could also find a like minded lady even in such a harsh, though beautiful environment. This was to happen to one of Major Brereton's fellow officers on the island of Barbados on 14 April 1811, when Captain W. Whitmore A.D.C., who Thomas had served with in the Royal West Indian Rangers married the 23-year-old Margaret Anne Olton in the Parish of St James, Barbados. Margaret was born in Barbados and will appear later in the life of Thomas Brereton, an appearance that would be seminal, though sadly all too brief.

Though conflict had calmed down in the West Indies after the conquest of Guadalupe the Royal Navy was still kept busy as it continued to patrol and stop any vessels that might be supporting the French war effort, or any engaged breaking the British ban on the slave trade. This was to erupt on 18 June 1812 as conflict restarts in the region by a declaration of war on Great Britain by their former colony the United States of America. This war was a continuation of the Napoleonic war, as the USA and France were allies and was brought about by amongst other issues; restrictions imposed on American trade particularly with supplying France, anti-slave ship enforcement by the Royal Navy, together with British support of American Native Indians against settlers expansion into Indian territory.

In response, Major Thomas Brereton together with his regiment is moved to the garrison of Mount Bruce Dominique. However, on the 22nd and 23rd of July and later on 25 August 1813, a hurricane strikes with such force it raises the fort to the ground, blowing people off the cliffs to their deaths in the sea below, and driving ships upon the shore. Over 3,000 people are killed, and Thomas is so badly injured that he is sent back to England to recover.

After a long arduous journey, Thomas is now back in London and in the spring of 1814, excitement swept through the city after the latest news that France had been defeated! This was followed swiftly by the abdication of Napoleon in April and on the 20th the reinstated King Louis XVII could be seen in London on his triumphal procession from Hyde Park. In May 1814, as well as Thomas's 22nd birthday to celebrate, the first Treaty of Paris was signed, the war with France finally seemed to be over, Rejoice, Rejoice!

To celebrate, all the crowned heads of Europe together with their generals who were part of the allied coalition arrived at Boulogne and boarded *HMS Impregnable* on 6 June 1814 to take part in a state visit to London.

These included the Russian Tzar and the kings of Austria, Prussia, and Sweden as well as others from various German States. Later on 11 June the Prince Regent welcomed the honoured guests taking them to the Opera House at Covent Garden and a lavish dinner provided by the merchant bankers of the City of London. On 20 June, a review of 12,000 troops in London's Hyde Park before a battle of Trafalgar re-enactment takes place upon the Serpentine and all to the strains of the National Anthem.

However, these celebrations weren't just for the nobility and the military, there was also much for the general public to see and enjoy themselves. There were many stalls, arcades and kiosks, together with follies and pavilions erected with cake and pie shops and taverns, to provide the public with refreshment. While military bands, acrobats, swings and roundabouts provided entertainment.

Later in July an announcement was made that in Green park on 1 August:

"It is the pleasure of HRH the Prince Regent to declare a Grand Jubilee in celebration of the recent victory over Napoleon culminating in the present Glorious Peace and in honour of the Centennial of Hanoverian rule."

Those who gathered there, were amazed to see Mr James Sadler a pioneering hot air balloon inventor who in 1784 was the first Englishman ever to fly in his *"fire balloon"*, now climb into the basket of his latest invention the gas balloon rising into the air far above the delighted crowds to open the festivities. Once air born he dropped programmes and favours as mementos of the occasion down to the cheering populace below. This was followed after dark by the military inventor of Congreves Rocket, Colonel Sir William Congreve, Second Baronet. The Colonel had constructed a Castle of Discord that disappeared behind a cloud of smoke and flames, only to reappear as the Temple of Concord whose upper part revolved to reveal in glorification the apotheosis of the Prince Regent and the triumph of England. While Congreve's fireworks lit up the scene in a blaze of colour, smoke and noise.

With all this triumphal praise of the military happening all over town, the soldier was now looked up to with even more pride and admiration. Thomas was now 22 years old and perhaps had recovered enough to start enjoying some of these festivities. He was living in Mayfair not far from Hyde Park and the other London parks where many of these celebrations were happening. Therefore, even if he was too ill to attend, he would certainly have heard them. There is evidence to suggest however that at least later in the year he was well enough to meet people. For Thomas, who was now in his prime and lucky enough to be in the capital just as the soldier was greatly appreciated, must have delighted in the praise for his chosen profession. He certainly cut a dashing figure in his red uniform as he strode the streets and taverns of London receiving the approbation of his fellow citizens, and so it comes as no surprise to learn that he soon catches the eye of a young lady called Catherine Bowe.

However, as the year ends and 1815 begins, these celebrations now seemed somewhat premature, because in February Napoleon escaped from Elba and resumed the throne of France, in a period known as the "Hundred days of Napoleon".

Nevertheless, four months later he was decisively and finally defeated at the battle of Waterloo in June 1815. He abdicated five days later and on 15 July he boards *HMS Bellerophon* off Rochefort, France and surrenders to Captain Frederick Maitland of the Royal Navy before he is taken far way to the remote island of St Helena in mid Atlantic and his finale exile. After which there is a final victory parade in Hyde Park of over 15,000 troops together with other celebrations and spectacles. No doubt, young Thomas would have participated in these celebrations and witnessed these spectacles perhaps even with Catherine by his side. Though Thomas was still an officer of his Majesty, and on the 20th July 1815, he is promoted to the rank of Lieutenant Colonel of the Royal Africa Corps.

However, later in the month we get an insight as to what Thomas and Catherine have been doing in his months convalescing, for on 31 August 1815 at St Georges, Hanover Square, Mayfair a baptism is recorded. It states that the father, Lt Colonel Thomas Brereton was living in Duke Street Mayfair and the mother is Catherine Bowe. Thomas junior seems to have been a "natural son" for I can find no record of any marriage. Perhaps Catherine Bowe was not of a class high enough for the well-connected Thomas to contemplate marriage to, or perhaps he promised marriage and then changed his mind, whatever the circumstances were, we simply do not know. However, one thing is certain; Thomas Brereton was now the father of a son and namesake. You might find it strange that a natural child could be baptised in a church, but in the Church of England, it was not only allowed, it was demanded under Cannon Law 68 and any clergy refusing could be suspended.

Sexual attitudes were also very liberal in Georgian and now Regency society, which everyone enjoyed fully without the later restrictions of the Victorians. Contraception was limited to crude condoms or various potions of herbs. The condoms were made out of linen soaked in a chemical or sometimes made of animal intestines, a method that had been in use for centuries. The famous Italian womanizer Casanova used them and referred to them as his "*English riding coat*". Nevertheless, whether you used a condom or a potion they were both fairly ineffective and so if you did indulge in sex, it was, as in this case usually followed by a pregnancy.

Therefore, a lot had happened since his arrival back in England, a son, promotion, and then he is further rewarded with the prestigious position as Governor of Senegal and Goree on the west coast of Africa. In November Lt Colonel Brereton and the Royal Africa Corps board the military transport ship the *Spring*. He is also joined on board by Major Piddie of the 12th Foot and Captain Campbell of the Royal Staff Corps along with Staff Surgeon Cowdrey. These last mentioned men under the Command of Major Piddie are to mount an expedition into the interior of Africa from its western coast to the river Niger.

1815 Senegal and Goree

Senegal is on the west coast of Africa which the British had captured in 1809 and installed Lt Colonel Charles William Maxwell as Governor. He remained until 1811, when Lt Colonel Charles McCarthy became Governor and served until May 1814 when the First Treaty of Paris was signed. This only lasted until Napoleon escaped from Elba in February 1815 and resumed the throne of France, However, he was finally defeated at the battle of Waterloo in June 1815 and a month later in July Thomas Brereton was promoted to Lt Colonel of the Royal Africa Corps and he became the third and last British Governor of Senegal. In November, the Second Treaty of Paris was signed. Which amongst other agreements also consolidated the British attitude regarding the issue of slavery by an addition which stated;

"The entire and definitive abolition of commerce so odious, and so strongly condemned by the laws of religion and of nature."

The island of Goree lies just off the mainland of Senegal, and has a tropical climate with only two seasons. The rainy season from June to October, which is hot, humid and stormy. And the hot dry season from November to May, where a cool ocean breeze and a dry and dusty west African trade wind, called the Harmattan, blows in fine sand from the Sahara. Temperatures can fluctuate wildly from very warm during the day to very cold at night.

This climate just like in the West Indies was not very healthy for Europeans particularly during the rainy season where Yellow Fever and Malaria were rife. The main town called St Louis is built on a rocky sandbank in the middle of the river Senegal about six miles from the river mouth. It is about two and a half miles long, and less than half a mile wide. The population at this time was 10,000, 500 of which were Europeans. They lived in about 150 houses of one storey built of brick, while the natives lived in traditional straw huts. The spacious streets were unpaved and often full of sand blown in from the Sahara by the desert winds which permeates everything, making it difficult to walk or breath; and where the narrower streets could become completely blocked and impassable

Lt Colonel Thomas Brereton arrived to replace Lt Colonel Charles McCarthy the former Governor who had left to take up his new post as Governor of Sierra Leone just as the previous Governor Maxwell had. Sierra Leone had been the centre for the British Naval campaigns against the slave trade since it was abolished and was also the site of the British anti-slavery arbitration court, as well as a site for resettling freed slaves. Goree itself is now famed as the centre of distribution during the slave trade, with its "House of Slaves", receiving many visitors each year, especially from the USA, including in 2013, President Obama, their first black president. However, Professor Raymond Mauny from the Sorbonne University in Paris has discredited this assumption, for in fact he discovered that only a few hundred slaves left from Goree and it was never a centre of distribution.

The Governors house in Senegal was, as one might expect, a little grander than the others available. It also had gardens stocked with many plants and vegetables, a vine, and even three fig trees. But in the poor soil and the hot, sand laden winds however, not all theses plants thrived, only those that were sheltered by walls. But though the accommodation itself might have been more appealing, this same climate that withered the plants was also a problem for ones health. Few Europeans could resist an attack of fever at sometime during their first two years, this was called "seasoning". Even those who had served in the West Indies as Brereton had, or in other parts of Africa like the Cape, were still not protected against this. In fact no one was immune to its effects even the black settlers and non commissioned officers resettled from Nova Scotia. For it had been noted, that those arriving from these places still fell victims, just as those arriving straight from Europe had. In addition, some of the white troops unused to such a climate took no care to keep out of the sun or the cold and wet and the excessive consumption of alcohol only exacerbated this. For after their rations were distributed on the 24th of the month they were often so drunk that they couldn't walk back to the barracks and would sleep in the grass where they fell, only to wake up drenched by the rain. Even the ones who made it home would often wake up hot and soaking with perspiration in their beds and so would seek cooler air outside to sleep. However, due to their stupor, they would not be sensitive to the cold that overtook them and so fever would quickly follow. One of the reasons that the men would drink themselves into stupefaction was to dull a clear perception of their dire situation.

The Royal Africa Corp was, as been stated, a penal regiment, composed of criminals and military miscreants from all the other regiments who had received a pardon on the condition that they served with the Royal Africans for life. However, once the reality of their existence became all too evident and was even more forlorn than many had ever imagined, with no exit except death, so far away forever from their country, families and friends, the lonely desperation of which, drove many to try and obliterate this and find comfort in excessive drinking and often declaring;

"a short life but a merry one".

Trying to discipline these desperate men was a difficult problem for any officer unlucky enough to be in command of them. In the 19th century, discipline was swift and merciless, even for minor misdemeanours and involved flogging in front of the regiment, which on average could exceed 1,000 lashes. There were also public firing squads or hangings for more serious crimes. Colonel Brereton would have been no different to his contemporaries in this respect and availed himself of these methods to maintain order and discipline. Nevertheless, even the death penalty held no fear for some of them as their life expectancy here was so short and even if they tried to return to Britain, they still risked execution on their capture. Only five years earlier in September 1810 a large section of the newly arrived soldiers had planned to mutiny and take control of the colony before deserting to America. Fortunately, the plans were discovered before they could be brought into affect and 15 of the ringleaders were tried and shot while several others implicated were removed from the colony to

Sierra Leone where they not only had disciplined regular troops but also a large militia to stop any recurrence. Major Maxwell wrote in his dispatch of 30 September 1810 about the situation and begged the Secretary of State not to send such desperate men to such a remote location without any regular force to prevent the reoccurrence of such unpleasant situations. However, the Major's warning were not heeded, even more pressingly, Governor Columbine of Sierra Leone refused to let them land and they were ordered to return to Senegal. Therefore, Major Maxwell had no alternative but to return them to their companies with the only measure available to him was to try and keep them under strict observation. As a result of this, Lt Colonel Torrens sent a letter in December 1810 to Robert Peel the Under-Secretary for War and the Colonies, requesting that Governor Columbine be instructed not to resist the redistribution of the miscreants amongst the regular disciplined troops to prevent any further mutinies. Maxwell was promoted to Lt Colonel in December 1810 and continued as Governor until he was appointed Governor of Sierra Leon and so was replaced as Governor of Senegal, by Lt Colonel McCarthy in 1811. Maxwell returned to England in July 1814 while McCarthy replaced him as Governor of Sierra Leone, but returned to Senegal in December to arrange the restoration of the Colony to France, under the recently signed Treaty of Paris, but this of course was postponed after Napoleon resumed the throne in March 1814. So in July 1815, Governor McCarthy returned to Sierra Leone only to find that of the four officers, who acted as Governor in his absence, two were now dead and the third Captain W. Appleton of the RAC was invalided back to England, only Captain Hyde of the West India Regt was still fit and active. As well as the deaths of these two officers in Sierra Leone there were also 23 Europeans and three African deaths amongst the non commissioned officers and men, totalling altogether 28 deaths in total during the year 1815. During this same year the death rate in Senegal and Goree is even higher with; two officers and 27 European NCO's and men together with two Africans in Senegal itself and 35 European and one African in Goree, a total of 67 deaths all in just the one year.!

(Details from; *Historical Records of the Royal African Corps;* by Major J.J. Crooks. Page 95–96.)

Lt Colonel Brereton had been lucky during his service in the West Indies, for though many of his comrades fell like flies around him, he managed to escape without fatal infection. Nevertheless, would his luck hold out here in Senegal when so many others had succumbed?

However, disease was not the only problem that he would face in Senegal, for as has been said he was still being supplied with the same class of soldiers in the RAC as Maxwell had complained of five years earlier. This resulted in a repetition of events while he was preceding to the colony in December 1815 with Major Piddie and Captain Campbell on board the military transport ship the *Spring*. During this voyage, yet another mutiny was frustrated after Brereton discovered that the mutineers were planning to murder him and the other officers before taking over the ship and sailing to freedom. Brereton acted swiftly and decisively and so the mutiny was put down before their plan could be implemented and those guilty were put in irons below deck. After they arrived in Senegal, the mutineers were taken ashore before being loaded onto the cutter *Active* embarking for Sierra Leone, but during this transfer they again attempted to mutiny and take possession of the vessel, but Brereton ever vigilant, managed to suppress the uprising and arrest several of the ringleaders who were later tried and condemned to death. However, before permission had arrived to carry out the sentence, they had already died under the relentless burning sun and the harsh climate.

(Details from; *Historical Records of the Royal African Corps;* by Major J.J. Crooks. Page 120.)

(And report in; *The Manchester Mercury*, Tuesday 30 April 1816.)

Nevertheless, Colonel Brereton, by a combination of firm discipline and fair leadership managed somehow to turn this desperate rabble of felons and ne're- do-wells into something approaching a disciplined military force and while he was engaged in this and the day-to-day running of the colony, a little expedition was setting forth from France.

For on 17 June 1816 at seven in the morning, a fleet of four French ships left the island of Aix on the west coast of France under the command of Captain Chaumareys in the frigate *Medusa*. It was from the island of Aix that Napoleon Bonaparte had finally surrendered, almost a year before in July 1815 after his escape from the battle of Waterloo the month before. King Louis XVIII of the Bourbon dynasty was then restored to the French throne and the Treaty of Paris was signed in November of that year in which the restoration of French colonies seized by the British was arranged.

Senegal was one such a colony and Viscount Hugues Duroy de Chaumareys was appointed as Commander in the flagship *Medusa*. This was more of a political appointment than for his knowledge or expertise as a naval man, and this was to have disastrous consequences. The new French Governor, Colonel Julien-Désiré Schmaltz and his wife Reine were also lacking in the necessary skills for this appointment and were somewhat selfish and arrogant, this would become apparent later in the voyage. A portent of what was to come occurred only five days later on the 22nd when a 15-year-old sailor fell into the sea and despite efforts to save him he was finally lost from sight and was never seen again.

These shortcomings were further to manifest themselves on 2 July when a supposed sighting of Cape Blanco was spotted, though others thought it was just a cloud of vapour. This supposed sighting of the cape was an indication to head west to avoid the notorious Airguin Bank. But Richefort persuaded the Captain that a more direct course he had chosen was correct and that he should do as directed and the officers of the ship were loath to offend de Charmareys by disputing his man's competence.

One of the passengers a Mr Picard, who had struck the Airguin Bank some eight years previously also voiced his concern. It was at this moment that ensign Maudet who was on watch, took a reckoning of the ships position and confirmed the worried gentlemen's concerns and reported to Richford that they were in fact on the edge of the reef. The Captain immediately altered course but the soundings now showed only six fathoms and not long after the ship ran aground. Efforts were made to free the ship, but as it had struck while at the high spring tide there would not be enough water beneath her again to help in her release until the next high tide, and so she would surely break up.

The only solution for them was to endeavour to continue the 60 miles to the shore in the ships boats, but that posed another problem as there were only six boats with space to carry 250 people but the *Medusa* had 400 including 160 crew. Therefore, to remedy this, the French Governor in waiting, decided that they should build a raft that would carry 150 men and their provisions which would be towed by the boats to the shore. These Provisions were hastily gathered on the decks, but in the confusion and haste most of it was left there, with only a large quantity of wine but no food and little water loaded onto the raft. One hundred and fifty souls embarked on this crudely constructed craft, which was three feet beneath the water at one end and even the middle section was awash, amongst these were one lone woman, who was the wife of one of the men. In contrast, Governor Schmalts was lowered reverentially into the best boat in a comfortable grand chair in which he sat giving orders.

The Governor his family and friends, including their luggage, travelled in relative comfort aboard the largest boat with 14 oars and yet only 35 people in total. The other boat, also with 14 oarsmen but without luggage, managed 42 people, and even the smaller Captain's gig took 28. But the worse boat was the long boat, which was in very bad condition, and possessed no oars whatsoever, but managed to squeeze in an astonishing 88. However, 17 men refused to board her as she was leaking at every seam, preferring to take their chance remaining on the stricken ship. This flotilla together with two other small boats all made their way from the *Medusa* promising to send help as soon as they landed on the coast. The overcrowded boat tried to unload some of their passengers onto some of the other boats, but all refused. It was not long however, before the inpatient Schmaltz grew tired of the drag that the raft was imposing on his boats progress, which he felt was just impeding their passage. After a distance of just six miles the ropes attaching them were purposefully let lose and they were left to the mercy of the ocean. Those on the raft thought that the rope had broken, and called out to alert those who were towing them, but the boats took no notice and continued to pull away from them. The poor wretches on the raft raised the French flag, and cried out *Vive le Roi* in an effort to awaken the patriotic conscience of their deserters, particularly Mr Chaumareys. Nevertheless, he just waved his hat dismissively in the air as the boats pulled further away in silence, broken only by the tortured cries of the people left on the raft, which grew more desperate as they realised that they were being abandoned to their fate.

Some days later and unaware of this tragedy being enacted off the coast, Governor Brereton was surprised to see three French ships arriving at Senegal claiming to be there to receive the Colony into French position, yet the new Governor and his flag-ship were nowhere to be seen. Therefore, the *Echo* corvette was sent to search for them and on the ninth not far from St Louis, the two boats carrying governor Schmaltz and Chaumareys were spotted and they were hauled on board. After they reached Senegal on board the *Echo*, it was then decided that the *Argus* should be sent to search for any other survivors, but the uncaring Schmaltz saw no urgency thinking most were dead anyway.

However, they were not, they had all somehow managed to land ashore at different times and places along the coast and by pure luck had managed to find each other and so it was decided that they should all join forces and find their own way to Senegal across the desert. However, it was soon noticed that the women and children were slower than the men, and after some time it was realised that a certain number were talking about leaving them behind. Mr Picard, whose family of course were all women and children, remonstrated with the ringleaders, and a hot dispute erupted that got so heated that some of the soldiers drew their sabres. Captain Bégnère of the infantry stepped forward and declared as Frenchmen, they could not abandon their fellow countrymen in the desert and should assist them instead. Fortunately, at this point providence shone on them and they encountered some Moors who traded them some asses to help transport the children and women and they also agreed to guide them across the desert to Senegal. On 11 July they reached another part of the coast, and after their tired asses had run into the surf to cool themselves, they continued their journey until a ship was seen just out to sea. The ship came in as close as it could, making it just possible for the brave Moors to swim out to it, and bring back barrels of wine and brandy, along with cheese and biscuits, as well as a letter from the Captain of the ship. The ship turned out to be the *Argus,* who were now searching for the raft and its survivors. After leaving the boat survivors with fresh supplies the *Argus* continuing along the coast for several days searching for the raft until the captain decided it was hopeless, and they should return to Senegal. For as with most people in St Louis, he too also though that they all must be dead. However, while returning, to their surprise and delight, they spotted the raft by chance and picked up the survivors, some of whom were only barely alive. It was now 17 July 1816 and of the 150 souls condemned to the raft only 15 remained and some of these looked closer to death than life after 13 days adrift and reduced to cannibalism to survive. There is a famous painting depicting the survivors being rescued, by the French artist Théodore Géricault called *The Raft of the Medusa*.

Now safely aboard the *Argus* the ship continued on its course for St Louis and cast anchor at 3 o'clock in the afternoon of 19 July.

Governor Brereton after being told of their arrival sent a large decked boat to convey them to St Louis and met them at the port along with several officers including some of their French compatriots. All those present, both English and French, were stunned to see their deplorable condition and many openly wept. But though weak, the survivors couldn't control their indignation to one of the French officers who held out his hand to them, one of the same hands that had caste them adrift to the mercy of the sea only two weeks before. All these raft survivors were placed in the hospital, but alas, too late to save some of them, for five died soon after landing. Governor Schmaltz arrived in the evening to see them and promised them all a guinea, and that all their needs would be met, but in fact, they received no money, and none of their needs were met by him. Others who were not in need of hospital attention were offered help by two French merchants Messrs Valentin and Lasalle. Later the raft survivor and surgeon Henri Savigny, complained about Governor Brereton's refusal to hand over the colony, accusing him of holding on to it so that the British merchants could have the benefits from the gum trade which was due to be commenced. It's possible Governor Brereton was loath to hand over the Colony to such a badly organised party who arrived in such great disorder and possibly wondered if such a rabble could run a colony when it couldn't even organise its own arrival properly. Savigny also came up with other possibilities, but in truth and despite Brereton's reservation about their competence, the reason were more likely to have been what he stated at the time, that he was still waiting for his orders to do so.

Meanwhile the boat survivors, who had been resupplied by the *Argus,* rested and had a meal from the supplies they had been given, and were greatly enrich, both physically and mentally. After this meal and a short rest, they then commenced their journey over the hot sands until six in the evening when Mr Picard started to feel very tired and wished to rest, his daughters and his wife agreed to stay with him, as the rest continued their journey. The three of them soon fell into a deep sleep. When they awoke some time later they were alarmed to see no sign of their companions, but as the sun was sinking in the West, to their alarm they saw several Moors mounted on camels approaching them. Mr Picard reproached himself for succumbing to his fatigue and allowing his wife and daughters to be exposed to such danger, and though they wanted to flee, the women were far to exhausted. As the Moors drew closer they could see their long beards and the terrified party feared the worst. One of the Moors dismounted and approaching them was heard to say:

"Be comforted, ladies; under the costume of an Arab, you see an Englishman who is desirous of serving you. Having heard at Senegal that Frenchmen were thrown ashore on these deserts, I

thought my presence might be of some service to them, as I was acquainted with several of the princes of this arid country."

So these poor wretches abandoned by their own countrymen were rescued in the burning desert by an Englishman, a Mr Carnet, a national of their former enemy. This party who had been convinced of their imminent demise were stunned to hear this declaration, but much relieved, they gratefully accepted the help and food he offered them. After this interruption, they carried on their relentless trek, through what appeared to them to be the base of some vast furnace. After some time they were able to rejoin their fellow survivors, before finding some respite under the shade of a desert acacia tree, in an effort to find some relief. However, to no avail, the sand beneath them was still burning hot, and the very air around them felt almost unbreathable. Mr Picard's eldest daughter looked up to the fiery sky and thought she had breathed her last, even wishing for the sweet release of death. Noticing her anguish, one of her fellow survivors a Mr Borner approached her with an old boot, which he had brought with him to carry water, and offered it to her. She grasped it gratefully, and poured the brown liquid into her mouth, and swallowed in large draughts to the envy of her companions, one of whom grabbed the boot in his turn, but the water left was so disgusting he could not swallow it; one wonders if it was any worse than the water just swallowed by Mademoiselle Picard.

After two more days of relentless strife across the burning sands of the desert their pace quickened with anticipation as they ascended a little rise and to their delight, they found the river Senegal lying before them shaded by lush green trees which housed brightly plumed parakeets and humming birds. This sight brimming with life and colour was such a contrast to the arid featureless desert to which they had become accustomed, that they stopped and looked breathless and spellbound by its rich exotic beauty.

After being led to a fresh steam by Mr Carnet to quench their thirst they relaxed in a shady grove while he went the rest of the way to St Louis and announce their arrival to Governor Brereton who arranged for them to be transported across the river to the capital St Louis. Moreover, at four o'clock the boats of the Governor arrived to pick them up with refreshment for all, on the two-hour journey to St Louis. The Picard family were on board a boat captained by a Mr Artigue captain of the port and an old friend of Mr Picard, who had already arrived earlier while the boats were being prepared, and provided them with provisions while they waited. He now returned with the flotilla to pick up the bedraggled but happy survivors, who after taking further refreshments sat and relaxed as the boats proceeded slowly to their destination. As the sight of the destination that they had fought so hard to see appeared, it filled them with delight and anticipation. Fine buildings and lush vegetation hove into sight, but as they grew nearer it seemed to dissolve like a desert mirage into the reality of a poor and ramshackle colony, not with fine buildings but soot blackened straw huts.

At six in the evening, they disembarked at the Port of St Louis to be received by the whole population, including Governor Brereton who arrived on horseback with several British officers and Mr Carnet. Governor Brereton was very moved by the fate of these poor wretches particularly the women and children, as were the people of the colony both black and white. Conspicuous by their absence were the new French governor in waiting and the French Commander of this disastrous expedition, who were nowhere to be seen. Governor Brereton immediately ordered that the sick be taken to the hospital and arranged for the rest to be housed by the local inhabitants. Mr Picard's friend Mr Artigue took the Picard family to his house but as there were many, Mademoiselles Picard and her sister Caroline were eagerly taken by two English women to the house of Mr and Mrs Kingsley, who received them very graciously. The two young ladies were taken to their quarters and were bathed and cosseted and dressed in fine linen from the ladies own wardrobe, the whiteness of which contrasted so markedly with the burned parched skin of the two French mademoiselles. After they had finished they returned downstairs to find the master of the house sitting at the dinning table with several English officers in conversation. On their entrance, all the men stood in deference to the ladies, as they were asked to join them by the master of the house for tea. One of these officers turned out to be French and was able to translate for them. So the two ladies related their sad and arduous journey, but the food they were offered after starving for so long, was still difficult to consume and all they could manage was to pick at some pastries and to sip some tea. The officers were astonished when they heard the story unfold, hardly believing that women and young children could have endued such depredations. The toll upon these two young ladies soon manifested itself however when they started to feel faint and complained of still feeling the vast ocean rising before them and the endless hot dessert sand which they had relentlessly struggled to cross. The officers noticing their malady and realising that the girls needed some rest decided it was time for them to leave. Therefore, the lady of the house took them up to their rooms, where they slid between crisp white sheets in a proper bed for the first time in weeks, and it wasn't long before they drifted contentedly into a deep and sound sleep.

The next morning, refreshed from their first uninterrupted sleep in a proper bed, the girls washed and dressed before visiting their father and the rest of their family. After returning to the Kingsley's, the girls were shown to the table where breakfast had been prepared for them and a stilted conversation began, as neither knew the others language, but some how they managed. It was shortly after breakfast that they learned that Governor Brereton had indeed not received any orders from England to give up the colony to the French. It was just at this time that there father arrived, to inform them that the French Governor in waiting, Schmaltz, had ordered him to go and take his whole family to Cape Verde nearly 200 miles away, until this matter was resolved. On hearing this all were affected, not least the Kingsley's who said they would not part with their new guests and would ask Governor Brereton's advice as to what he could do. The very next day, Governor Brereton's aide-de-camp arrived, and said that the Governor after seeing the wretched condition of the Picard family would give them all permission to stay in Senegal, including all the officers of *The Medusa* too. Two day before Schmaltz left, he was visited by Mr Correard one of the raft survivors, who heard him discussing sending a party to the wreck of the *Medusa* to retrieve the 100,000 francs on board that had been intended for the colonies treasury. As he heard this discussion Mr Correard was perturbed that no one had mentioned the 17 men who had been left on the wreck and whom they had promised earnestly that they would send a rescue party as soon as they reached land, yet now, they were forgotten and only the money was mentioned. He then spoke up about this, but the reply from someone in the room was:

"Pooh, seventeen! There are not three left. And if there remained but three, but one," replied he.

Mr Correard was very angry at such a callous remark, and replied that even if is just one was left, his life is more valuable than anything else on board the wreck, after which he left in disgust.

It was 52 days after the ship was wrecked that the rescue party finally arrived and to their amazement, three men *were* still alive. These survivors, who had been callously forgotten, were nothing more than living skeletons and two died soon after. The remaining one was murdered in his bed just before he was due to return to Paris and relate his tragic tale, the murderer was never found. When Schmaltz left for Cape Verde, the officers who were fit, felt duty bound to obey their own French Governor and so many reluctantly had to turn down Governor Brereton's generous offer and left for Camp Deccard at Cape Verde where many were to die of tropical diseases.

After twenty days at the houses of Mr Artigue and Mr and Mrs Kingsley, Mr Picard was worried that they might be too much of a burden on their generous hosts, so on 1 August they all moved into a small flat to the great reluctance of their erstwhile benefactors. Mr Picard then sent a letter to Governor Schmatlz asking if he could have some supplies for his family from the French administration, but an angry Schmaltz refused. Unable to source any help from the French administration or from anywhere else, Mr Picard was forced to borrow money and with so little for food, he could only afford the basic native meal of wheat granules for his family to survive. However, just as the meal was being prepared, Major Peddie of the 12th regiment of foot arrived unexpectedly just as the table had been set for dinner. He was astonished to see the family eating so poorly, saying; "How, Mr Picard? You being in the employment of your government, and living so meanly!" Mr Picard was very embarrassed to be seen providing such a poor meal for his family, but fighting back his tears, he replied that though he had requested the ration from Governor Schmaltz that were his right, he had been refused. He continued, trying to maintain his dignity by saying, just because they could not afford the food of the other Europeans in the colony they were still content with what they had.

Major Peddie much moved with what he had seen, and feeling only sympathy, but also noticing how he had embarrassed poor Mr Picard, apologised for his indiscretions, bid his farewell and left. The good Major however, who had travelled to Senegal with Lt Colonel Brereton was not going to leave the matter as it was, and immediately informed the now Governor Brereton. Who in turn, was so distressed to hear that this poor family who had suffered so much, should even now be suffering further. Therefore, he called in the Mayor, Mr Dubois, and made a proposal to him to alleviate Mr Picard's family from any more suffering. Mayor Dubois arrived at the Picard's home the very next day, and laid before them the Governors proposal to an astonished and very grateful man and his family. Governor Brereton proposal was to allot to Mr Picard, an English officer's allowance, of meat and bread, sugar, coffee, and wine and many other necessities. An amazed but very grateful Mr Picard readily excepted this generous offer, and within two hours it had all been delivered to his home. When word of the Families hardships spread around the colony even the poor negroes came with offers of eggs, and beans, and milk, yet the odious, arrogant, and lavishly appointed Schmaltz, who had been the mastermind of their misfortune offered them nothing.

Not as grateful however, were the French still housed in the Hospital, who were given standard British soldiers rations, but complained to Governor Brereton that though no doubt fit for fighting men, It was not good enough for men who had been through such depravations. In response to their pleas, the men were invited to dine with the British officers, whose offer they graciously accepted, dinning with them from then on. The survivors also received no aid from the French Minister of Marine when they applied for help to return to France. Therefore, these same British officers stepped in and raised the funds to help them get back to France.

Major Peddie who had earlier travelled to Sierra Leone to consult Governor McCarthy about his planned expedition into the interior from its western coast to the river Niger arrived back in Senegal in February 1816. The expedition left Senegal on 17 November 1816 and consisted of soldiers and civilians numbering 100 men and a train of 200 animals. They planned to travel into the interior to Kakundy to visit the King of Sego. However, before leaving, Staff Surgeon Cowdrey, one of his party, was struck down with the harsh climate and died. Major Peddie continued on the expedition but shortly after he arrived in Kakundy, he along with all the Europeans were struck down, and on 1 January he too died. The remaining expedition members were to succumb, one by one, Lieutenant Macrae of the Royal African Corps on 22 January, Mr Adolphus Kummer (naturalist) 1 June, and Captain Campbell 13 June, along with five other non-commissioned officers and soldiers, with all the Europeans dying before 12 July 1817.

(*Historical Records of the Royal African Corps;*
By Major J.J. Crooks. Page 99 and 102.)

The remaining British officers in Senegal were paid up until Tuesday 24 December 1816, and issued with passage money to return to Britain. However, Governor Brereton's luck finally ran out and he was also struck with the climatic malady, and like Captain Appleton before him invalided back to England, before he was due to surrendered the colony to the French on 25 January 1817.

The remaining detachment of the Royal Africa Corps comprising of:

1 Major,
2 Captains,

3 Lieutenants,
3 Ensigns,
1 Quarter Master,
1 assistant Surgeon,
20 Sergeants,
9 Drummers,
and 235 rank and file

embarked aboard the transport ships *Brilliant, London, and James* leaving on 14 May bound for Cape Town.

The total number of deaths in Senegal and Goree in 1816 during Lt Colonel Brereton's Governorship were;
2 officers
82 European Nco's
11 Africans
= 95 men in total

(*Historical Records of the Royal African Corps*;
By Major J.J. Crooks. Page 99.)

Based on two original French narratives from the survivors of the wreck and the records of the Royal African Corp which are;

Narrative of a voyage to Senegal 1816; By J.B. Henry Savigny.

The sufferings of the Picard family after the shipwreck of the Medusa, in the year 1816. By Charlotte-Adélaïde (née Picard).

(Further details from; *Historical Records of the Royal African Corps;* By Major J.J. Crooks.)

1817 Scarlett Fever, London

After yet another long journey, back to England in bad health Thomas Brereton was pleased to land once more in London, where in the healthier climate and with better doctors to serve him, he soon regained his health. Some time around January/February 1817, Thomas was feeling well enough to make the acquaintance of yet another young lady. Her name was Mary Harriet Pellett, who just like the young lady he met the last time he was in London must have also caught the *"scarlet fever"*, this was a popular saying at the time to describe the allure of a dashing soldier in his redcoat. In any case, she soon followed her predecessor in another respect too, as she also quickly became pregnant. Again, we can find no record of a marriage, so perhaps she too was socially or financially beneath him. Soldiers had a terrible reputation with women, as this popular song of the time illustrates.

In Woolwich town I courted Jane,
Her sister, and her mother,
I mean when I was there, they
Were jealous of each other.
Our orders came, I had to start,
I left poor Jane with a broken heart,
Then straight to Colchester did depart
The gay and rambling soldier.

The King permission granted me,
To range the country over,
From Colchester to Liverpool,
From Plymouth down to Dover.
And in whatever town I went,
To court all damsels I, was bent,
And marry none was my intent,
But live a rambling Soldier.

19th century English Folk song

Perhaps due to the harshness of life and his narrow escape from death he had adopted a *Carpe diem* approach to life. For nevertheless, despite his intimate relationship with Mary Pellett it was not long before he renewed his acquaintance with yet another and perhaps to him a more suitable lady. For later in the year he met an old friend, Mrs Margaret Whitmore, the now widow of his former comrade and friend Major W. Whitmore. Unfortunately, her marriage to Major Whitmore had only lasted six years and by 1815, she was widowed. Her husband had died in July of that year on the island of St Thomas, (now one of the US Virgin Isles) and a former Danish settlement seized by the British in 1801. Thomas Brereton had been himself involved in this action when he first went to the West Indies. His relationship with the widowed Mrs Whitmore was to become more serious though. She was the eldest daughter of the late John Allen Olton of Marylebone London. He had owned a plantation of 380 acres called Allen's in St Philip Parish, Barbados, which he had left to his son John. In addition, another in Surinam together with slaves that he left to his brother Henry in trust to be sold, so they were a very wealthy and well-connected family. After her father's death she had been left £10,000 in his will dated 1809, as was her younger sister Lady Rebecca Alleyn who also gained a title after having married in 1810 Sir Reynold Alleyne, Bart., the year before her fathers will was proved. £10,000 was quite a large amount to have inherited and is equivalent to almost half a million pounds in today's money.

Therefore, Margaret Olton was a very well connected and wealthy young woman and so one suspects, in Thomas's eyes a more suitable companion.

Nevertheless, on 28 October 1817 Mary Harriet Pellett gives birth to a son and he is named William Pellett Brereton, William, perhaps after Thomas's father, and he has his mother Mary's surname as his second name as was the custom of the time. The Brereton's had practised this custom for years and Thomas would continue it with his other children, as would William. The Pellett family must have been very important to this part of the family as their name is continued as a second name for at least three generations. William Pellett Brereton was to grow up and become my great great grandfather.

So along with the autumnal weather came yet another natural son, so perhaps Thomas felt it was time he married and put an end to his dalliances. After all, he now had two sons from two different women and he could not continue behaving in this fashion. Therefore, by the time Christmas comes along, he proposes to Margaret Anne Whitemore and she accepts.

Thomas now seemed in an indecent haste to get married. As curiously, on 1 January, New Years Day 1818, Thomas Brereton marries by licence, the former Margaret Anne Olton the widow of Major W. Whitmore of the Royal West Indian Rangers and Brevet Major and Aide-de-camp to Major General Munro.

Thomas and Margaret, who was still only 29 years old, married in London at St James's Piccadilly, a church built by Sir Christopher Wren and where the space around the altar is decorated with a carving by the famous Grinling Gibbons who also did the carvings at Hampton Court Palace.

Here you can see the altar at St James's, where Lt Colonel Thomas Brereton and his new bride Margaret stood and took their vows. The Church has changed very little since the 19th century and the Grinling Gibbons carving around the altarpiece can be clearly seen. St James is also where in 1757 William Blake the visionary artist and poet was baptised and who would later go on to illustrate the book of Gabriel Stedman that was used to influence the abolishment of slavery. Sam Coghlan, Thomas's cousin was a witness to his marriage as was a Georgiana Galliasa.

Margaret Anne was the eldest daughter and was named after her mother Anne who had died aged just 20 years old. There is a tablet in St James Church commemorating her death on 22 June 1804, so it was fitting that her daughter should marry Thomas there. Thomas, whose leave expired on 1 March, did not rejoin his regiment on time and was recorded as absent without leave. So perhaps he was having problems with Mary Pellett who had not baptised their son William yet; we might never know the truth. What we do know is that it was not until May that Thomas left for his new post in South Africa and a month later 0n 12 June 1818 William was finally baptised in St Marylebone, the same parish that the new Mrs Brereton's family was from. On the baptism register Mary describes herself as Mary Harriet Brereton the wife of Thomas Pellett Brereton, so had Thomas previously promised to marry her? If so, she was now obviously trying to protect her reputation and also didn't want her child to be recorded as illegitimate. A baptism usually occurred the next Sunday after the birth, so for Williams to be delayed until June, just a month after his father had left with his new wife, could this perhaps be indicative of a dispute between them and shows Mary as quite a determined young lady, prepared to fight hard for her reputation.

London at this time was flooded with soldiers due to the army numbers being reduced from 450,000 at the time the battle of Waterloo and now down to only 100,000 in total. Amongst these were a large number of unemployed officers living on their annual half pay of £155.20.0. Many of these were keen to be awarded a decent command so they would have some meaningful employment and enable them to go back onto full pay.

Therefore, competition was very stiff for any command that came along, and only the officers who had proved their worth were lucky enough to get the top positions. But due to Thomas's distinguished record he had come to the attention of none other than the King's second son Frederick, Duke of York, who was the Commander-in-Chief of the King's troops. Frederick had set himself the task of weeding out ineffectual officers and only promoting the best. In pursuit of these aims, the Duke was responsible for reorganising the British Army, abolishing the practice of selling commissions and setting up Sandhurst Military academy.

Sir John Fortescue the famous military historian said of him;

"Frederick did more for the army than any one man has done for it in the whole of its history".

So the Dukes recommendation of Colonel Brereton for the command of the frontier garrison at Grahamstown, South Africa, was in effect both flattering and also illustrates his opinion of Colonel Brereton as an officer of merit, much needed in the colony. An officer who could instil discipline and regimental pride in the rag tag of desperadoes still supplied as troops just as he had done before and more recently in Senegal. The level to which these Troops could stoop can be judged by these letters sent only a couple of months previously;

"Castle, 15 November 1817

Sir,

In compliance with your letter of the 13th instance. I have the honour to enclose you a statement of the different crimes committed by the last detachment which has lately joined the 1st Battalion 60th Regiment.

I am sorry to observe that there have been many defaulters in such a short period. 22 men have been charged with stealing. There has not been proved enough against Private Maloney, accused of stealing silver spoons out of the mess room. 21 men have been tried for making away with necessities; 10 men for absenting themselves without leave from their different guards; 11 men for being drunk on guard; 12 for striking non-commissioned officers in the execution of their duty; 13 men have deserted, and seven have been brought back. Six are still absent.

I need not include the great number of men sent to knapsack drill, or extra drill, and sent likewise to repair the Grand Parade for having been guilty of drunkenness or absent from regular parades, &ct.

Signed; G. Renaud, Captain. Comg. 1st Batt. 60th Regt. "

Enclosure with the above

"In addition to the crimes detailed in the accompanying papers, I have to add that a General Court Martial is now assembled by my order at Grahamstown (The headquarters of the frontier) for the trial of a man who having ill will towards one of his comrades deliberately (tho' sober) shot at him with his musket in the barrack yard. He was immediately seized, almost in the very act, and he declared he was only sorry he had not killed his comrade.

On the arrival here of the reinforcements for the 60th Regiment two accusations of sodomy on board ship were reported to me, and four men of that battalion have since confessed themselves murderers.

Signed; C.H. Somerset, General Commanding"

(*Records of The Cape Town Colony.* Page 414.)

Lord Somerset had also written to Henry Bathhurst the Secretary of State for War and Colonies, complaining about the numbers and quality of the troops supplied, as they were largely composed like the RAC of deserters, criminals and worthless vagabonds, who had been offered military service instead of long prison sentences. This was another result of the reduction of troop numbers after the Napoleonic wars that had ended after Waterloo. Reduction was a necessity however, as Great Britain was now in considerable debt, and so cutting military personnel was one measure to reduce expenditure. However, fewer troops were also making it increasingly difficult to police its ever-expanded empire. So now, four years later in 1818, in an effort to fill this gap, the government was again utilising prisoners and any other men of a rather dubious character. They along with over 500 deserters had been supplied to make up the numbers of the 60th Regiment alone.

These were proving to be more trouble than they were worth, as even when the ship containing the first of these arrived, a guard had to be placed on board as it was discovered that they had hatched a plot to seize the ship and make their escape just as they had in Senegal. In an effort to keep them out of trouble, it was thought prudent to place them as guards at the prison on Robben Island. The thought being that as it was difficult for the prisoners to escape through the shark infested waters the soldiers who were no better, would also find it difficult, or so it was thought. Nevertheless, even the notorious prison surrounded by sharks could not stop them, for when a whaling ship dropped anchor near by to load whale oil, they seized their opportunity. A group of convicts lead by members of the 60th Regiment rowed out and soon overpowered the captain and crew, forcing them into a long-boat before raising the anchor and setting sail undetected. When the alarm was raised, a naval ship pursed them until they disappeared from sight into the vast tempestuous ocean.

Lord Somerset must have had mixed emotions on hearing that the newly arrived and much needed reinforcements had deserted, but on reflection I expect he might have been more grateful than anything else to see the back of them.

"I cannot employ the description of soldiers of which the 60th Regiment is composed.... foreigners, deserters from all nations, grumblers, and of general desperate and bad character."

(Letter to Henry Bathurst, Secretary of State, 21 June 1817.)

Even Lt Colonel Brereton's own regiment the Royal Africa Corps, who he had left in Senegal West Africa when he was invalided back to England, had arrived before him and were also behaving just as bad as the 60th. They had been placed on the border for the protection of the colonists, but were more feared by them than the Xhosa raiders whom they were supposed to protect them from. They had committed many robberies and even murder, so it is hardly surprising. In addition, four soldiers had even deserted across the border with their arms and ammunition to join the Xhosa, just as two others from the same post under Lt Colonel Prentice's command had done previously.

Sir Henry Torrens was the Colonel of the Regiment and a very experienced officer who had served with the Duke of Wellington and since 1809 had been Military Secretary to the Commander-in-Chief, the Duke of York, and was responsible for spotting meritorious officers for promotion. So his response and opinion particularly regarding Lt Colonel Brereton just reinforces how well regarded he was at the very top of the military establishment, when he wrote that these Troops would soon be turned into useful soldiers:

"By the presents of active and intelligent officers who will soon proceed to join, particularly the Lt Colonel (Brereton) of the Royal Africa Corps, who was obliged to leave the coast from ill health."

(Letter from Major-General Sir Henry Torrens at House Guards to Henry Goulburn Esq. 14 January 1818.)

Therefore, it seems that there was plenty of work for Thomas to do in his new posting and a lot of promise to live up to.

1818 South Africa

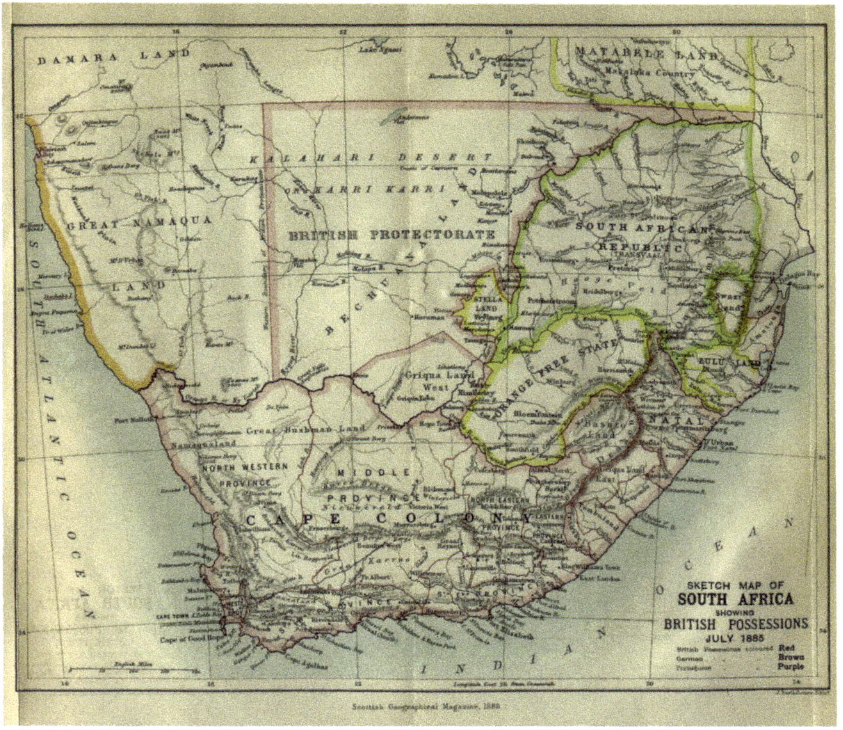

Sketch map of South Africa by J. Bartholomew, Edinburgh. Showing British positions July 1885. *Scottish Geographical magazine.*

Thomas, with his new wife and another prestigious posting, life was looking good. The newly wedded couple finally set sail aboard the *Minstrel* on 5 May 1818 from Gravesend in Kent with Captain Henry Bristow at the helm. The *Minstrel* was a three-masted ship with a carving of a man as its figurehead. It had been built in Hull in 1810, and was just over 104 feet long by 29 feet wide with a flush deck and square stern, and was a three and a half decked vessels of 351 tons. She was armed with 12 guns and was manned by 28 men, and was owned by Thomas Hall and

Sons of London who had previously been involved in slave transportation, but after the slave trade had been banned in 1807 they had employed them to transport convicts to Australia calling at the Cape on their way. The *Minstrel* had been used to transport female convicts only six years previously who had been convicted of such heinous crimes as stealing handkerchiefs and pickpocketing, its last recorded voyage to Australia was in 1825.

Details from , (Charles Bateson. *The convict ships 1787-1868.)*

(The Floating Factory; adventures of Thomas Hall and Company of London.)

Therefore, this ship was no pleasure cruiser and might even have been carrying convicts on this voyage too, but it was probably no worse than Brereton was used to. As it headed down the Thames and into the English Channel it tacked to starboard and followed the south coast past the Isle of Wight until it eventually reached Torbay in Devon. Twelve days later on the 17th the ship left Torbay and headed out into the open sea, during the trip the romantic couple would have had dolphins, sharks and flying fish to entertain them, when weather and seasickness allowed. No doubt during their conversations they made plans for their new life together in South Africa. And after three months of sailing through foul weather and fair, they finally arrived at Simons Bay on 15 August 1818*. Although by this time his leave had already expired on 1 March and he was listed as "absent without leave". However, the couple no doubt only had eyes for each other, and not for time and tide.

* (Cape Town Gazette)

The English had first visited the Cape in the 1500s when James Lancaster in the *Edward Bonaventure* and *Royal Merchant* landed at Table Bay and then again in 1601 aboard his ship the *Red Dragon* and started an extensive exploration of the Cape. In 1614 the British tried a small scale colony on Robben Island when Captain Peyton brought 10 men sentenced at the Old Bailey to banishment. This was done at the request of the English East India

Company so that the men could refresh passing ships. Later in 1620, Captains Shillings and Fizherbert raised a flag at Table Bay and claimed possession for King James. However, before this the Portuguese explorer Bartholomew Diaz had landed at Algoa Bay in 1486 and erected a large stone cross at the mouth of the Sunday's River and claimed it for the King of Portugal, this place is still called St Croix. Nevertheless, the first to realise its value as a stopping point from the east were the Dutch East India Company in 1665 as a place to supply their ships on route to and from the Dutch East Indies and so, the colonisation of the Cape began.

Originally their were many different tribes that lived in this region but the earliest people were the San who had lived in the region as hunter gatherers, but were later displaced and absorbed by the arrival of The Khoikhoi and then the Bantu who were both agricultural/pastoralists and are the same ethnic group as the Xhosa. Then in their turn the European settlers, who were not however exclusively of Dutch heritage, but also Flemings, Germans, Poles, Portuguese and French Huguenot's who after a few generation became the *trek boeren* or nomadic cattle farmers just like the African tribes that they were displacing.

There now followed almost a hundred years of misrule by the Dutch East India Company, as they seized more and more territory from the natives and constantly broke contracts with them. This ended their traditional life, reducing them to the labouring class of the colony, while others were either absorbed by the Xhosas or intermarried with the Europeans. The Dutch called the Khoikhoi people Hottentots in imitation of the click sounds that is characteristic of their language, but today it is considered offensive.

All this conflict between the *trek boeren or Boers* and the Xhosa's intensified as they moved east towards the Great Fish River resulting in armed conflict. The unruly Boers also tried on several occasions to overthrow the Dutch East India Company and just before the First Frontier War in 1795 they endeavoured to set up a republic at Graff-Reinet. Four years later the *First Frontier War* started in 1779 and was to last over a hundred years. The frontier wars were in fact a series of nine wars from

1779 to 1879, though you could argue that it was just one conflict, which increased and decreased in intensity during this time.

However, fate was on their side regarding the Dutch East India Company, as events in Europe took the upper hand after Holland fell under the control of the French during the formation of the Batavian Republic. Therefore, the British fearing the cape would also now fall under French influence took control after the battle of Muizenberg that same year, ending the rule of the Dutch East India Company. By May 1797 the British Governor Lord McCartney arrived with his secretary Mr Andrew Barnard and his wife Lady Anne Barnard the daughter of the Earl of Balcarres, who would started writing her famous letters and dairies which chronicled British colonial life. Nevertheless, in 1803 the British ceded control of the colony to the Batavian Republic under the terms of the Treaty of Amiens. However, in 1806 after the battle of Blaauwberg they again took control and in 1811, Sir John Craddock was appointed Governor and commander of the forces there. The problems that Sir John encountered were still being caused by the further expansion of the Boers into the Xhoas's traditional lands, and at the same time the Xhosa's had split into two groups when their Chief Ngqika fell out with his paternal uncle Ndlambe after he was reluctant to relinquish control when Nigqika reached his majority in 1795. Nigqika was described by a German traveller Heinrich Lichtenstein in 1803 as being a very handsome man and a Batavian officer Willem Paravincini di Cappelli wrote that he displayed spirit, determination and character and an unusual grasp of affairs, *for a kaffir.**

* (*A Proper Degree of Terror.* Ben Maclennan. Page 94.)

Kaffir is an Arabic word that means an unbeliever though today again, many find it more insulting than its actual meaning would justify. The British continued to use it at this time in its original meaning but expanding it to mean anyone who was not a Christian.

During Ndlambe's leadership, he had consolidated his power by absorbing smaller chiefdoms or expelling them from his lands. Therefore, because of his enhanced role, Ndlambe was reluctant to relinquish the power he had built up which resulted in Ngqika leading an attack on Ndlambe whom he defeated. However, Ndlambe escaped unscathed and went to hide amongst his mother's people seeking assistance from his cousin amaGcaleka chief Hintsa. When the two armies clashed, Ngqika was again victorious and captured both Ndlambe and Hintsa, and kept them as prisoners. This only caused more bad feeling between the Xhosa's during these simmering tensions increasing raids on the colony resumed.

In 1806 after the battle of Blaauwberg, Major John Graham of the 93rd Regiment of Foot was promoted to Lieutenant Colonel of the Cape Regiment taking with him some of his best officers including Captain George Sackville Fraser. This regiment was made up of around 300 Hottentots. Major Graham described them as tractable, honest people and splendid shots and who detested the Dutch as much as they liked the English. In 1811, Martial Law was declared along the frontier and Graham was sent with 800 British regulars and 500 Boer commandos to clear Ndlambe and his 20,000 from the Zuurveld (later called Albany) and to locate them east of the Fish River. Though Graham wasn't keen on the Boers, calling them; *"the most ignorant of peasants"* with a total lack of discipline and a known antipathy towards the Hottentots, one even refused to serve alongside the Hottentots declaring, *"I do not think I have been appointed to do commandos with Hottentots but with human beings"**. The Boers in return, did not much like the British either, especially after they outlawed the slave trade in 1807.

*(*A Proper Degree of Terror.* Ben Maclennan. Page 89.)

Nevertheless, Graham's task was completed by 1812, after which he created a string of 50 posts to defend the colony from incursions and on a deserted farm, he established Grahamstown as the Zuurveld's central military post.

The British also replaced Dutch as the official language of the Cape with English. They were also much more efficient administrators than their predecessors were. They introduced rules, laws and customs that would conflict with those of the Dutch. The most contentious of these was over the banning of the slave trade, which had the effect of making the lives of existing slaves much better, as they could not be replaced, so they became much more valuable and so were better looked after. In addition, local magistrates were encouraged to hear complaints by blacks and to seek redress for them; they were also given for the first time basic rights.

The Governor of the Cape since 1814, was the autocratic, His Excellency Lord Charles Somerset, a direct descendent of the Plantagenet Kings and a former General of the First West India Regiment that Thomas's uncle Andrew Coghlan had been a Major in. He was provided with a fine town house, a country house at Newlands, a marine villa at Camps Bay and a shooting lodge at Groenekloof all at public expense and a salary of £10,000 per annum around £730,000.00 in today's money.

(Figures and details from *South Africa*
by George McTheal. Page 148.)

When his Excellency Lord Charles Somerset became Governor, he inherited a fairly peaceful colony and so he sent the last Boer commandos back to their farms. However, this peace ended in 1815 when the Boers rose up against the British authorities. This was after a Boer farmer, Frederik Bezuidenhout, refused to appear in court for his maltreatment of a native worker. The British tried to arrest him but he ran off and was found hiding in a cave and when the British again tried to arrest him he fired upon them and during the shootout he was killed. This resulted in the Slachter's Nek Rebellion, which was quickly crushed by the British colonial forces and five men were hanged.

Sir Charles later planned to achieve peace with the Xhosa by reaffirming Nigqika as supreme Chief and entering into an agreement with him and the other Chiefs at a meeting on the banks of the Fish River in March 1817. The Chiefs all agreed to try to restrain any of their people from plundering cattle but if any did, these cattle would be restored to the victims. In addition, they agreed to allow the Colonial Government to restore any Colonial cattle found within their Kralls and if not, to allow them to take kaffir cattle to replace those stolen. These agreements were know as the *Spoor Laws* and helped to reaffirm Nagqika as the supreme chief by insisting all negotiation should be carried out only through him. As a sign of goodwill after his approval of the arrangement, Naqika was presented with a magnificent horse and many other gifts. Unfortunately however, this did not defuse the tensions between the Xhosa it just reinforced the animosity and jealousy towards Ngqika, causing a state of increasing tension. A tension the Boers were very ready to take advantage of escalating the tension even further.

Therefore, it was into this developing situation that Colonel Brereton arrived to take up his new post. On arrival, he reported to Sir Charles at the imposing Castle of Good Hope in Cape Town and produced an introductory letter from the Duke of York recommending him for the Command of the Frontier Garrison at Grahamstown. Later on 4 September 1818, he received a letter from Major Rogers the Military Secretary outlining his duties and commitments and the force to be placed under his command in accordance with the wishes of His Excellency the Governor of the Cape Colony. In this long letter were 22 separate points to which the Colonel was required to adhere too, as a guide and instruction to his mode of operation.

The troops under his command were to patrol 180 miles of frontier to protect it from the frequent incursions of the Xhosa's, who enter the Colonial territory to plunder Colonial cattle and in the execution of this act would frequently commit murder. To counter this, observation posts manned by a small detachment of troops were placed along the border along the frontier just to observe the movements but not for any aggressive purposes. Brereton was also told that the Xhosa should be considered as friends as it was only the acts of petty thieves or individuals who were responsible for this plundering and the Chiefs admit the injustice, and distance themselves from those responsible. He was also instructed to zealously encourage this feeling within the Chiefs. All negotiation should be carried out only through Chief Ngqika and not with the Xhosa themselves and Ngqika was also permitted to send to Grahamstown for any supplies he or his people required and could barter for any advantages they required.

His Excellency was keen to establish a settled society that would render the military presents on the border unnecessary by establishing amongst the settlers a feeling of security for themselves and their property and this in turn would encourage new settlers to arrive who would increase their numbers large enough to be able to protect themselves. To hasten this state of affairs it was necessary to patrol the borders vigilantly using the system of outposts already alluded to and by erecting signal stations as quickly as possible so that any infringements of these rules could be communicated swiftly and so any cattle theft could be dealt with before they could be driven back across the border

Colonel Brereton was also empowered with a warrant to assemble Court's Martial should he deem them necessary, but to resort to these measures as a last resort, as by his good management of the Troops and the prevention of any crimes would hopefully render these measures not often necessary. If he felt he did have to resort to a Court Martial he was not to convene one without reference to his Excellency and no sentence to be carried out until approved.

After receiving his orders and rejoining his regiment, The Royal Africa Corps, together with his new wife they preceded on the arduous 600-mile journey to Grahamstown to take up his position there. A few weeks later, they pitched camp upon a hill above the Drostdy (The official headquarters of the Landrost or Sherriff.) This overlooked the beautiful old town of Swellendam, at the foot of the Langeberg Mountains in the Western Cape. It was here after only eight months of marriage that Thomas was to descend from the ecstatic heights of love and happiness to the deep troughs of lonely despair. For unfortunately, Margaret's life, like her mothers before her was a short one, as on 8 September she died, apparently of a "fever ". There is no specific record of what malady claimed her life, but due to the time she died after her marriage, one is drawn to wonder whether she may have been pregnant? However, this is just a suspicion; there is no evidence to support it, though one of the biggest killers of healthy young women at the time *was* childbirth.

This was recognised by the Church of England, who even had a special service in their prayer book thanking God for;

"The safe deliverance and preservation from the great dangers of childbirth."

I repeat, at the time of writing there is no evidence to confirm or deny this theory, only circumstantial, but judging by all the women who we know came into contact with the virile Thomas Brereton who ended up pregnant, and with Anne's death after only eight months of marriage it does make you wonder. Nevertheless, one thing is sure, the newly married Margaret Brereton was alas, no more, and Thomas was alone again and heartbroken. His young bride was laid to rest in the northeast corner of the magnificent old Dutch Reformed Church on Voortrek Street, Swellendam of which only the gates and archway now remain of the original, the rest having been rebuilt in 1902. She was attended by the whole regiment, and the simple inscription is as follows;

"To the memory of Margaret Anne Brereton

wife of Lieutenant Colonel Brereton of the Royal Africa Corps

who departed this life on 8 September 1818 aged 29 years"

Therefore Thomas Brereton, at 36 years old, went from the elation of marrying his lovely young wife to the dark depth of losing her, all in the space of eight months. It is doubtful one could even imagine how he must have felt at this time

I laid her down in Swellendam beneath the sweating sun
The parched earth cracked open and swallowed her, our brief life of love was done.
In solitude, I gazed into her grave, as the dusty earth rushed in.
Which swelled my eyes with sweet regret for all that could have been.
And now I'm cursed to walk this earth alone, while she must lie within,
Oh tears, my mournful tears, cascading down after her, like falling stars into the dark
and empty void of space.

Later in the month Lord Charles also became unwell, for on 29 September, his secretary Colonel C. Bird wrote to Earl Bathurst to inform him of Dr Barry's concerns, saying that Lord Charles had been unwell for a week with typhus and dysentery and lately had become delirious. The doctor was very concerned and apprehensive as to the outcome, but fortunately by 1 October Lord Charles had rallied, and though still very week was out of fever, and so hopes were raised that he would recover and by the 17th he was back on duty writing letters to Earl Bathurst himself.

However, on 4 October, a rather sad and melancholy Brereton arrived to take up his new post at Grahamstown, where one wonders in such a God fearing age if he didn't feel that God was punishing him for his treatment of Mary Pellett and his new born son.

A few days later on 9 October, he had recovered his composure enough to write a thank you letter to his close Friend Lieutenant-Colonel William Ware, Deputy Assistant Adjutant General at the Cape, in which he writes;

My Dear Warre,

I arrived here on the 4th instance after as you can believe a most melancholy and miserable journey, when I received your truly kind letter of the 20th Sept for which my dear friend, I fear I shall never have it in my power to prove the gratitude I feel for such kindness. The arrangements you have made with Mr Buissance, I thank you far beyond anything I can say, together with the trouble taken by yourself to meet my most anxious wish, in alas, paying the last sad tribute of respect to the remains of my ever to be lamented dear wife – More my dear friend, I am sure your feeling heart will readily excuse on this most melancholy of subjects, – I endeavour to bear my misfortune as well as can be expected from a man labouring under so severe a trial of the will of divine Providence.*

I am sure you will learn with pleasure that already all here seems anxious to meet my wishes, and give me their support in every way I may have occasion to call on them, however a little more time will enable me the better to judge on these matters.

I do not intend visiting the Line of Posts before I have Embarked the Detachment of the 60th and such men from the Royal A Corps, as I find necessary for the safety of the colony, to transfer over to that Regiment, which arrangements will I hope effectively remove any further trouble or annoyance to His Lordship, or those of his Staff, in future from complaints against the Royal A. Corps – indeed I feel perfectly confident such will be the case, and that we shall soon merit the favourable opinion of those concerned – The day after my arrival at this Station, I ordered a Court of Inquiry to assemble for the purpose of investigating into shameful and scandalous reports that have been for some time abroad respecting Capt. Sparks and Lieut. O'Meara, in the very unpleasant business of Surgeon Lea and his family – the proceedings of which I shall forward when closed by His Lordship for consideration and approval – wonderful to think, the other party declines coming forward in any way whatever, and say they are much surprised how such reports could have taken rise.

I have directed the Qt Master of the Regiment to write to some merchant at Cape Town by this opportunity for a number of articles I find much wanting for the use of the Corps, which I request you have the goodness to endeavour to get sent by the Colonial Schooner, or some government vessel sailing for Algoa Bay, which will save the Regiment much expense, and me much annoyance by the delay that will otherwise take place, and prevent me from carrying my plans into effect, this trouble my good fellow I know you will excuse.

I have been here so very short a time that you cannot expect me to give you any information as yet respecting my important Command, when anything occurs that is worthy of notice, you may rely on hearing from me.

I am as yet without a House of my own, and of course a sad trouble to my friends here – Major Frazer has most kindly furnished me one for the present, and who I consider a very fine young man, and one that will be extremely useful to me in carrying out the duties of the Frontiere – Captain Trappes has hired a House for me, which must undergo some trifling repairs before I can possibly live in it, and which I am sorry to say must be paid for by the Government or myself, the latter I hope will not be required.

Soon after we parted I purchased four miserable Hacks quite out of condition- and on my arrival here, found neither corn or grass to give them, the country is quite parched up for want of rain and I fear when my miserable animals have to commence their work, that I shall find them little equal to the task.

I had two long letters from Rogers since my arrival, where he mentions your safe return to Cape Town, which I hope is unnecessary now to say, afforded me not a little satisfaction – he also says that Mrs Ware & family are still in Simons Town, where I hope from my heart they enjoy the health & happiness be assured my dear fellow I wish – and that you see some prospect of making arrangements for their safe return to England – when you must not forget your kind promise of passing some time with poor unfortunate me here. – and which you may rely will be one of the greatest satisfactions I can now have – and until then, I hope you will not forget also your promise, to write me a friend – a circumstance that will make me doubly happy – I shall write you most fully on my own affairs when I have a little more time, at present I do not wish to detain the post for a moment – I beg you will offer my sincere & best regards to Mrs Warre and sweet family. And that you will believe me to remain my dear Warre most faithfully yours.

Tho, Brereton

(National Army Museum London)

(Published in, *The British Army Cape Colony;* Soldiers letters and Diaries 1806–58. Page 43.)

*(Mr Buissance that Thomas mentions was a member of the Court of Justice and Receiver General of Land Revenues in the Colony; he was also the brother-in-law of the Colonial Secretary

C. Bird. He was later to have a spectacular fall from grace after discrepancies in monies collected by him failed to be deposited in the public treasury, this fall from grace also affected Secretary C. Birds.)

Lt Colonel William Warre.
Later, Lieutenant-General Sir William Warre C.B. K.T.S.
1784–1853
Portrait detail by kind permission of Miguel Potes,
Senior Manager at Symington, owners of Warre's.

You can still feel the warmth of friendship that transcends the years in this personal and heartfelt letter sent by Brereton to his dear friend Warre. Lt Col William Warre was the eldest son of James Warre of George Street, Hanover Square London, and was an experienced and distinguished officer, who had served under Wellington in the Peninsular war. He also fought with the Portuguese and was involved with the capture of Oporto from the French and for his services was awarded the Portuguese military order of *The Tower and the Sword*, and *Commander of the Order of St Bento de' Avis*. The Warre family were not strangers to Portugal however, as his grandfather also called William founded the Port Dynasty of Warre's, which is the oldest Port Brand in the world, and William was actually born there at Oporto, which he helped to liberate. A Port called *Warre's Warr*ior is named in his honour and was first produced in 1850, and is still available today. It is not impossible to imagine that the two men would have enjoyed a glass of Warre's port during one of their soirees together, and today it is still possible for us to also drink a glass to William and his friend Thomas Brereton.

William married in England, Selina Ann Maling in 1812 and a year later, 1813, he went to the Cape of Good Hope to take up the position of Deputy Quartermaster General. Therefore, he had served in the Cape for five years before Brereton arrived. He was to be much decorated in his lifetime, being made a Companion of the Order of the Bath in 1838, Knighted in 1839 and a Major General in 1841. So by the time of his death in 1853 he was Lieutenant-General Sir William Warre. Unfortunately, his replies to Brereton have not survived, but at least Brereton's letters to him have. He must have treasured them to keep them safe and leave them to posterity, so that we, in the far off distant future can again read them, and experience the men's close relationship that spans the years, making them human again and not just names lost in the mist of history.

Arriving in Grahamstown Thomas had entered a powder keg of disputes, distrust and anarchy, for what with the Dutch settlers unhappy with the British and their anti-slavery laws and the continuing cattle thefts. Also the British themselves, with their reduced number of troops and the disgraceful character of the reinforcements were making it difficult to deal with these issues. In addition, the Xhosa were unhappy with both, and who were still having disputes amongst themselves as a growing number lead by Chief Ndlambe were gradually being emboldened to take advantage of the situation. An uneasy truce had lasted through 1817 during which Nagika returned numerous cattle and horses to Grahamstown. But later when a small Colonial Dutch Commando led by Field Commandant Muller tried to seize stock traced to Ndlambe's Kralls he refused restitution and ordered them away justifying his right to keep the plundered cattle. In response on 8 January 1818, Major George Sackville Fraser of the Royal Africa Corps had crossed the Fish River with 300 infantry and 150 mounted settlers travelling for several days searching for Ndlambe to enforce the Kat river treaty demands. However, when they finally reached Ndlambe and his 2,000 warriors he realised that the cattle had been already removed and a standoff ensued during which Fraser noticed a group of warriors quietly surrounding them. Therefore, Fraser realising caution was the better part of valour, left and headed north into the lands controlled by Nagqika where he seized cattle from three local chiefs who Fraser had been informed were the ones responsible. Despite their protestation of innocence, he ordered his troops to take them. As the warriors tried to stop them, he ordered a volley of shots to be fired over their heads as a warning and to drive them back, but unfortunately several were killed in the operation. Fraser seized 2,000 head of cattle and on his return redistributed them amongst the colonists though only 600 were branded colonial stock. Nagqika's at once complained to Sir Charles Somerset who ordered Major Fraser to return some of the cattle, but only just over a hundred were. This caused resentment amongst Nigqika's followers who had wanted to take their own measures to return the cattle but had been stopped by Nigqika who expected Sir Charles to restore all the stolen cattle and when this was not forthcoming they angrily defected back to Ndlambe. These defections and the continuing disputes between the Xhosa Chiefs were to bring their simmering rivalries to a conclusion as to who was the supreme Chief.

As the tensions mounted, a raiding party from Ndlambe stole yet more cattle from one of Nigqika's chiefs possibly to replace those taken by Fraser and provoke a confrontation. Nevertheless, Nigqika's councillors warned him to be cautious and not to be drawn from their Great Place to pursue them, fearing that it might be disastrous to do so.

This situation was made worse by the fact that the missionary Joseph Williams, who had been the colonies eyes and ears in the district and confidant of Nigqika had suddenly died of fever on 23 August 1818.

Eager to take his place as Ngqika's spiritual council was Ntsikanna who had become something of a mystic and prophet after fusing his traditional Xhosa beliefs and the Christian teachings of Williams. Ntsikanna told Ngqika he had received a vision of foreboding, declaring;

"Abandon all thought of war with Ndlambe, otherwise you will bring down upon yourself fearful retribution, the nature of which I cannot describe, but I see the heads of the Gaika being eaten by ants."

This prophecy was later described in a Poem by Allan Kirkland Soga, published in 1897. Who was South Africa's first Black poet in English.

Ntsikanna's Vision

What thing; Ntsikanna, was't that prompted thee
To preach to thy dark countrymen beneath your tree?
What sacred vision did that mind enthral
Whilst thou lay dormant in thy cattle kraal?

Was it the sun, uprising in his pride,
That struck with glittering sheen Hulushe's dappled side,
By Chumie's laughing fountain hastening merrily,
To meet strong Keisi's waters rolling to the sea?

A Vision? Yea! That presence once had shone
Upon the men of Tarshish, down from the heavenly throne.
And in the holy light of His mysterious Word
The proud barbarian bows and worships God, the Lord!

Hark! 'Tis the sound of prayer, of savage melody –
Untutored voices raised to Him who sits on high;
Those hills and dales around fair Gwali's stream
Repeat again Ntsikanna's sacred hymn.

Wake, Gaika, wake! I see the gathering storm
By Debe's plain; Gcaleka's horse and Ndlambe's legions swarm;
Behold thy tribesmen scattered, thy warriors doom is sealed –
The word of God rejected – by prophesy revealed.

Nevertheless, despite these warnings, and even though Ngqika was by now suspicious that this confrontation had been arranged to draw him into a trap by Ndlambe. He finally conceded to the demands of his senior general and set off from his Great Place down the mountain, marching 28 miles until they reached the Debe river valley, near a place called Amalinde a name that was set to go down in Xhosa history.

The Battle of Amalinde

Amalinde is the name given to large earthworm mounds that rise three feet into the air with hollows in between. The worms that make these mounds are in fact the world's largest earthworms the Microchaetus rappi or giant South African earthworm; they commonly look more like the size of a snake than a worm and can reach a staggering 22 foot long. It was the mounds of these worms that gave their name to this spot and where a dreadful battle was about to take place.

However, in another part of the country and unaware of the eventful catastrophe that was about to happen, Lt Colonel Thomas Brereton sent another private letter to his friend Lt-Col Warre dated Saturday 17 October 1818.

My Dear Warre,

Your Most Kind letter of the first instance I duly received, and believe me sincerely regret to learn the account of Mrs Warre and my young friend's late attack of illness, and that Mrs W still continues delicate, which I trust the prospect of soon visiting England and friends will effectively remove.

I wrote you on the 9th such particulars of myself as time and circumstances would permit, and since when nothing particular occurred worthy of notice – at present everything goes on here perfectly quiet, and I trust during the time I may be obliged to remain, I shall be able to keep it so – all, & ever one, appears anxious to meet my wishes, which leaves me the greater hope that matters will go on well. As for the regiment, I feel perfectly confident Lord Charles Somerset will soon change his opinion of both officers and men, and I trust be fully satisfied with them. The proceedings of the Court Of Inquiry respecting Captain Sparks and Lieut O'Meara, I forward by this opportunity, which will I have little doubt clearly prove to His lordships full conviction, how unfairly and unjust those officers have been accused, and I trust induce him to direct a General Order to be issued, announcing their entire acquittal, which will not only be satisfactory to my feelings, but that of the Corps at large.

I must now my dear friend have your opinion and advice in what particularly concerns myself; you already know my intention to return to England, when I have established order and regularity in my present corps, which I see no difficulty in accomplishing ere long – therefore do you not think it advisable for me to write Lord Charles on the melancholy and unfortunate subject, which now obliges me to form so unexpected resolution, otherwise it may be thought I have not acted towards him, as his attention on that severe trial demanded; I therefore beg you will let me have your ideas on this point, by return of post; I do not intend to ask for leave of absence before Feby, or March, or until I have fully satisfied His Lordship as to the improved conduct of the regiment; after which I feel it will be impossible for me to remain in this country, unless to be the most miserable of men; during my stay I shall exert my utmost endeavours to bring into effect his Lordships wishes as far as concerns the command of this frontier.

By arrangements which my late melancholy misfortunes obliges me to now make, I am induced to hope, that I may have some chance of returning to England by the same ship, which will convey yourself and family (unless you are so fortunate as to get a Man of War) which would be to me a consolation I have not words to express – you will I am convinced write me candidly what I may expect. I do not wish my intentions to be made known before I have written Lord Charles – I understand I will have little difficulty in disposing of such articles of furniture &c. As I may wish here – I hope from my heart that you will be able to sell your estate to advantage – I still consider it certain, that you will ere long, have some satisfactory news from England and which may prevent your return for the present; should my friend, you will not hesitate to command me in every way you think proper, and which will be still to me a greater proof of your friendship & esteem.

I must now close this hurried scrawl, by requesting you will write me every particular – with my sincere wishes for Mrs. Warre and my young friend's better health. Believe me My dear Warre most faithfully yours.

(National Army Museum London. Published in *The British Army Cape Colony; Soldiers Letters and Diaries 1806–58*. Page 45.)

Lt Col Warre's wife whose illness is mentioned here was Salina Malling the sister of the Countess of Mulgrave. But despite returning home for her health, she was to die in February 1821 and of their seven children, three were to die at the Cape in South Africa.

The estate Brereton mentions that Lt Col Warre was selling was called *Sans Souci,* which is French and means; "without care". Perhaps named after the favourite summer residence of Frederick the Great King of Prussia, at Potsdam in Germany and where the king chose to be buried. Frederick was much admired in England and his military instructions were translated into English and formed the basis of army tactics for many years. This estate in Cape Town and its new occupants would play another important role in the life of Thomas Brereton. He did not know this at the time however, as he was still settling in and finding his way around. Nevertheless, while this letter was being written, in another part of the country a terrible battle was about to start that would also shape his time at the Cape. For by this time Ngqika's and his 5,000 warriors had reached the plain of Debe and in the distance they saw groups of warriors in exposed and vulnerable positions on the flat plain before them. Ngqika and his generals thought that they could easily crush them and deliver a blow to Ndlambe before passing through the passage of the Debe Nek on route to Ndlambe's Great Place. Ngqika made his way to higher ground to watch the battle as his warriors raced forward. As they reached the plain the warriors that they had seen, scattered and ran towards Debe Nek. They did not know it at the time but they were just decoys who had been placed there as bait to draw them into a trap. Ngqika watching events from higher ground on the mountainside could see more clearly events unfolding below and saw they were indeed being drawn into a carefully planned ambush. For as they reached the Debe Nek, where the plain channelled into a narrow pass leading to the Amelinde, the more ferocious and experienced warrior led by Ndlambe's son Mdushane, rose from their hiding places on the higher ground and raced into battle taking Ngqika's forces by complete surprise. Niqika watched in horror as a dreadful slaughter started to unfold before his eyes on the plain of Amalinde. His eldest son Maqoma charged courageously into battle time and time again but all to no avail, as the superior numbers (estimated as being 10,000) who also had the advantage of surprise cut relentlessly through the battle field. Maqoma was so badly wounded that he was eventually forced to retreat before he was taken captive. The battle raged all day and was the greatest and most ruthless battle ever fought between the Xhosa. Even when darkness descended the slaughter continued, for the tall grass that had hidden the warriors earlier, was now set alight so that the defeated could be hunted down and robbed before being ruthlessly killed. Even those that escaped detection died of their wounds and the cold where they lay. According to Xhosa tradition out of a total force of 5,000 of Ngkika's warriors around 500 were killed. Those that had managed to escape from the battlefield around sunset joined him on the mountain slopes, and then retreated to the Winterberg where they sent desperate messages to Lord Charles Somerset for assistance. In response to this request a week or so later in November, Major Fraser visited Ngqika in his mountain lair and assured him that Colonial forces would indeed honour their treaty and punish Ndlambe.

(Estimates of numbers and some details of battle from,
The South African Military History Society Journal.
Vol 13 No 5 – Jun 2006)

Although the continuing cattle thefts had escalated tensions on the border between the Xhosa and the Colony, it was this civil war between the Xhosa Chiefs Ndlambe and Ngqika that was the first serious clash and can be regarded as the start of the Fifth Frontier War. Therefore, with the success of defeating the colonists ally,

Ndlambe was encouraged to escalate his plans for the conquest of the whole Zuuurveld

On hearing the details of the various depredations against the colony, and then the ruthless attack on the Colonies ally Ngqika. Colonel Brereton felt that he should honour the agreement with Ngqika and Ndlambe must be made to pay dearly for his murderous actions. In order to do this he sent a letter to Lord Charles on 22 October outlining what had taken place and his proposals to deal Ndlambe a severe blow and show him such behaviour would not be tolerated.

He received a reply on 1 November 1818 from Major Rogers, in which his Excellency Lord Charles Somerset, agreed with his request to honour the agreement with Ngqiki. For Ndlambe was indeed guilty of these depredations, as the stolen cattle had been seen in his Kraals, but he had refused to return them to Major Fraser and had murdered two privates from the 72nd Regiment. Therefore, his Excellency had no difficulty sanctioning Colonel Brereton acting against him. He regretted however that the troop reductions had left them without regular Cavalry, which he considered essential, so the Colonel would need to enlist some mounted Burghers to fill this role, as Infantry alone would not be effective. Sir Charles also agreed with Colonel Brereton's plan to take this opportunity to punish Ndlambe severely, and that he was fully authorised to do so.

Nevertheless, he was also worried about the protection of the Colony while he and the troops were engaged in this action, and suggested he should inform the Boer commanders to protect the various district in case of attacks while the troops were away. Brereton was also told that Major Fraser was the best man at conveying Ngqikas true sentiments and that Hendrik Nootka the interpreter could not be trusted, as he had misinterpreted what Ngqika had said on more than one occasion. Williams the missionary who had also been a confidant of Ngqika had faithfully translated his wishes to the Colony, but after he had died there followed a lack of reliable information at a crucial time.

In the event of Colonel Brereton attacking Ndlambe he was urged to be quick and decisive so that there would be no escape, and once he was in custody it would do away with the prevailing belief amongst the Xhosa that the cattle retrieved in January belong to followers of Ngqika. In addition, if a considerable number of cattle fell into his hands he should restore them to their claimants providing they are not adherents to Ndlambe. After which the colonial sufferers should be recompensed and Ndlambe followers must be removed from the Kraals they now occupy and moved further from the Colonial border. After this is completed, all the Chiefs should be assembled and in their presence, it should be explained to Ngqika that all this has been affected through friendship to him and that it will continue, if the Colonial territory is left in peace and unmolested. However, if any repetition of plunder or murder takes place those Chiefs responsible will also be punished.

On 7 November 1818 Brereton wrote his last letter to his friend Lt Colonel Warre

Mr Dear Warre,

I have anxiously expected a letter from you for the last two posts, and must now only hope, the next will afford me that pleasure, having wrote three times since my arrival here.

I have by this opportunity written Rogers confidentially, mentioning my intention to apply for leave of absence, and to request he would let me know, what answer I am likely to get from Lord Charles, which of course you will not hear from him, – or do I wish you to appear to know.

I write also to say that I have been obliged to except Major Mackenzie's resignation to retire on Half Pay, and that I should be happy to recommend him for the Majority, provided it would suit his views, to take command of the Regiment in the event of my going home; as I must apply for some field officer for that purpose as poor Mackenzie is totally unfit, and was very near being the ruin of the Corps,– which I am proud to say improves in every respect, beyond my most sanguine hopes, and I am happy to think without one Court Martial, since my arrival, which is rather a new thing on the Frontier, and will I trust not escape the notice of those at Head Quarters.

Kings Gaika, & Slambie, are now in open war, as far as reports can be relied on from Gaika, and I only wait for proper instructions to take to the Field, in order to punish the villain Slambie, which I propose to do to the utmost of my power, if my hands are not tied, and left nothing to do, but harass troops without any earthly good.

I have commenced my operations of erecting telegraph along the front line, which I hope to have completed very soon, but in my opinion, it can be of no use to the service in this frontier, Captain Trappes is now out in that party.

I have at last got a house to live in, and one of the best here, but as my stay is to be so very short, I care very little about it, as when I hear from Major Rogers, I shall immediately apply for leave, and have my things advertised for sale, being determined to leave here if possible in March; – I hope you will not fail to let me know, if I am to have any chance of going home by the same ship which takes yourself & Family – and as I have already mentioned, if I can in any way be useful, I trust you will not hesitate to command me, as be assured my good friend, nothing will afford me more real pleasure.

I am happy to say every thing goes on here perfectly to my satisfaction, and no complaints or annoyance to Head Quarters; and hope they will be able to see the change themselves.

I have not been well for the last ten days owing to a severe cold, – be sure you write me a long letter by the next post, and believe me My Dear Warre with great truth faithfully yours

Tho. Brereton

(National Army Museum London. Published in, *The British Army Cape Colony; Soldiers Letters and Diaries.* 1806–58. Page 46.)

Brereton had no need to worry about getting permission to return to England as Lord Charles had also lost his wife only two years earlier and so knowing the heartbreak this entails would look upon his request favourably. Lord Charles would also be returning to Britain not long after Brereton for not only had he been dangerously ill himself throughout September to October, but his eldest daughter Elizabeth had also been taken ill and he was anxious to take her back to England himself for her to recover.

The transformation in the behaviour of the 705 Troops of the Royal Africa Corps and 156 men of the Cape Infantry Corps under his command would be much appreciated and would not go unnoticed. Brereton also mentions Major Donald Mackenzie of the Royal Africa Corps but the sentence is a little confusing and it seems in his rush he has left out the name of the Captain he wished to recommend for promotion to Major. Also when he refers to Gaika and Slambie he is of course referring to Ngqika and Ndlambe. The spelling of these names seem to be confusingly different depending to who is writing them.

However, though Brereton might have improved moral and discipline, Sir Charles was still worried about the actual numbers. For as early as 17 September, Lord Charles sent a letter to Major General Sir Henry Torrens, to inform him that he was still concerned about the strength, and inadequacies of the forces supplied to him, particularly the removal of the Cavalry. The total numbers of troops serving throughout the whole Colony on 25 November were only 3,400 including 168 officers of all ranks.

The Brereton Raids

On Major Frasers return to Grahamstown he was soon briefing Colonel Brereton on the latest intelligence and Ngqika's request for assistance. Lord Charles granted permission for Brereton to assemble a Commando in the greatest secrecy to avoid Ndlambe receiving any advance intelligence of the Commanders intentions. This was not possible however because Hendrik Nootka had not only been guilty of misinterpretation, he was also an informer who was reporting everything that was going on back to Ndlambe, though this was not realised fully at the time. Colonel Brereton gathered all available troops together with two artillery cannons and was joined by a force of mounted Burghers in order to punish Ndlambe and thwart his plans by driving him across the Keiskamma River and put a decisive distance between him and the Colonial frontier. The supplies and soldiers had to be gathered from different parts of the country, including Andries Stockenstrom and his mounted Burghers from Graaff Reinet and so it is doubtful that all this movement could have been kept secret from Ndlambe, even without Nootka's spying. So although ignorant that their movements were being reported, by the end of November all was ready and on 1 December Colonel Brereton lead his Commando out of Grahamstown and marched for two days before meeting up with Ngqika and his warriors on the banks of the Koonap river. This small force was to confront Ndlambe and his estimated 30,000 warriors, they marched for a further five days until they reached the banks of the Kat River which they crossed on 5 December 1818 and encountered the first signs of Ndlambe's people who they drove south capturing 6,000 head of cattle. Two days later on 7 December they had crossed both the Tyumie and Keiskamma rivers to enter the enemy's heartland and the punishment of Ndlambe and his people commenced as their Kraals were destroyed, and their fields burned. However, the people already knew of the advancing British and many had already escaped together with their cattle, and were hiding in the dense bushy valleys, hoping the British would be drawn in to follow them.

This was the preferred method of fighting by the Xhosa, which was to retreat into these dense valleys and then ambush the unsuspecting soldiers who would enter in pursuit, just as they had at Amalinde. This method also allowed them to take the advantage to themselves and deny the British their preferred tactics. Brereton was aware of this however and had honed his tactics in the similar terrain of the West Indies. He therefore, would not allow his troops to be drawn in; instead, he directed his cannon into the lush bush, terrifying both the warriors and their cattle, causing them to stampede in all directions and neutralising their intentions. Brereton continued his search for several days but there was no sign of Ndlambe, even his Great Place was deserted. However, Brereton was also finding Ngqika and his vengeful warriors hard to control who were in greater numbers than his force. No doubt Ngqika and his people were still angry after Amalinde and so they took out their savage retribution on any enemy warriors that they came across, including their women and children. Even the Burghers were becoming alarmed at their conduct and believed they recognised amongst them former foes and so were becoming concerned that they could turn on them too. Therefore, Brereton ordered that they should be relieved of their arms to prevent any more atrocities to the enemy, and to reassure the Burghers themselves.

"The British commander found it impossible to restrain the savage passions of the Gaikas, who were mad with excitement and joy at being able to take revenge, and were unwilling to show mercy when any of their enemies fell into their hands. He withdrew, therefore, before Ndlambe was thoroughly humbled."

(Dr George McCall Theal. *The History of South Africa* Vol 111. Page 153.)

Brereton's methods of laying his foes property to waste, is a typical military technique to subdue a troublesome population.

Indeed, it is very reminiscent of the methods used by his ancestors the *Normans* in the 11th century when they laid waste to the north of England in the *Harrowing of the North*, though this time in the 19th century Brereton was not genocidal. It was also used by his ancestor in 16th century Ireland, even to the extent of using his cannon where the geographical conditions made it impossible to engage them conventionally. Both these methods were used by Sir William Brereton, against *Silken Thomas* in 1535.

Nor did Colonel Brereton spoil the land to make it infertile as they had in the 11th century, or execute all his prisoners as Sir William had done in the 16th century. In fact, he restrained Ngqika and disarmed his warriors preventing them from doing exactly that.

By 15 December, Brereton decided to withdraw his forces and drove 23,000 head of recovered cattle back to the Colony. Only one soldier had been killed and one injured, it is not recorded how many Xhosa's were killed.

He also complied with the orders Lord Charles had issued him on 1 November, that he should restore the recovered cattle to their claimants providing they are not adherents to Ndlambe. After which the colonial sufferers should be recompensed, Lord Charles said that these two measures must be insisted upon and that Ndlambe must be removed from the Kraals he now occupies, all this was accomplished as instructed.

This action went some way to restore Ngqika's pride after his defeat in the eyes of his people, not only by the severe punishment netted out to his erstwhile victor but also by the 9,000 head of cattle that were presented to him by Brereton, who also restored him to the lands that Ndlambe had driven him from. The Xhosa prized their cows even higher than the lives of their own people and the possession of these cows cemented their authority and prestige. Only the Royal Chief could order the slaughter of a cow and they remained his property even though the lesser Chiefs and their people cared for them, receiving their milk and blood in payment. However, if they misbehaved, the cattle would be taken and they would lose this valuable privilege. Therefore, it was by the ownership of cattle that the Chiefs maintained their influence over the common people, who could use the cattle for both food and clothing, and the more you had, the wealthier and more influential you would become. The Xhosa chiefs used the possession of cows to reward and to punish the lesser Chiefs and there followers. Therefore, by taking these from Ndlambe and his followers, and restoring them to Ngqika, they were following Xhosa traditions and it was hoped the lesser Chiefs would flock to Ngqika leaving Ndlambe isolated, and no longer a threat to the colony. This was obviously, just what was expected as the Governments own paper claimed.

The Cape Town Gazette, reported triumphantly that;

"it is to be expected that this blow will put a final stop to the attempts to renew the former aggressions on the Colony."

Colonel Brereton however felt that as he had to call off the operation before it had reached its conclusion with the capture of Ndlambe, total success was still in the balance. For it now depended on how Ndlambe and his chiefs reacted. Would they be cowed into submission and submit to the will of the Colony as was hoped, or would they now seek retribution themselves? For after witnessing Ngqikas vengeance, he now wondered if the animosity between the two groups was so great that the minor chiefs might still be reluctant to return their allegiance to Ngqika, and indeed would Nigqika himself accept them? So on his return, he warned Andries Stockenstrom that he should continue with the; *"Utmost vigilance to be observed along your borders for some time to come"*.

Therefore, Brereton warned that this wasn't the only outcome and so the colony should be on its guard in case Ndlambe choose to continue, as those; *"Who have been so greatly punished may attempt an incursion into the colony"*.

(A letter from Colonel Brereton, quoted in, *A Proper Degree of Terror*, by Ben Maclennan page 179.)

The Brereton Raids, which this military operation came to be known, was as beneficial to Ngqika and his people, as it was a disaster to Ndlambe and his followers who were now stripped of all the symbols of power and prestige and the sustenance that they provided. Though, even at the time Brereton was criticised by some for the severity of his actions, notably the Rev Brownlee, and the controversial Bristolian Charles Leonard Stretch, who was also there at the time serving as an officer in the 38th Regiment of Foot and even some of the Boers viewed it as an extremely severe measure. This has been repeated in more recent times with contemporary South African historians like, Noel Mostert in his 1992 book about the Xhosa's called *Frontieres*, where he states that Colonel Brereton; "*Was to gain a fame of a similar sort after his return to Britain, when he became notorious for the brutality with which he put down rioters at Bristol*".

(*Frontieres* by Noel Mostert. Page 469.)

This of course is factually incorrect and the actual reverse of the truth, but just shows yet again, how false opinions can be written as "facts".

Nevertheless, something had to be done after the continuing depredations caused by Ndlambe and his followers, and after the massacre of hundreds of Ngqikas men, a severe measure had been necessary, and that is why Brereton proposed such, and was given Lord Charles approval to implement it. The numbers of cattle taken from Ndlambe in retaliation were large, but unlike with Frazer's commando the year before, Lord Charles did not request any to be returned. Instead, Brereton distributed the remaining cattle to the Burghers and Khokhoi soldiers who had participated in the raids, leaving the rest to be sold to cover the costs of the operation. These measures were designed to punish Ndlambe severely, for his brutal attack on Ngqika's followers and the Colony, and to force the lesser chiefs to realise that only under the protection of Ngqika and ultimately the British could they be safe. These methods did in fact bring about this desired affect, however, when Ndlambe's followers did turn to Ngqika, he angrily turned them away leaving them destitute with only one solution. Colonel Brereton had witnessed Ngqika vent his wrath upon his erstwhile persecutors during the recent campaign, and so his cautions were well founded. Lord Charles had demanded that no cattle should be returned to Ndlambe or his followers only Ngqika, however the animosity between the two sides was now so great, that after Ngkika refusal to help them, they declared;

"We are without milk and the new King (Ngqika) will not give us any, so we must get some from the white man's King who has taken all our cattle and left us to perish."

(Captain Charles Lennox Stretch, ACC, 378, *South African Archives*, Cape Town.)

Therefore, they had little choice but return to Ndlambe and continue their attacks on the Colony and Ngqika, forcing him to retreat from his recently restored land to the Kakaberg, so after a short lull the attacks resumed and they were soon back attacking isolated farms as well as besieging soldiers and settlers starting on Christmas Day 1818. Lord Charles now estimated that Ndlambe had around 30,000 men at his disposal, while Ngqiki had now only 10,000.

Yet the Colony's own supply of troops serving at the cape according to the returns of 29 January showed a total only 2,725

Comprised of;
Officers of all ranks 132
Royal Artillery 65
Sappers and miners 13
38th Regiment 771
72nd Regiment 858
Royal Africa Corps 659.
Cape Corps;
Cavalry 70
Infantry 157
Not including 71 Prize Negroes.

A few days later, on 4 February 1819, Captain Geithin of the 72nd Regiment, who had distinguished himself while serving under the Duke of Wellington, was reported to have been killed while pursuing some Xhosa's who had stolen 136 head of cattle from Farmer T. Dreyer along with a firelock and ammunition. The

Captain, more used to fighting in Europe had unfortunately pursued them with a troop of several mounted soldiers into the thick bush. Seemingly not realising that they were being drawn into trap, for the Xhosa's were there hiding; waiting to ambush them. After discharging his weapon at a decoy, he was surrounded and stabbed over 30 times before he fell to the ground, valiantly trying to defend himself with his discharged weapon. Two other soldiers died with him and all their horses and weapons taken along with the stolen cattle. In response, Colonel Brereton now recommended assembling a much larger force to act against Ndlambe, this time decisively and this time without Ngqika and his unruly warriors.

In reply to this, Major Rogers sent him a letter on 12 February; saying His Excellency was in agreement with his proposal, but wanted to remind him to keep all such measures secret because there ultimate success would depend on it. He also urged Brereton to deliver a decisive blow to Ndlambe and his chiefs by removing him from the border altogether and in the case of resistance, he should be destroyed or captured and his lands between the Keiskamma and the Colonial border given to Ngqika . In the event of the success of this mission it was pointed out that Ngqika might need to be protected, this time by placing a post nr the Keiskamma.

After receiving the various reports, Lord Charles sent a letter on the 15th to Captain Hercules Robison of *HMS Favourite* to ready his ship to take on board 200 soldiers to transport to Colonel Brereton at Algoa Bay to reinforce the frontier. There then followed a succession of letters to and fro, where the Captain said he could not comply with the request, because of previous orders, which in order to fulfil he needed to go before the monsoons arrived. Lord Charles replied finally, on the 17th in exasperation, declaring that Major Fraser had ridden 600 miles from the Frontier in only seven days, to deliver Colonel Brereton urgent request for reinforcements. In addition, that he had stated from the start that the aid was indispensible and that he expected the Captain to comply with his request urgently and wanted a reply by return by the same messenger he had sent to deliver it. So after this final statement of the imperious nature of his request and the forthright way in which it was delivered, the Captain finally conceded, sending a reply by the returning messenger which arrived by 5 o'clock. In which reply he finally agreed to comply, saying if he had known that Colonel Brereton requested the reinforcements to protect the Colony he would have complied earlier, but now he was no longer in the dark he was ready to co-operate fully.

During all this obfuscation and delay however precious time had passed and Brereton had at last received confirmation that his request for compassionate leave in March was to be granted, and he therefore would not now be available to complete the operation that he was preparing for.

So now, Lord Charles was in a predicament, as he was now in need of an experienced officer to replace him. However, as luck would have it, a ship arrived with reinforcement that included 29-year-old Thomas Willshire a brevet (temporary) Lt Colonel of the 38th regiment. So on 21 February 1819, Lord Charles sent a letter to the Colonel, newly arrived in the Colony, asking him to embark on board *HMS Favourite* together with his troops and proceed with them to Algoa Bay. Where he will meet Lt Colonel Brereton, who would acquaint him with the situation and furnish him with all papers and documents. After which he was to assume the Command of the Frontier forces that Brereton had been assembling there.

Willshire was seven years younger than Brereton and had joined the Army at the ridiculously young age of six years old. This was before the Duke of York had introduced his reforms to stamp out such practises. His father had purchased him a commission as an ensign in the 38th and then the rank of Lieutenant the year after when he was still only seven, he later spent most of his active service in Europe but arrived too late for Waterloo. He was 38 before he received the full rank of Lt Colonel on 30 August 1827 without purchase, while serving in India.

In a later letter, Lord Charles informed Colonel Willshire of Colonel Brereton's successful expedition against Ndlambe, though he was unhappy that he been unable to capture him and bring him back to the Colony to answer the charges against him.

However, he also informed Colonel Wilshire that the force that he was to take command of was now stronger and more efficient than any that had gone before it. This was due to the sterling work that Colonel Brereton had put in, disciplining the men and turning them into a reliable fighting force. Proof of which was that the Courts Martial that had been a regular occurrence before his arrival were now no more needed, indeed he had not needed to convene a single one since he resumed command.

Also by this time, the raiding by the Xhosa's on the colony had started to subside leading perhaps to a thought that the *Brereton raids* had indeed, finally achieved their goal. In his letter to Colonel Warre on 7 November, Colonel Brereton had expressed a hope that his efforts would not go unnoticed at Headquarters. Well he need not have worried, for indeed they had not and in recognition on 14 March 1819 Lt Colonel Brereton was presented with a handsome engraved sword and gilt scabbard valued at 200 guineas (*£12,576.00 today) by the Royal Africa Corps;

*(National archives historical currency converter)

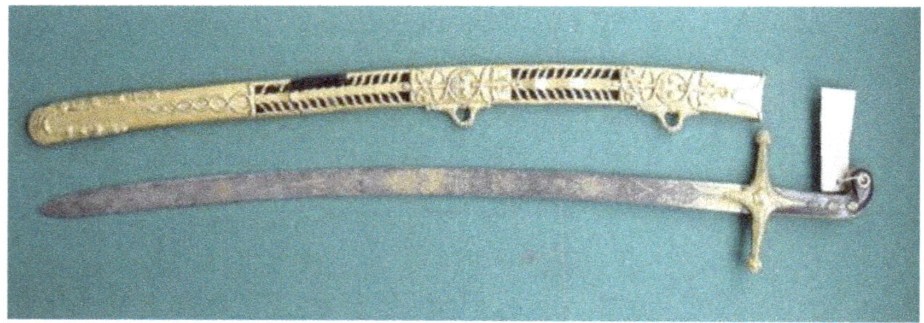

Picture by kind permission of Fleur Way-Jones Curator emeritus:
Albany Museum Grahamstown, South Africa.
H 312 Albany Museum (History Collection)

The engraved inscription read :

"Presented on March 14th, 1819, by the Officers of the Royal Africa Corps to Lieut.-Colonel Thomas Brereton on his departure for Europe, as a testimony of the high sense they entertain of his character as an officer, for the discipline he established in the regiment during the short space of time he was with them and for

their sincere attachment to him for his amiable and gentlemanly demeanour by which he endeared himself to all under his command."

Colonel Brereton must have made a big impression on the RAC when you consider the low esteem with which they were held before his arrival. It was a month later, on the 16 April that he received official permission from Sir Charles to return to England on compassionate leave. Alas, too late to return with his friend Colonel Warre, as he had hoped, for the Colonel and his family had already sailed three days earlier on the 13th, aboard the *Lady Raffles* bound for Portsmouth.

Nevertheless, with Colonel Brereton now gone, Willshire set about making his plans to punish the Xhosa rebels and capture Ndlambe or if not, destroy him. He planned to commence on 1 May after he had assembled his force, but before this on 21 April, he received a message from the Xhosa's at his new command in Grahamstown declaring that they would *"breakfast"* with him the next morning.

Though Ndlambe and his followers had been comparatively quite up to now, they hadn't been idle, they had been assembling their forces in readiness to attack. However, before doing so, they would try to test him and see if he was up to the task by attempting to split his force and lure him into an ambush. Unaware of this, Willshire led a detachment of 25-mounted soldiers out towards Botha Hill where he had been informed cattle theft were taking place. However, once they had arrived and crossed the stream he noticed a group of Xhosas at the summit of a ridge and decided to pursue them. Unfortunately, he was unaware he was being led into a trap, for as they advanced up the slop the Xhosas attempted to encircle them. Willshire only just realised in the nick of time and just managed to escape back across the stream only to find 5,000 Xhosas following them. It now dawned on him that the cattle theft was just a ruse, for the Xhosas were not there to steal cattle but to divide the troops and attack Grahamstown itself. He therefore, ordered the troops back to the town, arriving only 10 minutes before the enemy's first appearance on the hill to the east of the settlement. There they waited until between 10,000 and

15,000, warriors were assembled according to the official figures. Willshire force in the town numbered only 350 but they did have guns and ordinance, but now, so did the Xhosa's.

The Battle commenced with a few random shots being fired from both sides before a sudden chilling battle cry the warriors swept down the hill in a cloud of dust. The British waited anxiously until they came into range before their cannons commenced belching out fire and smoke, adding to the confusion. The fighting was fierce and it was not long before the Xhosa's had taken control of the barrack square and the hospital. Nevertheless, just as all was looking hopeless a troop of 130 Khoikhoi arrived to join the defenders and soon after the Xhosa were driven out of the town, leaving many of their dead littering the streets and the surrounding countryside.

Amongst the dead, which historians numbered as high as 1,400, were found the two bodies of the men sent by Nigqika to guide Brereton in his raids only months previously.

The night after the battle Colonel Wilshire was discussing the battle at dinner with one of his officers, Captain Charles Stretch, remembering that at the time, he thought that the battle was lost saying;

"He would not have given at one time of the fight a feather for Grahamstown."

(The Journal of Charles Lennox Stretch. Page12.)

Later on 25 of April, unaware of the resurgence of hostilities, Lord Charles Somerset sent a letter to Earl Bathurst, requesting permission to return to England himself in order to accompany his daughter who had been taken ill and had been advised to return for treatment. He also asked for his urgent plea to return to be passed on to Sir Henry Torrens, so that once permission had been granted by the Prince Regent, he too could be relieved of his Military Command.

Nevertheless, after hearing of the battle at Grahamstown he realised his departure would have to wait until Ndlambe was finally and severely dealt with. Therefore, he instructed Colonel

Wilshire, that the force he would inherit would be the largest ever assembled in the Wars against the Xhosa. Containing "2,000 armed and mounted burgers"*, 1,100 regular infantry, 32 men of the Royal Artillery complete with field pieces, 183 Khoikhoi cavalry men from the Cape Corps, and 150 Khoikhoi ex Cape Corp soldiers recalled for the duration, in total he had over 3,465 men just for this campaign. This was many times the amount of Troops previously available to Brereton in his Commando operation in December, when the records for January showed a total only 2,725 troops in the whole colony.

*(figures quoted from a letter from Lord Charles to Sir Henry Torrens, dated 22 May 1819. Page 202, Records of the Cape Colony.)

Nevertheless, due to the affects of the heat on his newly supplied horses Willshire had to abandon his 1 May deadline and so it was not until July that he was ready to retaliate. However, even with all these resources, and though he tried relentlessly until 15 October, concluding almost a year after *The Brereton raids* and costing many times the amount to implement, he still failed to capture Ndlambe. Just as Colonel Graham had failed in 1811–12 even with his force, which was the largest in the colony previous to Wilshire's.

Willshire however, also brought back 13,000* head of cattle as punishment and managed to capture Makana, Ndlambe's general. Nevertheless, Ndlambe himself was never captured and died of old age in 1828 aged 90.

*(figures quoted from Encyclopedia of African Colonial Conflicts page 17)

A dispatch with the Prince Regents permission dated 7 July reached Lord Charles but as Willshire was only just leaving on his mission he did not send his reply until the 6 November 1819 after Willshire had returned but in this reply, he said that he was very anxious to leave before the hot season in January, February and March. He felt that if he stayed it might have the most fatal consequences for his eldest daughter Elizabeth's precarious state of health.

Sir Rufan Donkin, would be taken over as Governor, while Sir Charles was absent, and Sir Charles was relieved that it was someone of his experience and talent. This would certainly relieve his mind while he was absent, for according to Sir Charles, Sir Rufan had said; *"he shall pursue precisely the line I have adopted in every branch of the administration of this Government"*

(Letter from Sir Charles Somerset to Earl Bathurst. Cape Town, 6 November 1819. Page 367, Records of the Cape Colony).

The New Governor Sir Rufan Donkin, was a very distinguished officer, who just like Colonel Brereton had also recently lost his wife and was truly heartbroken, suffering both mentally and physically due to his woeful loss. His wife was buried quickly in India, as was the necessity due to the great heat, but he had her heart embalmed and took it with him when he embarked with his small son to the Cape, where he had been invalided. His arrival in the Colony was fortuitous for Lord Charles, just as Colonel Willshire's had previously been, allowing Lord Charles to finally return to England.

1822 Commander of the Cape Town Garrison

On his return to England, Thomas Brereton had the unenviable task of telling his late wife's family about the sudden death of his new bride and then sorting out any legal affairs. During this time, he no doubt met up with Colonel Warre and his family but it is not recorded if he had any contact with his two sons who were now eight and five years old, but one would like to think that he did in the time he spent on leave.

On 12 August 1819, he transferred to the 53rd The Shropshire Regiment of Foot. On 29 January 1820 King George III had died and his son the Prince Regent had assumed the throne, as George IV. The next month Colonel Brereton transferred on 24 February 1820 to the half pay of the Royal York Rangers.

Back in South Africa the Fifth frontier war had ended and the Government had been persuaded of Lord Charles plans to create a buffer zone between the Xhosa and the colony manned by British settlers instead of the small and reducing number of troops supplied by the Government. In Britain due to the ending of the war with Napoleon's France there were many unemployed and because of this wages had been driven low by oversupply. When the Government was made aware of Lord Charles proposal, they not only saw this as an opportunity to resolve the Cape Colonies problems, but also these problems closer to home. Therefore, in Parliament they voted to allow 50,000 to apply but 90,000 did before just 4,000 were selected.

Lord Charles who had left for England on 12 January 1820 after Sir Rufan Shawe Donkin had assumed Command as Governor and had promised to follow his predecessors system and plans. To implement these he was soon heading to the interior to facilitate the arrival and establishment of the area set aside for them between the Sunday and Fish Rivers. This would act as a populated buffer zone between the Colony and the recently embattled Xhosa's.

Sir Rufan then later journeyed from Cape Town to Algoa Bay to welcome and supervise the landings of the settlers who arrived in 20 ships. Soon a canvas town was formed to temporarily house the settlers while they waited to be conveyed to the Albany district that had been set aside for them. The new settlers included many ex Army officers on half pay, tradesmen, farmers etc.

After four months at sea the settlers were bursting with energy and were soon investigating their new surroundings with awe and optimism before organising balls and diner parties as well as discovering with wonder the many plants and strange beasts. A 15-year-old daughter of one of the settlers wrote a diary about her experiences and described how she met an Ostrich "A very majestick bird". On 11 June Sir Rufan laid the foundation stone of Captain Moresby's house, the commander of the sloop *Menai*, who had been given the land in recognition of his services in landing the settlers and the house that was erected there later became a hotel called Markham's in honour of Sir Rofan's late wife Elizabeth Markham. After the ceremonial laying of the foundation stone, a party was organised to celebrate. The fifteen-year-old diarist wrote;

"June 11th, 1820 A dance at night,– gathered flowers to ornament the room. The dance – Captain M. spouted a very beautiful, long and affecting speech, – about us not being likely ever to meet again – he made us cry. We danced till daylight, and then had a kind of breakfast, after which, and a great deal of beautiful singing, we put on our clokes and went to Captain Moresby's garden by daylight he took a spade and gave to each of the Ladies an acorn to put into the ground that the Oaks which grow there may keep in remembrance the many happy hours which we spent at Algoa Bay".

(*The journals of Sophia Pigot*. Page 6.2.)

A year later on 9 August 1821 Lt Colonel Brereton returned to full pay by exchanged with Lt Colonel Yates of the 49th (or the Princess Charlotte of Wales, or the Hertfordshire) Regiment of Foot which was stationed in Ireland at the time. Some detachments were at Banagher where Colonel Brereton's family were from, so perhaps he visited them while he was there. The day after he joined the regiment, orders were received to reduce the establishment from ten companies of 65 men to eight companies of 72. By 2 November 1821 all detachments united at Waterford and the whole regiment of 576 men embarked on the brigs *Skeen, John, Hope and Betsy*. As the ships went down river, the *Skeen* ran aground causing the headquarters to move ashore until she could be refloated on the next day's tide. But by 5 November all ships had reached Bristol where the regiment disembarked and marched in detachments on the seventh, eighth and ninth, right across England, from Bristol in the west, to Chatham in the east. They arrived on the 18th, 19th and 20th and were inspected by the Adjutant General on the 23rd and the next day in brigade, after which they were favourably reported on. Colonel Brereton's friend Colonel Warre would later become commandant of the Chatham garrison in 1837. On 3 December the left wing embarked for Cape Town South Africa, on board the Indiaman vessel *Thomas Coutts,* and on the 7th the remainder on another Indiaman vessel the *William Fairlie*. However, bad weather delayed them on the downs and then at Cowes, Isle-of-Wight for seven days until they finally headed out to open sea on 11 January. Thomas together with the left wing finally reached Cape Town in the *Thomas Coutts* and disembarked on 4 March 1822. The other ship the *William Farlie* was put into quarantine on Robben Island due to an outbreak of measles until they recovered. On his return to Cape Town, Lt Colonel Brereton was appointed to the Command of the Cape Town Garrison in the imposing Castle of Good Hope.

However, a lot had changed since he had left only 18 months before. Sir Rufan on assuming control of the Government of the Colony had discovered discrepancies in the financial records and had instigated a full inquiry. One of the charges was that Lord Charles had paid himself 45,000 Rands more than he was entitled to. An incensed Lord Charles returned in 1821 just before Colonel Brereton. The return journey would have taken them to St Helena for supplies, Saint Helena was in the possession of the East India Company and their ships like the ones that the 45th Regiment were on, would call there on route to Cape Town. St Helena is also, where Napoleon Bonaparte was being kept in custody but in May, he had died. This death must have been welcomed in the Colony because of all the rumours on his impending escape had kept them tense ever since he had been brought there in October 1815, but it would also have less welcome consequences.

(Details of the 45th Regiment from F.L. Petre. *The Royal Berkshire Regiment*. Vol 1. Pages 115–116.).

When Lord Charles Ship arrived in Table Bay on his return Sir Rufan sent a carriage down to meet him and announce that dinner would be served for him and his family as soon as they landed. Nevertheless, the carriage returned empty without even a letter of thanks, just an announcement that they would land early the next morning. Lord Charles did land the next morning and entered Government house just as Sir Rufan had left to receive him. This rather arrogant attitude would only exacerbate the problem between the two and would lead to more problems later.

This was not the only controversy that Lord Charles had been involved in, there was also the strange story about 22-year-old Dr James Barry, an outstanding surgeon and intellect. He had also arrived at the Cape around 1817 the year before Brereton, and was appointed Military Hospital assistant, but soon found favour with Lord Charles by saving his daughters life and so was promoted physician to The Governors Household and was given furnished rooms there. Lord Charles was a widower, and rumours soon started to circulate about their unnaturally close relationship. This led to a lewd piece of graffiti, which alleged that the writer had seen Lord Charles and the Dr Barry in the act of buggery. The flamboyant Dr Barry, with his squeaky voice and slight build would strut around wearing very thick three-inch soled shoes and a cocked hat. Or sometimes ride about the place in uniform with a parasol accompanied by a black manservant and a black poodle called Psyche. Lord Charles would often invite him to his hunting lodge the Round House along with Brereton's friend Colonel Warre, of whom Lord Charles said, *"was a good-natured fellow but the worst shot he had ever seen*". Dr Barry was obviously an entertaining fellow who also cultivated an image as a ladies man and with a short temper he was often challenging other men to duels. He returned to the Cape in November 1821 after Colonel Brereton had left and was still there when he returned in 1822 and had been promoted to the role of Colonial Medical Inspector of the Colony. He later performed a pioneering caesarean operation on a woman in the Cape, saving both her and the baby's life and would remain in the Colony during Lord Charles stay. When Dr Barry died in London after a dysentery epidemic in 1860 and his maidservant Sophia Bishop laid out the body, she discovered a long hidden secret. Dr Barry was not a man at all, Dr Barry was in fact really a woman, called Margaret Bulkle. No doubt, Colonel Brereton would have met the colourful doctor in his role as Army surgeon and known of the scandal in the still small community. Perhaps it was in his new capacity as Commander of the Cape Town Garrison that Col Brereton also met another Cape Town notable the 48-year-old Honourable Hamilton Ross, who was a founding Member of the Legislative Council in Cape Town. Earlier as a 24-year-old, Hamilton Ross had come to Cape Town like Colonel Brereton in the performance of his duties as a Captain in the British army. Arriving in 1795, he fought at the battle of Muizenberg after which he followed the retreating Dutch to Wynberg Hill and later after a forced march joined up with reinforcements and attacked Cape Town Garrison on 14 September. After the defeat of the Dutch on the 16th, Hamilton Ross and his troops were the first to enter Cape Town and is credited by several writers as the one responsible for hauling down the Dutch flag and raising the Union Jack over the garrison.

The Honourable Hamilton Ross
1774–1853
(Picture by permission of the Special Collections Library, University of Cape Town, South Africa.)

The Cape now in British hands Captain Ross was put on garrison duties and while there, he made the acquaintance of a young Dutch girl called Catharina Vandenberg who was the daughter of a rich Dutch Surgeon called Jocubus Johannes Vandenberg. The young officer fell in love with Catharina and asked her father if he could have his permission to marry her. Unfortunately, his proposal was rejected by Vandenberg, who threatened that he would deny his daughter her inheritance if she married without his permission before her 18th birthday. Meanwhile Catharina's Mother Elisabeth died in April 1798 and her father told her he intended to marry a woman who had been in the habit of whipping her and that he also intended to marry Catarina to her new stepbrother. Interestingly, a

South African descendent told me during my research that there was a rumour in the family that Catharina was badly treated in this way because she was of mixed ethnicity. This is also confirmed in the diary of Lady Bernard but who states that it was in fact Catharina's grandmother Arendse who was of mixed heritage.

After her father's refusal, a defiant Catharina then threatened to marry Captain Ross regardless of her father's threat of disinheritance. However, all looked lost as the young Captain had to leave Cape Town with his Brigade aboard *HMS Sceptre* in September 1798 bound for Madras, India. Nevertheless, Catharina was a very determined young lady who was already pregnant with his child and so two weeks later the 17-year-old Catharina left to join him in India chaperoned by a fellow officers wife. On 22 January 1799 they married at Fort St George Madras before giving birth to a son George Robert Ross, just six months later on 6 June 1800.

In 1802, the couple and their young son George returned to Cape Town as man and wife, with Hamilton now retired on half pay from the Army and with his wife's inheritance, he set up the first British business at the Cape, Ross and Co, which was very successful. He not only became very rich in his own right, but also influential by his contribution to the political, economic and cultural life of the Colony. For as well as his position on the Legislative council, he also sponsored the setting up of the Cape of Good Hope bank and a shipping line, with offices in Adderley Street in the commercial centre of town and warehouses on the waterfront to unload and supply his ships. Therefore, his elopement against the wishes of his in-laws had turned out to be a very good choice for all concerned. The happy couple went on to have five more children one son and four daughters. Colonel Brereton must have been delighted to make his acquaintance particularly as Hamilton Ross had bought his friend Lt Colonel Warre's property *Sans Souci* at Claremount before he had returned to England in 1821. Therefore, Colonel Brereton continued to be a frequent visitor there and also at his town house, Mount Nelson where he would hold many parties. A previous guest had been none other than the Duke of Wellington in 1805 when he stopped there on his return home from India with his brother Richard the Governor-General of India. During these visits, he would have met Hamilton Ross's children, and it seems his fourth child, the 18-year-old Olivia, made a big impression on him.

(Details from the letters of Lady Bernard. Published in, "*South Africa a Century Ago*" *(1797-1801)*. Part I. Page 74.)

However, more trouble was brewing for Lord Charles who was now also criticised for not visiting the new settlers, who after the elation of their arrival were now aggrieved because the Colony was not as wonderful as they had been led to believe. Also after the death of Napoleon and the loss of trade to St Helena and the Garrison there, trade from the Colony was lost and the economy declined. Lord Charles was paid the enormous amount of £10,000 per annum around £419,200.00 in today's money and he was also very extravagant. Moreover, when he was criticised in the Cape Town press by Thomas Pringle he tried to control and censure it. By 1826 with all this criticism from many quarters, he was called home to answer the charges against him. None of the charges were proved however, but he never returned to the Colony and died a few years later of a stroke at Brighton after returning from a horse ride.

During his tenure, Lord Charles had managed to turn public opinion against him and the whole sorry tale ended up by changing Colonial policy, not only in the Cape, but throughout the colonies, bringing about profound legal and constitutional transitions in imperial governance. Which resulted in his eventual replacement as Governor of the Colony, being paid only £6,000, just over half of what Lord Charles had received.

However, before all this trouble had erupted in December 1822, Lord Charles had granted Colonel Brereton leave, and this was extended by the Duke of York on 14 February 1823, before he resigned from the 49th Regiment on 19 June 1823, and his position as Commander of the Cape Town Garrison. He was replaced by Colonel Napier before he left South Africa for the last time and returned to England. But why did the Colonel leave his prestigious post and resign from his regiment and return to England?

1823 England

King George IV was now in the third year of his ten-year reign, which was illustrated by his extravagant lifestyle. George had built Brighton Pavilion remodelled Buckingham Palace and Windsor castle, but his selfish behaviour and wasteful extravagancies made him unpopular and left him obese and addicted to laudanum, an opium derivative. The Earl of Liverpool was still Prime Minister and had been since 1812, after replacing Spencer Perceval who had been assassinated while entering the House of Commons.

Lord Liverpool had steered the country safely through the Napoleonic wars and the War of 1812 with the United States of America. However, during Liverpool's paranoid and repressive government, simmering tensions were brewing and they reached a climax during a peaceful Reform rally of 60,000 men, women and children, who had gathered in St Peter's field, Manchester. They had arrived to hear the radical orator Henry Hunt speaking of Reform and the Repeal of the Corn Laws which had made bread almost unaffordable for the masses while the land owning two per cent prospered from it. A jumpy military overreacted after the yeomanry tried to arrest Hunt and the 15th Hussars led by Lieutenant Colonel Guy L'Estrange and Major Joseph Thackwell misread the situation. They led an attack without warning on the unarmed gathering resulting in 15 deaths and over 600 injuries. The brutality that resulted so soon after the famous battle of Waterloo where the 15th Hussars had fought was compared unfavourably and so it became known infamously as the Peterloo Massacre.

Lord Liverpool and his government's attitude were made clear by its total endorsement of the massacre. Even the Prince Regent, declared his approval of the; *"prompt, decisive and efficient measure for the preservation of public tranquillity"*.

Moreover, despite many calls for an official inquiry none were granted and instead Lord Liverpool's response was to impose the oppressive Six Acts Legislation which limited free speech and the right to gather for a peaceful demonstration. This just reinforced the masses distrust of the Government which the majority had no vote in electing and so the call for Political reform escalated.

Arriving in London at this time was Colonel Brereton, and we get an indication as to why he had resigned his Command and Regiment and travelled to England so suddenly, because when Thomas arrived in London in July, he was not alone.

Arriving with him was Olivia Ross, the now 19-year-old daughter of the Honourable Hamilton Ross the rich Cape Town Merchant. The young Olivia must have been truly spellbound to have arrived in London on the arm of the dashing Colonel Brereton dressed in all his military finery. In addition, London was far removed from the small provincial colony of Cape Town, with its still small population. London was the largest and most populous city in the world and the capital of a vast and powerful empire. One expects she was truly taken aback to see so many people trundling through the streets in pursuit of trade and commerce, and passing such large magnificent buildings, like nothing she had ever seen in her native South Africa.

The couple moved into accommodation in Seymour Place Camden Street, Old St Pancras. However, not long after their arrival on Tuesday 15th they married by Licence at St Marylebone with the bride's mother and father in attendance, a legal necessity as Olivia was still under the age of 21 and therefore considered a minor by law. Nevertheless, why did they travel to London to marry rather than her family home in Cape Town?

The excepted norm is usually for a bride to marry near her parental home where she will ready herself in the bosom of her family. It is even considered unlucky for the groom to see his bride before the ceremony. Also the brides extended family and friends would all be close at hand, indeed as would have been the groom, Colonel Brereton, who of course had also been in Cape Town at the time, so why London?

The answer to this question becomes apparent just eight days later, for on Wednesday 23 July 1823 a daughter, Catherine Leticia Brereton is baptised in London.

However, it was customary to baptise a child on the first Sunday after birth, though this is not always adhered to as in this case. Catherine must have been conceived at the earliest, sometime around October 1822 in South Africa. Not long after this in December, the Colonel is granted leave and this leave is extended in February 1823 by the Commander in Chief, Frederick, Duke of York. After which, Colonel Brereton resigns from his regiment altogether on 19 June, and now we know why!

For it seems the amorous 41-year-old Colonel had been having a relationship with the then 18-year-old who had then become pregnant. In an almost perfect re-enactment of Olivia's parent's elopement, this would no doubt have been a scandal in Cape Town amongst the gentility. So we can guess that a plan was hatched that Olivia would have the baby in secret before leaving for England, probably in one of her father's own ships and getting married in London far away from any unwelcome gossip. One can speculate that a similar event happened with Thomas at least twice before and possibly three.

Later that same month, in July, Lt Colonel Brereton took up his new appointment as, "Inspecting Field Officer for the Bristol Recruiting District". This was even further away from any prying eyes and it is here in Bristol that *a* Catherine Leticia is baptised again on 10 June 1826, at St Augustine the Less not far from Colonel Brereton's recruiting office in College Green. This church was built in 1240 but like so many in Bristol, it was damaged during German bombing in the Second World War and was subsequently pulled down in the 1960's. The 2nd May 1826 is often quoted as her birthday, but she would have been around three years old by then? It seems inconceivable that they would pretend that she was born three years later just to avoid the embarrassment of admitting that they were not married at the time. Alternatively, it could be that with the high mortality rate amongst children in this period, it could be possible that this first child died and a later child was christened with exactly the same name. This assumption is further reinforced by the discovery of an announcement in the local press; Bristol Mirror Saturday 6 May 1826;

"May 2nd at Hambrook House near this City, The lady of Col Brereton a daughter.

So events had moved swiftly for the Colonel of late, he had left his prestigious Command in the burning African sun at Cape Town, returned to the temperate climate of England and was now a married man again with a young wife and now a baby daughter to look after. This is the reason he needed to find another position and a permanent home to bring up his new family and that quest had lead him to Bristol. Of course, Colonel Brereton had been in Bristol only two years previously with the 49th Regt when they disembarked from Ireland on route to South Africa.

Bristol is on the west coast of England and can trace its name back to Anglo Saxon times when it was known as Brigstowe, which means a settlement, by a bridge. This is very much like Thomas Brereton's hometown in Ireland, which also originated as a settlement by a bridge, but that is not the only connection between Bristol and Ireland.

Bristol had a long history as a slave trading port, but it did not start with African slaves, it started long before that. Many earlier cultures practised slavery even within the British Isles including the ancient Britons followed by the Romans, Anglo Saxons and Vikings. In fact, the Vikings were northern Europe's leading slave traders and both the Saxon and the Vikings settled and ruled parts of England at one time. The Vikings not only settled in England but also in Ireland and founded the port of Dublin for the trading and distribution of English slaves from Bristol. After the Norman Conquest this trade was stopped by William the Conqueror, who replaced slavery with Serfdom.

Later after the conquest of Ireland by King Henry II all English slaves were freed by royal decree and in a complete reversal of fortune Dublin then became a colony of Bristol.

(Saxon Slave Market by Jean Manco.
First published in *Bristol Magazine*. July 2006.)

In the 18th century Bristol was again trading slaves but this time from Africa and between 1725–40 Bristol became the major British slaving port. During the years 1739–48, there were 245 slave ships leaving from Bristol (about 37.6% of British trade).

In 1769, Granville Sharp was the leading defender of Africans and published a pamphlet called: *A representation of the injustice and dangerous tendency of tolerating slavery in England,* in which he declared that any person that came to England to live became a subject of the King and thereafter was protected by the law of the land which included *Habeas Corpus* which prevented forcible arrest or imprisonment.

In 1771 he successfully defended an American runaway slave called James Somerset by putting Somerset's case before the Lord Chief Justice of England, Lord Mansfield. Somerset's lawyers worked free of charge though his case was vigorously contested by the powerful West India planters, who declared that "negro slaves" were chattel, and that Somerset was a slave according to the laws of Virginia and Africa. Mansfield was fully aware of the implication that his decision would entail and this would not go down well with the influential West India planters, declaring, "Fiat justicia, ruat coelum" (Let justice be done, though the heavens fall). Announcing his decision in June 1772, he stated that though the laws of Virginia may support slavery, English law did not, therefore slaves became free upon entering the British Isles and so Somerset was declared a free man. Though this ruling was a great step forward in clarifying English law it was not the end of the matter and was mostly ignored by the powerful and influential West India planters, who still found ways to get around its enforcement.

Granville Sharp formed; *The Society for Effecting the Abolition of the Slave Trade,* in 1787 and was later responsible for getting William Wilberforce involved in Abolition

(Dates and figures from; *Understanding Slavery.*
Memoirs of Granville Sharp. © 2011. London 1820.)

The Mayor of Bristol at this time (1823) was John Barrow and the Sheriffs were John Savage and Charles Pinney who like many Bristolians owed his wealth and prestige due to being a slave trader and owner. Both Savage and Pinney would go on to be Mayors of Bristol themselves, the latter infamously.

Though Colonel Brereton no longer commanded his own regiment, his new appointment as Inspecting Field Officer for the

Bristol Recruiting District was a large prestigious one, consisting of the counties of Gloucester, Wiltshire, Somerset, Dorset, Devon, Cornwall, and parts of Hampshire. In this position Lt Colonel Brereton would be assisted by his staff which would include his Adjutant, Lt Hodges; Paymaster W.H. Philips. and Surgeon, I.Q. Short (Dept. Insp.)

The King had ordered that each district throughout the country should have its own militia with its own General Officer Commanding them and an Inspecting Field Officer for superintending the troops of the local Yeomanry and the Volunteer Corps in the district. Both the Yeomanry and the Militia came under the Home Office, though Horse Guards appointed the Inspecting Field Officer.

Brereton would be continually employed visiting, and supervising the drill, and exercises of the Corps under his inspection during the time of the year appointed, so that they would be fit, ready, and properly supplied for service.

The Brereton family originated of course in the west of England, and so perhaps Thomas had chosen this appointment purposefully because just a few miles away was the town of Bath where his relative Major William Brereton had been master of ceremonies at the Lower Rooms, until his death 10 years previously in 1813. Also his son Major General Robert Brereton, whom Thomas had served as Brigade Major in St Lucia who was also now deceased, but his widow and their children were living at 5 The Vineyard, Bath. In addition, Thomas's beloved uncle, Colonel Coghlan and his wife Sarah also lived there. In fact the Coghlan family as we have seen also had a long associating with Bath, as Andrews sister, and Thomas's aunt, Mary Coghlan, c1761–1821, had lived there for many years and as Viscountess Mount-Earl she had died there at 24 Circus only two years previously in 1821.

Therefore, Bristol was not only close to Bath and close to family; it was also a convenient transit point to visit Ireland just across the Irish Sea. In addition, he was not the only Brereton living in Bristol itself either. For Major Robert Brereton, the natural son of the aforementioned deceased Major General Robert Brereton also lived in Bristol, living at 6 Hope Square, Clifton, just up the hill from the town.

Thomas himself set up home at the rather grand Hambrook Court, Winterbourne, just over eight miles away from his office in College Green Bristol.

Hambrook Court, was a large house owned for many years by Thomas Baynton an eminent surgeon and medical writer and his family.

It must have been very hectic with all these exciting changes going on in his life, however later in the year it must have pained him and brought him down to earth to hear the dreadful news about the fate of Brigadier General McCarthy. Brereton had replaced McCarthy as governor of Senegal in 1815 and his career in some ways mirrored his. For McCarthy had been promoted to Lt Colonel of the Royal African Corps and then Governor of Senegal and Goree in 1812 just as Brereton had, in both respects in 1815. Therefore, it must have been shocking for him to hear that while commanding a detachment of the Royal African Corps on the Western Cape he had been attacked while waiting on a riverbank to rendezvous with his main force. However, they soon ran out of ammunition and were overwhelmed by a large Ashanti force of over 10,000 men. His Colonial secretary J.T. Williams was later taken prisoner and kept in a hut with the severed heads of both McCarthy, and Ensign Wetherell, who had tried valiantly to protect his commanding officers body.

McCarthy's skull was later seen gruesomely gold-rimmed and used as a drinking vessel by the Ashanti rulers. This was a terrible end for a man who, like Colonel Brereton also fought in the West Indies and had not only been the Governor of Senegal and Goree, but when Brereton took over in 1815 McCarthy left to become the Governor of nearby Sierra Leone. Sierra Leone was where the British crown established a settlement for freed slaves and black American who had fought for the British in the American Revolutionary war which ended in 1783. Five years later Granville Sharp together with black American ex slave Thomas Peters were involved in helping to settle 400 freed slaves, who were all given £12 by the crown. The capital city of Sierra Leone is still called Freetown to this day.

While he was Governor, McCarthy took a strong interest in the welfare of the natives and liberated slaves, arranging support and education for them. His concern for their welfare even extended to corresponding with the abolitionist William Wilberforce and campaigning for the end of the slave trade altogether. Therefore, it is ironic that he should have been killed and his remains used so disrespectfully by those he had tried so hard to help.

After hearing this news, Colonel Brereton must have been grateful that he had managed to serve his time there without meeting such a gruesome end. Thankful, with his new wife and daughter, he must have been very happy and thought how providence was at last shinning on him as he contentedly settled into the day-to-day work of his new command, and his new role as husband and father.

Four years later the happy couple were soon blessed with another child, this time a son, on 12 April 1827 *.

*(*The Morning Post*, birth announcements Friday 20 April 1827.)

Less than a year later in January 1828, the Duke of Wellington resigned as Commander-in-Chief and was appointed Prime Minister of a more hard line Tory Government, and the Duke appointed his former aide-de-camp, Lord Hill as Commander-in-Chief.

Later that same year, perhaps due to his growing family and the expectation of yet another child, Colonel Brereton advertised in the local press that he intended to vacate Hambrook. Which he did, taking his growing family to an even grander abode, the three story eight-bedroomed mansion called Clifton Wood House which was built in 1720 and altered in the 1800s, it sold in 2015 for over £4million It was at this impressive mansion that on 2 October 1828 another daughter was born. This daughter was named Mary Sarah Coghlan Brereton, (named after his two Coghlan aunts in Bath). Clifton Wood House was about six miles closer to Bristol and was the former home of the ship owning and banking family of Levi Ames, former Mayor of Bristol. Later the next month on 27 November 1828 his Uncle Col Edmund Coghlan Lt Governor of Chester died. Col Coghlan was buried at St James, Piccadilly, London; coincidentally this is also the same church that Colonel Brereton married his first wife Margaret less than ten years earlier in 1818.

The mourners at the service included Edmunds younger brother, Colonel Andrew Coghlan and his only son James Coghlan. It is not recorded whether his nephew Colonel Brereton attended, but it is likely that he did and if so it must have brought back many painful memories to be once again in the very Church he left so happily less than ten years previously.

Also attending were a number of mourners from the United Service Club. The now deceased Edmund Coghlan, like his nephew Col Brereton had previously served as an *Inspecting Field Officer* but in his case for the Waterford recruiting district in Ireland.

The remembrance of his first wife's tragic death must have brought a shudder to the Colonel who no doubt took comfort in his new happier circumstances.

However, death was ever present for our 19th century ancestors, and happiness just a fleeting shadow.

For his infant son had died the year before not long after birth, and then only three months after the birth of his last child Mary, yet another tragedy struck him to the very core.

For in the early hours of 14 January 1829, his dear wife Olivia still only 25 years old also passed away, she was tragically even younger than his first wife. Thomas must have been devastated after only six years of marriage to yet again be burying his dear wife.

Olivia Brereton was buried in the church of St Andrews Clifton, where his daughter Mary had only recently been christened. With the happy memories of that day in his mind, he must have scarcely believed he could have returned so soon with Olivia, not for a joyous occasion as before, but this time to say his last goodbyes and bury her.

The grief stricken Colonel, reeling from yet more deaths in his young family, wrote in the fly leaf of the family Bible;

"14th of January, 1829, 3 o'clock in the morning my beloved wife, Olivia, died at my house, in Clifton Wood."

What curse is this!
That strikes me to the core,
To see my love, die in full bloom once more.

While cold death, hangs like a shadow over me
Devouring all that I hold dear

What curse is this!
That cuts me to the very bone,
And runs me through the heart, once more I weep alone.
But no tears of grief can wash away my pain,
For my heart is broken
And will never love again.

After the death of his first daughter and then his son and now his beloved wife, perhaps as grand as it was, Clifton Wood House seemed almost cursed and it was hard for the Colonel to live in a house that had only brought him pain. Therefore, he decided it would be better to move yet again into a house where these precious memories would not haunt him so.

Eventually he found a suitable house about three miles away on the east side of Bristol called *Redfield House,* off the upper Bath Road and therefore closer to his relatives in Bath. Perhaps more importantly it was only a couple of miles away from his recruiting office in College Green. This substantial three-storey property was a former School known as *Redfield House Academy.* It was set in its own extensive grounds of some eight acres, all enclosed within a wall and with a frontage on the main road of some 1,200 ft. The entrance on Redfield Road was through a gothic styled lodge doorway along a long and twisting drive past the outbuildings and stables on the right-hand side until finally it turns into a roundel in front of the house, which lies sideways to the main road. Therefore, the house was very secluded being 110 feet away from the nearest boundary wall.

The main three-story building was an oblong flat fronted structure of some 50 feet long by 25feet deep with bay windows on the ground floor. The entrance was through a columned porch into the entrance hall with the adjoining doors leading on to the well-appointed dinning room and parlour, and a large 26feet by 17½ feet drawing room whose bay windows looked out over the meadows towards Bristol itself. To the rear of the property was the kitchen and scullery, beneath which in the basement were extensive beer and wine cellars stocked to accompany the meals prepared above and served in the nearby dining room. Also to the rear of the property, stained glass French windows opened onto the lawns where the children played and beyond that were the fruit gardens, a meadow, as well as an asparagus garden. On the first floor, four comfortable bedrooms and dressing rooms were situated and further up the next flight of stairs a further two bedrooms, two attics and yet more rooms.

To the right of the building and adjoining it was an additional two-storey dwelling house measuring some 25 feet square. Further outbuildings comprised a large two story brewhouse of 27 feet by 13 feet, a coachhouse, three stall stables, as well as a dairy, piggery, and two gardeners cottages beyond which were paddocks and fields for the grazing of horses and dairy cows while to the left of the house were further outbuildings. The Colonel also took his staff along with him, which included Mary Anne Pitchforth his loyal housekeeper, who had worked for him since he had been the Governor of Senegal in 1815. Mrs Pitchforth would take on some of the duties of his late wife by helping to look after his two young daughters. In addition, his young footman James Wilson, who had worked for him since he had moved to Bristol; as had his gardener and coachman.

(Details of the house and grounds from; The printed Ordnance Survey sheet Gloucester LXXII 13.15 of Redfield House.

Houses and People in Old St George, by William T. Sanger. Published by Messrs Jeffreys, Son and Co, Baldwin Street, Bristol. Further details from Bristol Newspapers, and Directories of the period.)

Though the hurly-burly of moving into this new home must have helped to temporarily take his mind of the dreadful reality of his wife's premature death. Nevertheless, in the quiet moments when he was alone with his thoughts, it must have weighed heavily on him to realise he was alone yet again. Fortunately, he also had his military routine and official duties to attend to which helped to fill the hours, hopefully leaving little time to dwell on personal grief.

The next year on 26 June 1830, King George IV died at Windsor Castle after a life of excess, he weighed an incredible 20 stone and his waist extended to over 50 inches around. Though he had 11 illegitimate children still living, his only legitimate child, Princess Charlotte of Wales had died 13 years previously. The current (2015) Prime Minister of Great Britain, David Cameron is a descendent of one of these illegitimate children.

After King George IV death, his younger brother Prince William, Duke of Clarence, succeeded him as King and reigned as William IV.

Later on Tuesday 19 October 1830, an article in the *Bristol Mercury* announced that Nangeon's Hotel, Clifton, had received orders to prepare for some very special guests. The new Kings sister-in-law, her Royal Highness the Duchess of Kent, and his niece, the 11-year-old Princess Victoria, who would of course later become Queen Victoria, would be staying at the Hotel.

The young Victoria was the daughter of King William's younger brother Edward Augustus, the Duke of Kent, who had died 10 years previously in 1820. However, the Hanoverian brothers had many illegitimate children and even Victoria herself at the time was rumoured not to be the child of Edward at all, but Sir John Ponsonby-Conroy, her mother's private secretary and the comptroller of her household. Sir John himself also believed that his wife Elizabeth was secretly the illegitimate child of Victoria's father the Duke of Kent.

Many people at the time had also said that the elderly Duke of Kent was actually too old at the time when Victoria was conceived. This all lead to gossip at the court, referring to Victoria's family at Kensington Palace as the, "Conroyal Family".

Victoria later admitted catching her mother and Sir John the year before when she was aged 10 years, engaged in what was rather diplomatically reported as, "*some familiarities*".

Even Prince Ernest Augustus, the Duke of Cumberland had spread rumours that the two were lovers and even his brother HRH the Duke of Clarence referred to Conroy rather disparagingly as "King John".

Sir John Conroy and the Duchess took a very controlling influence over the young Princess. They isolated her and would not allow her to play with other children except Sir John's own. In addition, they demanded that the Duchess should rule as Regent if the Princess assumed the crown before her 18th birthday. They also embarked on a series of royal tours with Victoria in order to expose her to the people. It was during one such tour that they would be visiting Bristol on their way from Malvern to Bath. On hearing of the Royal intentions, the Corporation of Bristol went into frenzy and a sent an invitation to a formal reception at the Mansion House. However, unfortunately due to the strict planning of their tour they had to decline the invitation. Nevertheless, the Royal party replied that they would very much like to receive the Mayor and corporation early on the Thursday morning. As news of the Royal visit swept through the City, a large crowd assembled at Clifton on the Wednesday evening to greet their arrival, where the entrance of the Hotel was illuminated with variegated lamps and the Royal coat of arms encircled with laurel. All the houses of the neighbourhood had their lights burning, which rendered the dark October night into an almost magic scene of twinkling lights, as the expectant crowds waited the Royal arrival.

At half past five the crowds were disappointed to see the approaching carriages were only the royal staff, but then an hour later as the Royals carriage finally appeared the expectant crowds could contain themselves no longer and exploded with spontaneous cheering with the gentlemen waved their hats with great enthusiasm. Colonel Brereton in his capacity as *Inspecting Field Officer* of the District was there to greet them in full ceremonial uniform with feathered cocked hat and his sword awarded him by the Royal African Corps hanging proudly by his side. On entering the hotel, the Royal party appeared at a window at the front to greet their spellbound subjects and Sir John Conway held a light before them so that they could be seen by the crowd below. Later while the Royal party dined a band played popular airs on the green opposite and the evening was ended by a firework display. No doubt, many in the crowd would tell of this magical night for many years to come.

The following morning, Thursday, at 9 o'clock, the Mayor John Savage now in his second year in office, together with all the civic dignitaries of the City met at the Council House in full ceremonial attire before leaving in a procession to Clifton for their audience with the Royals. On reaching the hotel they were escorted into the dinning room where they waited until Sir John Conway announced that her Royal Highness and the Princess were ready, before leading them into the drawing room where the Royal party received them most graciously. Sir John first introduced Mayor Savage and then in turn he introduced each member of the Civic party, which included some names that would be come infamous only a year later. These names included; Alderman's, Daniels, Fripp, George Hillhouse, Abraham Hillhouse, Barrow, Camplin and Goldney. Amongst the Sherriff's, were Protheroe and Claxton, Nicolas Roach, Charles L. Walker, Francis Savage, Daniel Stanton, Charles Payne, Thomas Riddle, Hugh Danson, J.E. Lunell, George Bengough and a Mr Charles Pinney who himself would be Mayor this time next year.

Later after the Civic dignitaries had departed, the Royal party took to their carriage and went on a tour of the local beauty spots. On their arrival back at the hotel, they sat down to an elegant luncheon before finally leaving Bristol at a quarter passed two on their way to Bath. As the Royal carriages clattered through the streets the church bells rang out and the populous cheered waving their hats as they passed. Even the upper windows of the houses were crowded with spectators anxious to see their Royal guests as they passed through the City which was bedecked with flags flown on all the churches and even the ships in the harbour. Later in honour of its Royal guests, Nangeon's Hotel would afterwards be known as, *The Royal Hotel.*

After all his years abroad serving in the most inhospitable climates in the world Colonel Brereton must have felt at least his professional life was more pleasant and at least their was no chance his skull would end up as a African Kings drinking vessel, like his comrade McCarthy's had.

Reform or Revolution

The people of Bristol must have been delighted to see the Royal party and their future Queen visiting them and must have looked on in awe at all the pomp and ceremony that accompanied them. As they stood in the crowd watching all this colourful display parading down the very streets they knew, and probably seeing for the first time in their lives such splendour. They even saw their own dignitaries in their ceremonial finery parading through the town, and later would no doubt have heard of the sumptuous dinner that they had all enjoyed.

However, when the event was over and many had returned to their modest homes and had time to reflect, no doubt the difference between their own meagre existences and the lavish lifestyle of the upper classes must have rankled with the majority. Especially as the last two years of harvest had been very poor, and due to mechanisation many were now unemployed. Even the rising ranks of the middle classes, though better off monetarily than their poorer brethren, still had no political voice either. In fact, the very Bristol dignitaries that they had witnessed parading through the streets and representing them and the town, had not been elected by the majority of the population of Bristol. They were appointed by a small clique of their own class, predominantly West India traders and the same names would be appointed to various civic roles year after year. This realisation of the starkly different lives lived by the upper classes had fuelled the revolution in France and the same discontent had been brewing in Britain. The call for political reform was rising throughout the land and everywhere you heard the call Reform! Reform! Nevertheless, the governing aristocracy that had been in control for centuries were not going to give up power without a fight.

In Bristol despite having a population of 104,000 only 6,000 had the vote and the rising middle and working classes still had none. This was at a time when places such as the new industrial centres like Birmingham, Manchester and Sheffield with fast growing populations around the 250,000, had no Parliamentary representation *at all*. Yet Bristol still had two MPs, due to its former glory as the second city of the kingdom and although it was declining, it retained these seats. Even Sir Charles Wetherell the Bristol recorder who was an MP through his seat in Boroughbridge Yorkshire, which despite only having a population of 947 still returned two MPs to Parliament one being Sir Charles. But there were even worse examples like Gatton in Surrey that had only seven voters yet also returned two MP's as did Old Sarum in Wiltshire the former seat of William Pitt the elder whose family actually owned the borough until 1802, but by the 1830s no one actually lived there yet they still returned two MP's to Parliament. These were know as the *"rotten boroughs"* and with such great inequalities in the voting system it is not hard to see why the clamour for reform was so widespread and why the people were demanding it when places like Manchester that had grown rapidly since the industrial revolution had no MPs at all. The meeting in St Peter's Field had been organised to discuss this but had turned into the *Peterloo Massacre* instead.

This only fuelled unrest that grew throughout the country, the repeal of the anti- trade union *Combination Acts*, and the *Corn Laws* which artificially inflated the price of bread, together with the *Test and Corporation Acts*, under which religious minorities faced discrimination, were all major issues

After the death of King George IV on 26 June 1830 Parliament was dissolved by law, and a general election was held which the Tories under the leadership of the Duke of Wellington had won, but by only a small majority which lead to a number of defeats. And so they were forced to resign in November, and the new King William IV appointed Earl Grey of the Whig party to form a government of; *"peace, retrenchment and Reform"*.

This was the first time any Whigs had been in government since 1807. The difference in political philosophy between the Tories and the Whigs was that the Whigs believed that political power and authority came from the people up, while the Tories believed power came from the privileged ruling classes down to the people. Earl Grey was determined to push ahead with reform to; *"prevent the necessity of revolution"*. The Whigs had been promoting reform since Charles Fox in 1780 and Earl Grey himself founded an organisation advocating parliamentary reform in 1792. This group, known as *"The Society of the Friends of the People"*, included 28 MPs. and in the same year petitioned for reform but it was defeated by 256 to 91 votes. A year later in 1793 he introduced another Reform bill saying;

"a man ought not to be governed by laws, in the framing of which he had not a voice, either in person or by his representative, and that he ought not to be made to pay any tax to which he should not have consented in the same way."

This declaration of no taxation without representation, goes all the way back to the Magna Carta of 1215.

Magna Carta was signed to give the barons more rights from the King, though the common man wasn't even thought of at that time, so six hundred years later they were still waiting for it and even this latest bill was also defeated by 282 to 41 votes.

Charles Grey, Second Earl Grey, married Mary Elizabeth Ponsonby (1776–1861), who bore him ten sons and six daughters: Because Mary was virtually always pregnant Grey travelled alone and had many affairs. The most famous is perhaps Georgiana Cavendish, Duchess of Devonshire with whom he had a daughter named Eliza Courtney who was brought up by Earl Grey's parents as his sister. Colonel Brereton also had a connection with the Duchess through his mother's family the Coghlan's, who also had another connection with the Ponsonby's. Thomas Brereton's maternal Grandfather James Coghlan had left £7,000 per annum* through the maternal line of inheritance to the Honourable Frederick Ponsonby, Third Earl of Bessborough. Whose mother was Lady Caroline Cavendish, daughter of William Cavendish, Third Duke of Devonshire and his daughter was none other than Lady Caroline Ponsonby, wife of William Lamb and lover of Lord Byron.

*(*King James Irish Army List*. Page 367.)

William Lamb of course was at this time also a prominent member of the Government and by the time of the reform riots he had succeeded to the title and become Lord Melbourne and appointed Home Secretary. He also employed his younger half brother George, as his undersecretary.

He was born William Lamb, his *"father"* was Peniston Lamb, First Viscount Melbourne and his mother was Elizabeth Milbanke also a close friend of Georgiana, Duchess of Devonshire. William was the second of six children, four boys and two girls, but his older Brother Peniston, and possibly his younger sister Harriet, were the only children fathered by Peniston Lamb senior. All the others were the children of Lord Egremont, except the third son who was fathered by King George IV and so named George. It seems Peniston Lamb senior was comfortable with this arrangement as his older son, also named Peniston assured his descent. Unfortunately, Peniston died aged only 15-years-old, and so his estate and title would now go to his second *"son"* William, who of course was no blood relation. The distraught Viscount allowed William to assume the title Lord Melbourne, but he drastically cut his inheritance from that which his true son had enjoyed.

(Details from, *Lord Melbourne* by L.G. Mitchell. Page 6.)

William Lamb himself had previously married the 19-year-old Lady Caroline Ponsonby as mentioned, who was also related to Georgiana, Duchess of Devonshire, being her niece; she was also the cousin by marriage of Annabella, Lady Byron. Lady Caroline Ponsonby now became Lady Caroline Lamb and you will no doubt remember this name from the recent Coghlan connection. Their Marriage was at first a happy one, and they had two children but only their son George Augustus Frederick survived, though he suffered from what is believed to have been autism. As William Lamb's political career gathered pace the couple grew more distant and seven years after her marriage at age 26 she met the young 24-year-old poet Lord Byron falling madly in love with him, she even sent him a cutting of her pubic hair. Unfortunately, it was a destructive relationship and she coined the descriptive phrase of Byron as; *"Mad bad and dangerous to know"*.

Yet the entanglement of these aristocratic dynasties was deep, Byron's confidante and close friend was none other than William Lamb's own mother, Elizabeth Lamb, Viscountess Melbourne herself.

As Home Secretary Lord Melbourne as he now was, gained a reputation as a procrastinator and when any measures were finally announced they were often described as lacking any merit. Melbourne himself though a Whig politician, was because of his class an anti-reformer.

The other important office at this time we should consider is that of Commander-in-Chief of the Army. This roll had been given to the Duke of Wellington's junior officer General Rowland Hill in 1828, Hill had served under the Duke in the Napoleonic wars. Wellington himself had been C-in-C at the time, but when he became Prime Minister he had to relinquish the post, after all the 12 members of his cabinet told him that this was not possible for him to continue in both. Therefore, if the Duke himself could not do it, what better than to have a person in position who would follow all the Dukes orders to the letter. Therefore, Rowland Hill was given the appointment over the top of more experienced and senior officers, and so was informed by the Duke to keep it to himself for the time being so as not to upset those who would by seniority have expected the appointment themselves.*

*(*Wellingtons Right Hand Man*, by Joanna Hill. Page 179.)

Wellington of course held very strong opinions on military and political matters, and regarded Hill very much as his protégé. So would often instruct him on what course of action to take and Hill rarely disagreed with the Duke's recommendations.

Another man who will be prominent in this tale is Major Mackworth who in turn was one of Rowland Hill's aide-de-camp at Waterloo and who he reappointed to this post on half pay in 1830 after he became C-in-C. Hill also appointed Lord Fitzroy Somerset as his secretary who was the younger brother of Lord Charles Fitzroy Somerset, Governor of the Cape Colony, South Africa, who Lt Colonel Brereton had served under. He had also served with Wellington and had lost his right arm at Waterloo. Fitz as he was called was however not a brilliant soldier and would later go on to command the troops in the Crimea and be held responsible for the famous disaster that was the *Charge of The Light Brigade*. When Earl Grey became Prime Minister in late 1830 he didn't, as would be expected, appoint a Whig man of his own as C-in-C, he kept on Wellington's man who himself was of course also a Tory and anti-reformer. Therefore, though Grey himself was pro-reform the two men who would play a pivotal role in events were in fact anti-reform as were many others in influential positions.

As these calls for reform were spreading around the country, Colonel Brereton must have noticed the rising discontent and wondered what the outcome would be if political reform was not delivered. To defuse this situation, as soon as Grey became Prime Minister he had further plans for reform drawn up and on 3 February 1831 these proposals were announced. The Bill was passed by the House of Commons on 22 March, by a majority of 136. However, despite a powerful speech by Earl Grey, the Bill was defeated in the House of Lords by forty-one. Therefore, Earl Grey resigned and asked the King to dissolve Parliament and call for new elections so that he could return with a larger majority.

King William IV reluctantly agreed and dissolved Parliament in person on 22 April. At this time, there was not a single election day, but separate elections in the various constituencies around the country so these elections were held from April until June 1831 before the results were known which only lead to a longer period of uncertainty.

This uncertainty only added to the discontent around the country, manifesting itself throughout May, and into June. In Merthyr Tydfil Wales, frustration turned to demonstrations and then violence. Merthyr was just 62 miles from Colonel Brereton across the Bristol Channel. The population at this time in Merthyr was 22,083 and many workers had been laid off or had their wages cut, all at a time of rising prices. To try to combat this and give themselves a voice, they had organised themselves into a Political Union calling for the change in the Corn Laws and for political reform. Therefore, when they heard that the Reform Bill had been rejected and the reform government had resigned, a demonstration in May attended by 5,000 people was organised. During this demonstration their political impotence and frustration soon turned violent and stones and missiles were thrown at anti-reformers and their property and in response two of the ringleaders were arrested. The next day an angry mob of 3,000 marched to the house of a Mr Stephens an anti-reformer flying a flag dipped in ox blood, this red flag was destined to become the symbol of working class protest throughout the world. As the violence escalated a local Magistrate J.B. Bruce signed up 70 Special Constables and sent a request to the Military Authorities at Brecon for troop reinforcements. He later assembled his 70 Specials outside the Castle Inn where they remained for four days together with 52 soldiers of the Royal Glamorgan Light Infantry from Cardiff and a detachment of 80 soldiers of the 93rd Sutherland Highlanders. The mob surged forward disarming some of the soldiers while stabbing and beating others with clubs. Some of the soldiers inside the pub seeing that they were losing ground fired a volley and killed three rioters but the fighting still continued for a quarter of an hour before they were beaten away leaving the cobbled streets covered in blood while screaming women looked for their menfolk amongst the many motionless bodies littering the area. Sixteen soldiers were wounded and 24 rioters killed, where there bodies, just as they would later in Bristol, were spirited away so as to not bring any recriminations on their families.

On 4 June the Eastern Glamorgan Corps of Yeomanry Cavalry and the Royal Glamorgan Militia arrived in Merthyr. Together with the Swansea Yeomanry Cavalry under Major Penrice along with Fairwood Troop. During clashes at Penydarren House the Magistrates had tried to calm the situation and reach a peaceful conclusion, but yet again they had been unsuccessful and so had lined up the Cavalry in front and behind in a defensive formation to protect the house. While some of the rioters confronted them brandishing their stolen sabres and firing their muskets. Meanwhile the main body of the crowd met up with one of the delegations from the Magistrates and though what took place is not recorded, it lead to the mob reinforcements dispersing with only a little violence.

Later on 6 June a crowd of 12,000 supporters marched from Monmouthshire to meet the Merthyr Rioters at a local common for a mass meeting. Taking the initiative the Magistrates decided to mobilise their troops and take the fight to the protestors so 110 Highlanders, 53 Royal Glamorgan Light Infantry Militia and 300 Glamorgan Yeomanry Cavalry, a total of 463 troops. *

* Figures from the *Newgate Calendar* on the riots.

With this formidable array of force levelled at them, the mob's nerves finally gave way and they slowly started to drift away peacefully without a shot being fired. Which was just as well, as the next day Tuesday 7 June, 400 infantry troops arrived at Newport from Plymouth, with a certain Major Mackworth arriving post haste from London to take command. Later at 8 pm a further two detachments of the 3rd Dragoon Guards also arrived from Trowbridge, all too late however, as the riot was now over.* With his services not needed Major Mackworth set himself up at the now liberated Castle Inn, where the most serious rioting had started, and wrote a report to Lord Hill the Commander in Chief.

* From *Monmouthshire Merlin*, 11 June, 1831 Newport – Military.

With the rioting over, the Home Secretary Lord Melbourne was anxious to set an example and hanged 23-year-old Richard Penderyn in Cardiff. Penderyn had been found guilty of stabbing a soldier despite a petition of 11,000 signatures claiming he was innocent. But it seems Lord Melbourne was fully aware of his innocence because forty-three years later in America a man called Ianto Parker confessed on his death bed that it was in fact he who had stabbed the soldier.*

* (This confession was reported in the *Western Mail* in 1874 and is referenced in the South Wales Police Museum. Later a prosecution witness James Abbott, admitted that he had committed perjury at Penderyn's trial in order to secure the conviction on the express orders of Lord Melbourne himself.

The Cardiff Five: Innocent Beyond Any Doubt. By Satish Sekar. *Judicail Murders in Cardiff. Vindication.* Page 182.

This is also mentioned in many other accounts such as Wales online and on BBC Wales; *"In the Footsteps of the Chartists".)*

Total number of Troops deployed 463 plus the regular cavalry, which arrived just as the magistrates had defused the situation. That does not even include Major Mackworth and another 400 infantry and two detachments of the Third Dragoon Guards who arrived too late. The population of Merthyr at the time was 22,083.

Details of the riots from;

The Newgate Calendar, The Merthyr Tydfil Rioters, June 1831.
And the account of Welsh historian Robert Saunders.
Also the South Wales Police Museum.

Colonel Brereton no doubt heard about the rioting in Merthyr and not long after, rioting broke out even closer in the Forest of Dean only 35 miles from Bristol. This started when the local foresters began breaking up fences that were restricting their ancient rights. Their leader was a man called Warren James who had tried to reinstate their rights legally but to no avail and so threatened to break down the forest enclosure from 8 June when the 20 years enclosure act would expire. Edward Manchen a local magistrate arrived after the fences where attacked with 40 special constables and a warrant for Warren James arrest, but after arriving at the scene of destruction where 200 foresters were present he decided to err on the side of caution and not issue the warrant. A fellow magistrate Henry Davies asked the foresters what they wanted and they handed him a piece of paper which said *"King William and Reform; our rights and nothing but our rights"*. He was soon joined by 80 foresters tearing at the enclosed and breaking it down, while a further 100 stood by cheering them on. Outnumbered the magistrates tried to reason with them to no avail and so at 7.30am they decided to read out the Riot Act. In response, the forester stated their own rights under the 1668 Forestry Act. After 20 minutes, another Magistrate read the Riot Act a second time but the forester continued unabated. Powerless Manchen retired and sent a letter to the Commissioners of Woods in London asking for military assistance and he forwarded the request to the Secretary of State for War who arrange for troops to be sent together with two Police officers to liaise with the civil powers. On the Friday, the ever-present Major Mackworth arrived with 50 men of the Monmouth Militia but just as in Merthyr previously, his efforts were in vain. As the Magistrates declared that;

"We do not doubt your ability," but our object is not to murder the peasantry, but to show them such a force as will convince all but fools and idiots that resistance will be in vain".

(*Warren James and the Dean Forest Riots*,
by Ralph Anstis. Page 103.)

After much derision by the local inhabitants, Major Mackworth marched his troops out of the town and back to Monmouth. On Saturday 11 June, Manchen wrote a letter to Lord Melbourne formally asking for military assistance and saying that Major Mackworth and the Monmouth Militia were not strong enough to use against the rioters without much bloodshed, though there was no mention of the 40 Specials he already had. By this time, much of the enclosure fences had been destroyed, and so the foresters turned their attention to the destruction of the recently introduced turnpikes. But before this could be started a report that regular mounted troops would be arriving the next day, lead to Warren James making a speech to reassure them;

" not only the King but the Duke of Beaufort is on our side – he is the poor man's friend, and will see us righted."

Just after Sunday service in the local town of Coleford, a squadron of the Third Dragoon Guards arrived from Dorchester in their dashing red uniforms with loaded pistols and flashing sabres. They were ready for trouble, but were surprised to see the town quiet and peaceful. The next day Major Mackworth and the Monmouth Militia returned with their numbers now augmented to 70 men and shortly afterwards 180 men of the 11th Regiment of Foot also arrived from Plymouth, so the Militia were again sent back to Monmouth.

(Details and troop numbers taken from; *Warren James and the Dean Forest Riots*, by Ralph Anstis. Page 107.)

Their first priority was to arrest Warren James and interrogate him to find out if he would reveal his patron. In pursuit of this objective, they assembled outside the *Angel* Inn at 11pm, with the special constables and the two police officers from London at the head. They were followed by a large body of Woodmen and then the Marquis of Worcester, a body of Magistrates, and several gentlemen of the district, followed by the imposing presence of the Third Dragoon guards, and fifty infantry men lead by the ever present Major Mackworth. James was later discovered hiding in a local mine and arrested before he could escape. Declaring, *"I am betrayed by treachery,"* but *"I have nothing to fear,"* before being taken to Coleford and where in the early hours he was interrogated by the Duke of Beaufort and his son, together with the Magistrates apparently to discover who his advisers were, but James refused to incriminate anyone. Warren James was later tried and convicted of felony, but rather surprisingly not of a misdemeanour, but he was still condemned to death. This was later commuted to transportation and in a letter written by Lord Duncannon the Commissioner for Woods to George Lamb (Melbourne's brother) the Under Secretary of State responsible for shipping convicts out of the country the following was received.

My Dear George *19 August 1831*

Warren James the Dean Forest rioter has been convicted and will probably be transported, and it is most desirable that he should soon be sent out of the country – Mr Milne will call upon you and explain the circumstances, which make this very desirable.

Yours truly Duncannon

PRO HO17/7pt 1

This letter seems very intriguing, why the haste to remove James so expediently? Was it because they feared that he might incriminate the nobleman who he claimed had supported him? The reason was obviously too delicate to contain in the letter, and we have no idea what was said at the latter meeting between Mr Milne and the Under Secretary George Lamb. Nevertheless, on the back of the letter was added by Lord Melbourne himself, *"Lord M regrets circs are such,"* he then ordered that James should be removed as soon as possible. He was to follow this method three years later with the Tolpuddle Martyrs but in their case, it did not calm the uproar and so the Government had to admit defeat. Warren James was duly transported in irons on the convict ship *Elizabeth* on 18 October 1831 and after a long and arduous journey dropped anchor at Hobart, Van Dieman's Land (now called Tasmania) on 14 February 1832. Warren James settled into his new life of hard labour, which he expected would continue until his death, but a few years later a letter was on its way from London that would change his situation completely.

Lieutenant Governor Arthur, *Downing Street,*

16 February, 1836

Sir, I have the honour to transit to you herewith a free pardon, which the King had been graciously pleased to grant to Warren James, who was sentenced to transportation for life at the Gloucester summer assizes of 1831, and sent to Van Dieman's Land in the convict ship Elizabeth; and I have to desire that you will take the necessary measures for giving to Warren James the benefits of His Majesties pardon.

I am etc

Lord Glenelg

(PRO CO 40/12)

Warren James must have been stunned to receive this unsolicited pardon and must have asked the question, why? But there was no answer to be given, perhaps it was something to do with the Duke of Beaufort who he claimed had sponsored his actions in the Forest of Dean, there must have been a good reason, but what was it?

We simply do not know, but we can speculate that it was the consequence of political intervention by Government, as had been seen in Merthyr. However, whatever the reason, he was now a free, though poor, man in a strange land without friends or family and without the means to return to his beloved Forest of Dean and the bosom of his family. Unfortunately, he was never to return and he died four years later on Tuesday 26 October 1841 after a long and painful illness far from his family and friends.

This episode just highlights further the Machiavellian politics behind the Government and Lord Melbourne in particular who were ready to sacrifice the lives and freedom of their fellow countrymen in order to achieve what they desired and maintain the privileged status quo.

Reform Bill Rejected

These riots that had spread around the country after the rejection of the Reform Bill in the House of Lords, led to fresh elections staged at the end of April 1831. And were probably instrumental in returning the Whigs committed to reform sweeping the board and forming the first majority Whig government in 14 years. This political change was also mirrored in Bristol with two Whig members being elected for Parliament for the first time since 1774.

Even though Earl Grey was re-elected with an increased majority and soon after an amended bill also passed in the House of Commons it was again rejected in the House of Lords on 7 October 1831. News of the Bill's latest defeat soon reached the populous and more demonstrations and violence ensued, starting in Derby that very day. Two days later Nottingham Castle was set on fire and burned to the ground. Disorder and violence spread all over the country, at the houses and seats of the nobility as well as the Bishops who were both implicated in the Bills defeat in the House of Lords. In London, the Duke of Wellington's house was targeted by a mob of protesters who threw stones and broke windows. In addition, a huge march ended at St James Palace where a petition was handed to the King.

In Bristol however, although there had been many rallies and protests, there had been no great displays of violence, though there was a growing mood of anger. No one had forgotten that Sir Charles Wetherell the 61-year-old recorder of Bristol had stood up in the House of Commons in the summer of 1831 stating contemptuously that the people of Bristol were not in favour of reform. This despite the fact that there had been several petitions from them saying the complete opposite, the last one with nearly 20,000 signatures. Therefore, this made it inevitable that on his arrival there would be a demonstration of their displeasure, not to do so, would be an admission that he was right. In addition, though Sir Charles was the recorder of Bristol, he didn't live there, he lived in London, and his constituency was in Yorkshire, so how could he pontificate upon the opinions of the people of Bristol?

In Queens Square, Bristol's local meeting place there had been three rallies held in October alone. All attended by many thousands of people, where Sir Charles was roundly denounced, along with two local Bishops who also had voted in the House of Lords against the Bill. One of them George Law, the Bishop of Bath and Wells, was greeted as he arrived to consecrate the Church of St Paul's in Bedminster by a large baying crowd carrying banners and shouting there disapproval of his voting against the wishes of the people. He was rushed inside and after a tense ceremony left hastily through the seething crowd to his coach which was pelted with missiles of mud and stones amid a torrent of abuse which left him visibly shaken. It was now becoming apparent to the Corporation and the former Sherriff and now Mayor Charles Pinney, that the arrival of Sir Charles might be met with even more disapproval when he arrived later in October to open the assizes.

As the time for Sir Charles visit approached, the populace were becoming more and more vocal in their condemnation, and with so few prepared to come forward to police his arrival. Mayor Pinney decided to send a delegation to London to request Military assistance, but this was also destined to inflame the situation as no one had thought to ask the City of Bristol's elected representatives. Therefore, it is no wonder that very few of the Citizens of Bristol were prepared to help police their city when the Magistracy who were asking for help treated them with such contempt. When the delegation reached London however and met with Lord Melbourne he would give no reply before he had invited the two city representatives Mr James Evans Ballie MP and Mr Protheroe to be present at the conference. Mr Ballie, (the brother in law of Pinney) was indisposed so could not attend but Mr Protheroe did and attested his reluctance to employ the Military and thought that an effective civil force should be employed instead. He also said however that he felt it was proper and necessary to allow people to voice there disapproval of Sir Charles in any legal way possible regarding his behaviour in Parliament and his misrepresenting them on reform, as long as they respected the office he held as a Judge. By law, it was the responsibility of the local Magistracy to provide local policing and not the job of the Military. The Military could only be sent after all order had broken down and even then, it was strictly controlled and they could only act after the specific request and physical presence of the Magistracy to authorise their response. Melbourne had even sent a circular to all Magistrates reminding them of such, and telling them to meet all threats of violence with firmness.

After a similar request, he had expressed his opinion to Sir Thomas Gooch, saying; *"It is impossible, and if possible would be highly objectionable to post troops in every town the neighbourhood of which may be threatened with riot"*.

(Letter from Melbourne to Gooch, 13 December, 1830; Custance 36.)

Also the available number of troops was only 29,000 and so it was impossible to police the whole country, and in any case it was not the Army's job, instead they should rely on; *"the firmness of the Magistracy... to repress any similar ebullition of popular feeling."*

(Letter from Melbourne to Sir G. Clerk, 16 April 1831;ibid GD/8/3332/2.)

Melbourne had only sent troops to Merthyr and the Forest of Dean *after* the rioting had started and not before to act as a peace-keeping force, as he was now being asked for in Bristol. Troops had only been employed after the Magistrates best efforts had not quelled the unrest. For his opinion was also that; *"It was always safer to allow violence to proceed somewhat too far rather than to run the risk of being accused of uncalled for interference."*

(Melbourne to Lord Talbot, 18 August 1832; ibid, box 89/60.)

However, the Corporation spoke as one, and disagreed with what had been said by Mr Protheroe and pleaded with Lord Melbourne to concur with their request. So Lord Melbourne finally gave in and agreed with the majority and so consent was reluctantly granted. However, only a token force would attend, and they should be kept out of sight and only be used if a breach of the peace was committed and their attendance was completely necessary.

So having attained the attendance of the military, the Magistrates still needed to fulfil their duty and recruit constables to keep the peace while Wetherell attended the opening of the assizes. Unfortunately, however, this was not an easy task, for the citizens embittered by his misrepresentations were more inclined to take part in protesting against his remarks and arrival than they were in protecting him. Even the Bristol Alderman and the common council had been unable to appoint watchmen and night constables due to widespread hostility to an increase in the local rates to finance them.*

*(*History of Criminal Law* by Leon Radzinowicz. 1956, Vol 4 page 208.)

Sir Charles was also pressed to cancel the opening of the assizes at such a volatile time, and instead postpone the event until tempers had cooled, but he refused and the opening would proceed as planned.

Colonel Brereton had been in Bristol now for eight years and had watched this growing discontent spreading across the country even as his own personal tragedies had unfolded. Nevertheless, as the superior officer of the district it would fall on him to command any troops supplied to assist the magistrates, even though 15 years earlier Lord Anglesey had remarked in a letter to the then Home secretary that;

"Men from the vicinity of a disturbance were useless in suppressing it," adding that, *"it is very revolting to the feelings of any man to be called upon to attack his neighbours and possibly his kinsfolk"*. *

* (PRO HO42/160)

Therefore, this was yet another difficulty the Colonel would have to deal with on top of his wife's tragic death less than two years previously and his own health declining.

The Army surgeon serving under him for the district had been replaced 13 months ago by Dr Augustus Loinsworth. Colonel Brereton had met the good doctor 20 years before in the West Indies, but since he had taken up this new post under Brereton's command, the doctor had known him more intimately. The Colonels constitution had always been a robust one, but though he managed to avoid dying from fever while serving in unhealthy climates like the *Soldiers Graveyard,* and in Africa, he did not get away scot-free. For as he got older, he had developed a severe liver disorder, which was no doubt directly related and possible magnified by the mental strain of his wife's sudden untimely death. "severe liver disorder" would probably today be known as cirrhosis of the liver, and one of the main causes that Brereton would have been exposed to was the Yellow Fever virus, which can cause acute hepatitis and lead to cirrhosis of the liver. A chronic hepatitis infection can take a few weeks to many years to develop and in some cases up to 40 years to progress to cirrhosis, during which the patient might show no apparent symptoms. Cirrhosis can also be exacerbated by alcohol consumption, but Dr Loinsworth said later that Colonel Brereton's drinking habits were moderate. However, even a moderate drinking habit is bad if you have cirrhosis and after the premature death of his wife, perhaps the Colonel had sought some comfort there.

When the symptoms do appear, they can start with fatigue, nausea, and abdominal tenderness, and as it develops, the toxins it releases into the blood can affect the brain, causing changes in personality, with difficulties concentrating and sleeping. Though I can see no evidence that the Colonel was adversely affected as he continued with his duties, so it seems his condition was not in these advanced stages.

After examining him, the doctor had tried to convince Colonel Brereton to take things easy, but being the dutiful old soldier he was, the Colonel refused, saying he could still complete his duties and could survive a little fatigue.

On hearing about the various riots around the country slowly getting closer and closer he must have known Bristol would not escape. Sir Charles may have ignored them before, but Brereton had seen all the local rallies denouncing him and felt sure that on his arrival they would leave him in no doubt as to their feelings once, and for all. Therefore, despite what Lord Anglesey had said previously, it was probably no surprise when on 25 October Colonel Brereton received a letter from the Quartermasters Guard informing him;

"that in four days one Squadron of the 14th Dragoons would arrive at Clifton and a Troop of the 3rd Dragoon Guards at Keynsham, both with instructions to report to one, and to follow which orders might be given by the Magistrates of Bristol".

(PRO HO 52/12)

Therefore, on receiving this letter Brereton reported to the Magistrates in order to hear what instructions they had. The Magistrates first instructions were concerning the billeting of the men in the town, the 14th Dragoons were to go to the New Cattle Market and the 3rd Dragoon Guards to the New Gaol on the 29th both on the outskirts of town but in the vicinity of Sir Charles' processional route. The day before, the 28th, Brereton arrived at the billets with Mr William Ody Hare the under Sherriff as arranged. Brereton suggested it would be advisable for a Magistrate to be present with the troops in order that they could issue any orders without delay or confusion. This request however was rejected by Mr Hare, who said a written request would be sent in event of any need. The rejection of this proposal and the resulting lack of any organised communications or firm location on behalf of the civil authorities was an indication of things to come and would weigh heavy on future events.

Fuel to the Flames

Saturday 29 October 1831

From 6am as usual, Colonel Brereton now aged 49 had been at his recruiting office at 9 College Green in the pursuit of his regular duties. This office would also serve as a command post during the period if he was needed by the Magistrates and would be manned 24 hours a day so he could always be contacted. He would also not be retiring home at night during these extra duties; instead, he would be sleeping for the duration at his Adjutants house also situated close by in Unity Street.

An hour and a half later at 7.30am Charles Pinney the newly appointed Mayor of Bristol arrived at the Council House. Mayor Charles Pinney was a very wealthy 38-year-old West Indies trader, a man of small stature who suffered from a deformity of his back.

After meeting his Clerk, the 55-year-old Daniel Burges, they spoke for a minute or two and then crossed the street to the Exchange Building. On entering the Exchange, the Mayor was greeted by the 46-year-old Under Sherriff William Ody Hare, whose task had been to recruit some men to serve as Special Constables to supplement the 100 Parish Constables and the same number of nightwatchmen. These men were needed to guard the route that the Bristol Recorder Sir Charles Wetherell would take as he entered Bristol in his ceremonial coach and later to maintain order. There was no Police Force at this time in Bristol, and even in London it had only been formed two years previously in 1829.

These Special Constables were usually recruited from the respectable classes but on this occasion as has been stated it had proved difficult if not impossible, so William Hare had to pay to make up the deficit.

Therefore, the Specials now included some 119 hired men as well as the volunteers, around 300 men in total. Amongst this rag tag of hired men were some who should not have been there at all, and some were later reported to have even joined the rioters.

Nevertheless, perhaps by organising them into groups and assigning the few responsible men into leadership roles this motley crew could perform the task in hand. Unfortunately, no such organisation or deputation took place, nor did any Magistrates accompany them to instruct and control their movements as was required and indeed performed in the recent rioting elsewhere. Therefore, this ill-disciplined force was equipped with a short staff and unleashed on to the streets of Bristol with just a pep talk from the Mayor whose only leadership was to tell them to act with firmness and moderation. He then left the Exchange to return to the Mansion House to change into his ceremonial robes. The men also left to take up their positions along the route that the 61-year-old Recorder Sir Charles Wetherell would be entering the City later in the day.

By 8am dressed impressively in his long blue greatcoat and cocked hat Colonel Brereton met up with the squadron of the 14th Light Dragoon in their blue uniforms comprising around 60 men under Captain John William Gage who had been camped outside the town at Clifton for three days.

The 14th Light Dragoons

Illustration from page 1; *Historical Record of the Fourteenth, or the King's, Regiment of Light Dragoons.* Compiled by Richard Cannon (1847). Parker, Furnivall, & Parker. 30 Charing Cross Road, London.

The name Light Dragoon reflects the fact that both horses and men were smaller than the Heavy Dragoons. These troops had been widely used in the suppression of rioting around the countryside and had recently been employed supporting the civil power at Dowlais Iron Works near Merthyr Tydfil in Glamorgan, Wales. Later on 20 August, one troop had moved from Abergavenny a market town in Monmouthshire to Llandudno on the coast, owing to rioting in Carmarthen, and in September, they had operated in various other places. It was during these sorties that the 14th would earn their sobriquet of "*The Bloody Blues*" due to their brutality.

By 9am the Colonel accompanied them down to their billet in the Cattle Market, Temple Meads. The name Temple Meads came from the nearby Temple Church built by the Knights Templar in the 12th century and the Anglo Saxon word *meads* meaning meadow.

Around the same time, one troop of the Dragoon Guards of around 30 men in their red uniforms under Captain William Henry Warrington arrived. These were the same troops who had been lately employed at the suppression of rioting in the Forest of Dean.

The 3rd Dragoons Guards

Illustration from page 112; *Historical Record of the Third, or Prince of Wales' Regiment of Dragoon Guards*. London: William Clowes and Sons 1838.

They had been camped at the other side of Bristol and as they rode into the town they were joined on the bridge by Colonel Brereton who rode with them to their appointed place outside the New Gaol. The Colonel instructed the Captain that his duties would take him to other parts of the town but that he would keep in constant communication with the Magistrates and that he must not move his troop from the gaol or furnish any party without his direct order or a requisition signed by two Magistrates. The total numbers of troops now under Lt Colonel Brereton's command totalled around "80–90 Dragoons"* these were of course far fewer than those supplied in Merthyr, the Forest of Dean, or recently in Nottingham, all with far smaller populations. In addition, these troops were mounted with no infantry; unlike those supplied in any of the aforementioned riots and this was to prove a contentious issue during the next three days.

* (80 according to Colonel Brereton's suicide note perhaps reduced through injuries.)

The Colonel then rode back to his post at the recruiting office to continue his duties there, and wait in readiness for any such requests from the Magistrates. While the Magistrates themselves waited for the imminent arrival of Sir Charles Wetherill, who was now on his way to open the assizes after spending the night in Bath.

Sir Charles had decided to leave Bath early in an effort to bypass any protests, and so had brought forward his arrival by two hours so he would now arrive at 10am instead of 12 noon. However, it was 10.30 before he arrived at the Blue Bowl Inn not far from the city centre, which was two miles closer than he would normally have changed coaches. Yet another ruse to avoid any crowds or protesters but unfortunately, Saturday was also market day and in the crowded city, word had spread rapidly. Not surprisingly, for as the traders arrived from early morning, many from Wales, they would have been gossiping with the locals about Sir Charles Wetherell's pending arrival and also bought news of the disturbances in their own localities as well as from others around the country. They would have no doubt also witnessed the arrival of armed troops at the New Gaol, where a large curious crowd had already assembled. In addition, the trooping of the specials from the exchange through the main streets to police the route would just have confirmed their suspicions, so a crowd of around 2,000 were already gathering. Into the half-mile Temple

Street the pavements were filling with spectators anxious to get a glimpse of the reviled Sir Charles and as the coach approached Bristol Bridge the coach found it ever more difficult to make its way across into the High Street. Sir Charles was treated to the sight of closed shops and thousands lining the streets and hanging out of the windows just as they had the year before to watch the Royal procession but on this occasion not with joy but disapproval and all anxious to get sight of the hated recorder. As the coach finally reached its destination, the Guildhall in Broad Street, where the crowds were so dense it made it difficult to alight from the carriage in a dignified fashion. So the formal welcoming ceremony had to be abandoned, Sir Charles on finally stepping out tried to recover his dignity and address the crowd but it was a futile gesture that was rewarded with hissing and booing and so he was rushed into the Court House and safety. Once inside he hurried into the Courtroom and sat at his judicial place on the bench, no doubt feeling a bit perplexed by his undignified entry, but quickly composed himself. Unfortunately, no one had expected the crowds to be so large and vociferous, so no one had thought to limit their numbers attending, which would have been wise in the circumstances. Once in they roared and hissed and the noise was such that nothing could be heard. The Town Clerk, Sergeant Ludlow then rose and announced;

"That he believed there was not an individual present who had come there for the purpose of insulting the commission of the King: that with respect to reform...."

(*Narrative of the Bristol Riots* W.H. Somerton)

However, at the mention of *reform* his remarks became inaudible as the noise from the crowd became unbearable. Sir Charles looking very terse grabbed the Town Clerks gown and pulled it to get his attention, and in doing so remonstrated with him about introducing the word reform, into the proceedings. After some sort of order was established the proceeding continued, but they were accompanied by more disruptions, and some constables were sent into the crowd to get the worst offenders.

Sir Charles trying to take the initiative and restore his authority announced that any one interrupting would be charged with contempt. This however had the reverse affect and the crowd became even more vociferous. It was under these trying disrupting conditions that the ceremony preceded, and so it was with relief that with "*three Cheers for the King*" the Court was finally adjourned until 8am Monday morning.

After a short wait of half an hour Sir Charles, the Mayor and John Edgar the City sword bearer entered the ceremonial coaches for the short drive to the Mansion House where a large official banquet was being prepared for them in honour of Sir Charles.

Along the narrow streets more jeering faces appeared calling out their disapproval to the occupants. All apart from a small group who cheered, but this was an exception in a sea of insults. As the coach carrying Sir Charles stopped outside the Mansion House, it was again targeted with a few more stones raining down and this time one of the glass lamps was shattered but no one was injured.

It must have been with some relief that at about 12pm, Sir Charles along with the Mayor, the first Citizens, the Sheriffs, Recorder, Aldermen and Councillors found themselves being safely escorted up the sweeping stairs by the Mansion House footmen to the opulent first floor dining room, where they could at last relax for a while.

Meanwhile outside, Alderman Abraham Hillhouse instructed the Constables to endeavour to arrest anyone who was throwing stones and so the Constables pushed into the protesting crowd arresting those who they suspected were responsible. Nevertheless, they completely disregarded the orders of the Mayor earlier, with reference to their behaviour while on duty and as there was no one there to maintain discipline they acted as they pleased. Intoxicated by success they ventured into the crown another five times to make arrests and mercilessly bludgeoned any one who resisted or tried to reason with them. One man was beaten so badly on the head that he could no longer stand and had to be taken to the infirmary. This by many people was considered the turning point, as the crowd before this had been very vocal with only a few stones in the way of violence, but after these incidents, the mood changed noticeably, and was to get worse later as darkness fell. Numerous observers at the time felt that the crowd would have started to dissipate after they had protested had not this violence been metered out to them. Instead, the crowds were growing larger by the minute from about fifty or so earlier, now about three thousand strong. Not all actively engaged in protest but not doing anything to intervene either, many feeling enraged by what had just taken place. The condition of the young man at the infirmary started to circulate with stories about him suffering from a fractured skull. This further enraged the crowd, along with the knowledge that the vilified recorder and the out of touch Corporation were seemingly oblivious to their protest and instead banqueting on the finest food and wines. All paid for by the very disenfranchised people outside who were being beaten by their lackeys. This was in complete contrast to all the previous riots where a Magistrate had been in control, monitoring the situation and instructing and organising any response and reassuring the protesters that their voice was not being ignored. Many at the time thought that if this had been the case here in Bristol it is very likely that the rising violence could have been halted at this point. Earlier in May at Merthyr, Magistrate J.B. Bruce had organised the Constables and intervened for the peace of the town when he saw trouble rising. However, In Bristol not one of the Magistrates intervened, let alone the Mayor, which just lead to an escalation of tensions.

The following contemporary map of Bristol was printed in 1828 and is reproduced here by permission of Bristol Reference Library. It shows the location of Colonel Brereton's recruiting office in College Green near the Bishop's Palace as well as all the other relevant locations.

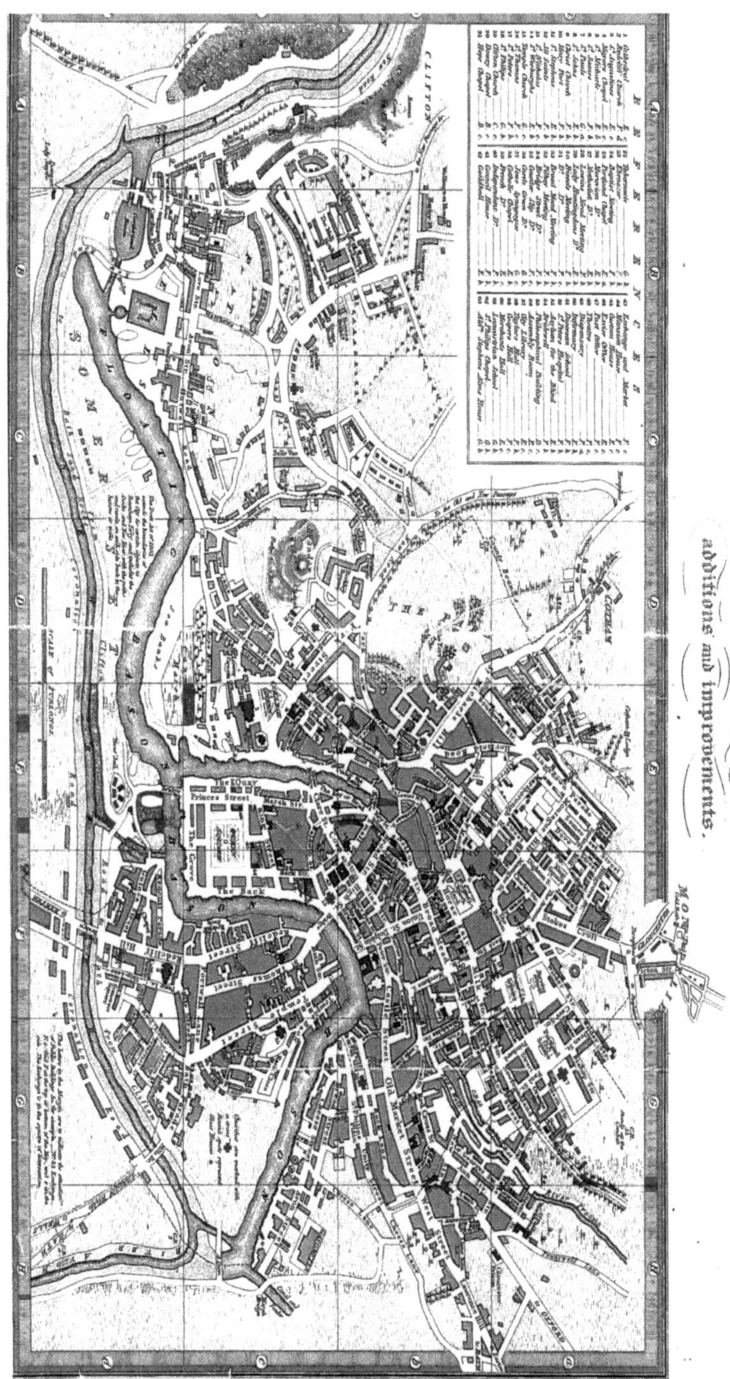
BRISTOL, CLIFTON and the HOT WELLS
additions and improvements.
The Quay
Princes Street
The Grove
The Back
E 23553

At this point, the mob took to prising the cobbles from the street and pelting the Constables guarding the Mansion House. This resulted in the Constables once more surging into the crowd, pulling out one or two who they thought might be responsible and giving them a good beating with their staves. As this went on and more innocent people were arrested, this further antagonised the crowd some of whom had only come out of curiosity. Mr James Townsend, who had been assisting behind the carriage of his master, Mr Sherriff Lax earlier, witnessed what was going on while taking off his ceremonial livery inside the Mansion House. Moreover, he felt compelled on a few occasions to remonstrate with the Constables who treated their captives with much brutality, even after they had them in custody inside the hallway.

This brutality just escalated the tension so much so that, by about 1pm, a cry of *"To the Back"* (The Welsh Back) a nearby Quayside where large piles of faggots were stacked. Armed with these they attacked the Constables driving one into the river where a boatman had to rescue him.

A fierce battle now commenced with the Constables taking the upper hand and forcing the mob to flee, littering the ground with the fallen and their makeshift weapons. One man was beaten so seriously that it was reported he later died. It was thought by many at the time that if the Magistrates had ventured into the crowd and urged the demonstrators to go home, while keeping the Constables in check much could have been prevented, this had not only happened in Merthyr and the Forest of Dean it had also happened before here in Bristol in 1810 as W.H. Somerton pointed out in his narrative;

"Sir Vicary Gibbs who had made himself particularly obnoxious to the reformers of that day, was recorder of this city. A similar multitude had collected on occasion of his arriving to open the Commission of Assize. J.H. Wilcox Esq, was then Mayor, and his conduct, in going amongst the mob, who remained in front of the Mansion House many hours, entreating and exalting them to disperse, was attended with the happiest results."

This unhappily was not to happen on this occasion however, as the new Mayor Charles Pinney was not made of such stern stuff, and seemed to be intimidated by the protesters, or perhaps he just could not be bothered, preferring to keep himself away from the common riffraff outside. Indeed, as the violence intensified instead of taking charge he was seen less and less.

However, though the Mayor was not up to controlling events, the heavens were, for by this time the constant rain and cold conditions had cleared the streets, even if the seeds had been sown for later retribution. Therefore, an uneasy calm descended on the streets of Bristol, and it was during this calm that some members of the Corporation felt it prudent to make themselves scarce too, leaving the Mansion House and retiring to their homes. The Mayor however, and a few others stayed on with Sir Charles, though the Mayor had already felt it wise to send his wife and her mother out to a Hotel in Clifton just in case.

Though the streets were now quiet and calm, those driven from the area were now refreshing themselves in the local alehouses, which only fuelled their resentment. At about 3pm word reached them that the people who had been arrested earlier were being taken to Bridewell Gaol. Therefore, they decided to intercept them in Nelson Street, attacking the Constables beating one to the ground and seriously injuring him before releasing all the prisoners. The seed of resentment sown early in the day were now ripening and bearing its first fruit.

Oblivious to any of this, Colonel Brereton was still waiting at the Cattle Market with the 14th and after hearing nothing from the Magistrates thought it would be prudent to make his way to the Mansion House and see if there were any orders for him to issue to the troops. By the time he arrived, there was a large crowd gathered, but he had not noticed any predilection to violence. After reporting to the Magistrates and asking if they had any orders for him, he waited some time before the Magistrates decided that the troops were not needed and should be withdrawn to their quarters, it was now about 4pm, dark and wet. Around this time, Brereton received an urgent message from Captain Warrington of the Third Dragoon Guards who had been stationed at the New Gaol and been exposed to severe weather for upwards of 10 hours without refreshment.

Colonel Brereton suggested that instead of having the troops billeted in various parts of the city it would be more practical to have the troops together and close by his office in College Green. So the 14th were now to be billeted at Fisher's horse repository off College Street and the 3rd at Leigh's Horse Bazaar off George Street, both within 200 yards of each other and closer to his command post. On receiving approval, Brereton immediately dispatched orders to the 3rd at the New Gaol and the 14th at the Cattle Market. With the orders dispatched and the troops retiring for rest, Brereton decided it was also time for him to retire to his lodgings at number 2 Unity Street, the home of his Adjutant and refresh himself. Brereton had arranged that his office at 9 College Green would be manned 24 hours a day and with his quarters also close by and the troops within 200 yards he was well organised to respond to any orders sent by the Magistrates who would always know where he could be found.

It is just at this time that the Magistrates make a vital mistake regarding the Constables guarding the Mansion House. As they were also ordered to go and refresh themselves at the same time as the troops, leaving the Mansion House almost completely unprotected. This just as the crowds were increasing in numbers and anger and so realising that a window of opportunity had opened before them, they were quick to take advantage surging forward yelling; *"Give us the bloody Recorder, we'll murder him"*. The remaining Constables managed to drive them away, while others in the crowd sang *"God save the King"*. Those driven away rearmed themselves and started to pelt the Mansion House with stones and the small number of remaining Constables retreated inside to the sound of breaking glass.

One of the chief Constables John Cossens advised the Mayor to call for the troops but when the Mayor tried to get his fellow magistrates support for such action, he was told that as Chief Magistrate it was his sole responsibility. The hapless Mayor replied that he was used to doing everything in committee and so did not feel comfortable to take the decision on his own. At this point Sir Charles interrupted and said he thought that military action was not necessary. Therefore, the Mayor realising there was no support for such action, belatedly showed some initiative and for the first time went outside to address the crowd. His sudden appearance supported by some officials surprised the crowd into silence as they waited to hear what he had to say. He began by urging them to leave quietly, and was rewarded by three cheers. Encouraged by this response he continued, but instead of reassuring them that their opinions and grievances were understood and would be addressed, he foolishly admonishing them for the, "*impropriety of your conduct*" and then threatened them that the Magistrates did not want to use stringent measures unless they had to. At this stage of events, using threatening language was possibly the worst thing he could have said, for this just angered the crowd further, who now started throwing missiles at the Mayor and his party knocking off the hat of one and breaking more windows. This onslaught caused them to withdraw smartly into the Mansion House, as more missiles struck the door as it closed behind them.

Followed by the crowd who now surged forward and tried to push their way into the building, but were beaten back by the remaining Constables. With the situation rapidly deteriorating the Mayor now re-emerged heavily guarded in a vain effort to control the situation, but he had already wasted his opportunity and reinforced the protesters conviction that he was just as out of touch as Sir Charles Wetherell. Therefore, this time the crowd was not struck dumb, and instead roared their disapproval loudly. In an effort to get their attention, the diminutive Mayor had to stand on a chair so he could be seen and tried to calm the situation, but as no one took any notice he decided his only option was read the Riot Act;

"Our sovereign Lord the King chargeth and commandeth all persons, being assembled, immediately to disperse themselves, and peaceably to depart to their habitations, or to their lawful business, upon the pains contained in the act made in the first year of King George, for preventing tumults and riotous assemblies. God save the King."

The punishments for ignoring the Act were severe – penal servitude for not less than three years, or imprisonment with hard labour for up to two years.

In the melee however, it is unlikely that anyone heard a word of what he said, and those that did paid no attention. Other than showering him with stones, and a top rail torn up in the square, which narrowly missed his head. His secretary Burges was not so lucky being struck both on the head and stomach, forcing them all to make an undignified retreat back into the Mansion House.

It was now 5.30pm, just as the troops were arriving at their respective stables where soldiers and horses would be sleeping. Nevertheless, just as they were preparing to refresh themselves, Colonel Brereton received a dispatch from the Mayor requesting the troops to proceed to Queen Square, where the Magistrates were assembled at the Mansion House, which was now under attack. Colonel Brereton now wearing his forage cap, put himself at the head of the wet bedraggled 3rd Dragoon Guards under Captain Warrington, who had only just arrived at the billet, but would not be getting their much needed rest. Instead, the Colonel lined them up in College Green and waited for one Troop of 14th under Captain Gage to arrive, and lined them up on the left ordering all troops to load pistols and carbines before they left at a quick trot.

Meanwhile back at the Mansion House the mob had taken the upper hand and stormed the building forcing their entry through the doors and windows. Smashing all the furniture on the ground floor and placing a quantity of straw in one of the rooms doused in turpentine in preparation to set the building alight.

The remaining Constables now greatly outnumbered, were reaping the seeds of hate they had sown earlier and were viciously beaten, some even receiving broken limbs. Nevertheless, even though some were badly hurt, they still managed to stop the mob from gaining access to the upper floors, where the Mayor along with Sir Charles and various dignitaries were busy barricading the windows and doors with upturned beds and various bits of furniture that they could lay their hands on.

However, with the mob attempting to set the house alight and with the kitchen now abandoned and the food for the banquet left cooking on the open fires they were obviously worried about being trapped without the means of repelling the crowds or escape.

It was at this time that Sir Charles was persuaded that as the situation was rapidly deteriorating and his life could be in imminent danger he should take what measures he could and affect a hasty escape. In addition, it was reasoned that once the people knew the object of their disapproval was no longer there, perhaps the disorder would cease and the situation might improve. Sir Charles whose entrance into Bristol was with all the pomp and ceremony that the second city of the Empire could muster was now leaving in a much more undignified fashion. For the 61-year-old Recorder left not in his ceremonial clothes but in disguise, wearing the borrowed clothes of a humble coach driver and without a hat, the recognised symbol of the upper classes. He scrambled out of the dining room window onto the roof followed by a few others including Charles Gardiner a Special Constable and Captain of a merchant ship. A female in the next house provided a ladder down onto the roof of the stables where they hid in a hayloft and finally when safe to do so, over a wall into an alley. In his drab attire and without a hat he blended into the crowd and made his way to Gardiners House in Kingsdown by about 6.30pm, and left Bristol altogether at around 10.30pm taking a boat across the Severn for Newport arriving at 2.30am in the morning. Sir Charles whose provocative arrival had been so brazen and in the full sight of the populous now left humbled and under cover of darkness leaving the city in growing chaos and turmoil behind him.

As Sir Charles was making his escape, the mob were busy building barricades at the Squares entrances and vandalising the gas supply. This was in order to put out the street lighting in anticipation of the military's arrival. With the mob's meek relinquishing of their sticks earlier it was thought that they would flee with the arrival of the military but with their successes and realisation of how small the force against them was, in contrast to their own increasing numbers, the mood was changing.

It was around 6.00pm as Colonel Brereton and the Troops arrived in Queen Square with the two Aldermen who had delivered the Mayor's request for assistance. It was obvious that the Mansion House had been ruthlessly attacked previous to the troops arrival, but there was no sign of riotous behaviour as they trotted across the square. Indeed the crowds cheered as though they were being delivered from the clutches of the mob themselves.

The troops drew up and formed in front of the Mansion House, which was now clear and in the possession of the Constables. Colonel Brereton dismounted and on entering, was informed by a Magistrate that the Riot Act had been read three times and to use his best endeavours to preserve the public peace and disperse the mob.

The Mayor also confirmed this, but was vague and gave no clear orders as to how he wanted it done, neither did he, or any other magistrates go with the troops as was the law, to authorise and supervise their movements. Within half an hour, the other Troop of the 14th under Captain Musgrove arrived and lined up with the others outside the Mansion House. Therefore, Brereton ordered them to go about the square and the adjoining streets and carry out the Mayor's request by maintaining order while dispersing the mob without drawing swords or using violence. This was the new system in dealing with civil dissention strongly recommended by Headquarters and would also be used by Colonel Thackwell of Peterloo fame, in Nottingham during the recent reform riots there.

In response, the crowds chanted "King William and reform" as the Colonel rode through the crowd continuingly urging them to return to their homes if they wanted to avoid any injuries.

Queen Square is a very large square of nearly six acres in size, encircled by a cobblestoned road running around the perimeter and enclosed by iron railings in front of the buildings. On the other side of the road, a post and rail fence, over which lies the grass square with it's cinder paths intertwining the trees, and leading to the centre where the statue of King William sits. Some of these rails had been broken up to use as weapons and barricades in an effort to limit the mounted troop's movements, and they with other debris littering the road and pathways would certainly make it difficult. The cobblestones with their smooth top and irregular shapes were not ideal for trotting along on a horse, especially when it had been raining most of the day rendering them slippery. Proof of this was to manifest itself during the evening when a Dragoon's horse slipped and fell seriously injuring its rider.

Colonel Brereton had also complained;

"The Constables were of little or no service in dispersing the mob, and although I Insisted that magistrates would order the wardens guarding, who surrounded the enclosure of the square to be cut away, so as to give room for the troops to act, yet I could obtain no attention to my request, and so was left at the disadvantage of having to act against a mob which had constantly the means of placing a barricade between themselves and the Troops".

(Colonel Brereton's statement, *The Court of Inquiry.* Page 6. HO 50/12)

This again was because there were no Magistrates present in the square to organise the wardens. In addition, the mounted Dragoons were not usually deployed on their own in these situations but rather in unison with other troops such as infantry, just as they had in Merthyr, the Forest of Dean or indeed Nottingham. So in Bristol, in addition to their limited numbers, they had no ground forces to clear barriers or go where horses couldn't. These mounted troops were best placed to act in large open spaces, Queen Square was a large space but it was hardly open, so they were always acting at a disadvantage. The Constables could have supported the Dragoons in place of the infantry if they had been disciplined and trained properly and had been instructed by the Magistrates but as we have seen, they were not. However, despite these difficulties and without any assistance the Colonel's persistent warnings were working and the mob started dispersing without the use of any force.

"Colonel Brereton, the Commanding Officer of the District, was particularly conspicuous throughout the whole evening, in exhorting the mob to retire to their homes, and in cautioning them of the dreadful consequences which would otherwise ensue."

(W.H. Somerton *Narrative of the Bristol Riots*)

The Colonel returned regularly to the Mansion House to report on the dispersal of the crowd and asked if there were any other orders for him? At which the Magistrates would retire to another room to have secret conversations, and after some discussion returned and gave more vague and indecisive orders. This was to be the pattern for the whole operation.

It was around this time, about 7o'clock that an all too familiar face appeared, Major Digby Mackworth, the half pay ADC to Lord Hill.

However, unlike his two previous appearances at other recent riots he was apparently not on official business and so was dressed in civilian cloths and not accompanied by any troops. He had been apparently *"visiting friends"* in Clifton, and on hearing of the disturbances had decided to offer his assistance to the Mayor

At 42, Digby Mackworth was seven years younger than Colonel Brereton and had joined up in 1807 as an 18-year-old subaltern in the infantry. He served in the 7th Fusiliers at the battle of Albuera during the Peninsular War of 1811 and was one of the few that escaped the unparalleled slaughter. He was captured by a French patrol and during his captivity; he had been lodged with General de Richepanse and fell in love with the general's daughter who he later married. He later served at the battle of Waterloo in 1815 when he was 26 serving as a junior Aide-de-camp to Lt General Lord Hill, responsible for carrying despatches to and from Wellington. He remained on Lord Hill's staff until the end of the war when he retired on a Captains half pay and where he appeared to have remained. In 1828 when Lord Hill became Commander-in-Chief, he asked Mackworth to resume his role as his aide-de-camp but still on half pay. He later reached the rank of brevet (temporary) Major of the 8th Light Dragoons and in August 1830 full Major (*London Gazette*). Earlier this year in June 1831, you may remember he had been employed by the Government at Merthyr Tydfil and later the same month in the nearby Forest of Dean.

He was to resign in January 1837.* *United Service Gazette* January 1837. This was the year before he succeeded his father to the family title and became Sir Digby Mackworth, Fourth Baronet, he died in 1852

As he made his way across the square, he had little trouble in entering the Mansion House and on climbing the stairs asked where he could find the Mayor. Once acquainted with the Mayor and the remaining Magistrates, the Major offered his services and looking around the house and later claimed that;

"There was a total want of organisation amongst the civil force".

He also claimed he had suggested organising the men in to four divisions and placing them in strategic places around the building which was completed by about 9 o'clock. Although Thomas Sheppard a local merchant and special constable claimed that, it was he, and not Major Mackworth who had suggested this idea, and that he had also offered to command one of the detachments of 25 specials.

* The Waterloo Roll Call.
* *United Service Gazette*, January 1837

Nevertheless, it's more important that at last some organisation was carried out rather than who was responsible. However, the Major's recollections of the events published in his rather egotistical *A Personal Narrative,* detailing his role were to prove contentious at a later date as some felt he had exaggerated his part, while others wondered on whose orders he had attended in the first place while "visiting friends".

"By an amazing coincidence, Lord Hill's ADC, Major Digby Mackworth, happened to be in Bristol as a private citizen at the time of the riots and got himself embroiled. After the event, some people felt he had taken too much on himself, when it was a matter with which he was not officially involved, but he escaped an official enquiry."

(*Wellingtons Right Hand,* by Joanna Hill. Page 181.)

But how much was this just "*an amazing coincidence*"? Mackworth had been sent post chaise to Merthyr and then to The Forest of Dean to take the command of the troops that had arrived to suppress these riots. Yet in Bristol, he arrived in plain cloths and without any troops to offer his services. Was this as innocent as we are lead to believe, or was there some other more devious intent?

Mackworth was later to declare;

"In less than five minutes by a trifling, but combined operation, the whole vicinity of the Mansion House was cleared; and thus it remained till the following morning, except that now and then the Constables were annoyed by stones thrown from the by-streets, barges and a few from the tops of houses. Not withstanding this, nine prisoners captured by the civil force were safely conveyed to the gaol. Three privates of the 14th were wounded by stones, one severely so, and a subaltern much hurt by his horse falling under him".

(*A Personal Narrative of the Bristol Riots,*
by Major Digby Mackworth)

We must however distinguish at this time the difference between the crowd and the Mob. The majority of the crowd were just watching what was going on but it must be noted passively supporting the mob; who on the other hand were much smaller but also more active and involved in the violence. So it was very difficult to extricate the mob from the crowd. To charge into the crowd with drawn sabres and firearms would not be a solution even if it had been sanctioned by the Magistrates, which it had not. However, at his trial the Mayor stated that he was;

"desirous that the troops should fire on the mob, but was dissuaded from giving the order by the advice of Major Mackworth and Colonel Brereton."

Though at the same time the Colonel is reported by Major Mackworth as asking the Mayor's permission if he could fire, and it was *he* who advised against it, not the Colonel. Also in a letter to his sister Mrs Mary Ames written on the Sunday morning and not discovered until long after the trial the Mayor admits;

"I have forbore ordering of the troops to fire".

(From the Pinney Archive, DM58, University of Bristol Library
Special Collections.)

So as the Mayor had explicitly forbade the use of firearms it was the Colonel's duty to obey. Also he didn't want to use more force than was necessary against an unarmed populace and end up hurting innocent people, as this would only turn them against the soldiers, just as indiscriminate violence by the Specials had done earlier. Also foremost in his mind was the example of Peterloo an example he was anxious not to repeat. Especially as this small military contingent was now the only barrier to outright anarchy and so this was to be avoided at all costs.

Brereton was later to state;

"I felt I confess, a strong sense of the responsibility which devolves upon a military man when called to the assistance of the civil power, and a thorough conviction that such circumstances he cannot fairly be required to proceed to extremities against the populous except under the express authority of a Magistrates order, and if practical with the sanction of the Magistrates presence. Military operations and the means of civil coercion are widely different, and there is ample experience to show that the officer never escapes a heavy measure of blame who allows the feelings habitual to him in his military capacity, to have their full effect in dealing with an unarmed multitude."

(Colonel Brereton's statement. The Court of Inquiry.
HO 52/12. Pages 6/7.*)*

However, the Colonel's present course of action was indeed working as the crowd significantly decreased and so around 9pm the3rd Dragoons Guards and Captain Warrington were finally able to step down. Along with Captain Gage's troop of the 14th Dragoons, though Captain Gage remained with Captain Musgrove's troops in Queen Square. These remaining troops continued to police the square and by this stage, much of the crowd had taken the Colonel's warnings and left the square. This left the more militant mob exposed and who were more persistent in remaining. Therefore, by about 10pm, with these still not dispersed despite Colonel Brereton's constant warnings of the consequences, the Colonel decided it was now time to enforce his demands, and so he now ordered his troops to use force for the first time to clear them, but to use the flats of their swords as much as possible. This method of crowd control was the recommended army practice for the time, start off with persuasion and then slowly increase the amount of force if and when needed.

However, as soon as the troops were lined up in readiness and drew their swords to carry out these orders the mood of the mob changed as they realised that force was about to be used against them. Therefore, they began pelting them with bottles, stones, and pieces of iron causing serious injuries to two soldiers. Nevertheless, despite this, the troops carried out their orders and in about half an hour, the square and the adjacent streets were all cleared. Those not lucky enough to escape were arrested and taken prisoner, and some were injured. However, some of the persistent offenders, still refusing to go home had taken refuge on barges and were assailing the pursuing troops with impunity from there. Captain Gage rode up to the Mansion House and seeing the Mayor asked for permission to use pistols. The Mayor apparently now hesitated and seemed unsure (according to Captain Cage). Colonel Brereton asked again, *"Am I to fire, Sir?"* then Major Mackworth came in and strongly advised against it. Saying; *"Firing was a bad mode for cavalry to adopt and that shots meant for rioters might hit innocent people."*

(Statement of Major Mackworth at
The Trial Of Charles Pinney.)

After which the Mayor again refused to sanction their use, even after Mr Harford a Special Constable offered to take 25 men down to flush them out if the Army would cover them but the Mayor was again uncertain and Alderman Daniel was also worried in case some innocent people were killed. As for it being market day there were many market boats from Wales and he was very worried that a great many lives might be sacrificed.

So Captain Gage left, saying;

"He could no longer allow his men to attempt clearing those particular parts because the mob there could assail them without the men being able to reach the mob".

Then the Colonel told the Mayor that as it was late he felt that if the remaining protesters were left unmolested they would soon get tired and return to their homes, saying he would be answerable for the peace of the city and would continue to patrol it during the night.

"Doubtless Colonel Brereton had seen enough of the indecision of the Magistrates, and of the irritating conduct of the Constables, to place much confidence in either; his suggestion was adopted, and, it should have been added, entirely succeeded. But surely such timidity and indecision justify Col Brereton in hesitating to fire without an express order."

(J.T. Manchee; *The Bristol Riots*)

Later at 10.30pm Brereton arrived to report to the Mayor his latest appraisal of the evening only to be confronted by the Town Clerk Mr Sergeant Ludlow pointing out the soldier who had been injured when his horse fell and two other soldiers who were also suffering from injuries caused by missiles thrown by the mob saying;

"Does that look if the crowd are good humoured?" He then asked, "Have you any instructions from the Horse Guards or the Home Secretary which prevent you from carrying out the directions of the magistrates?"

Authors Note;

(Strangely these events were remembered in reverse order by Ludlow and were repeated unquestioningly in both Geffrey Ameys book, *City under Fire*, page 44 and Peter McDonalds *Hotheads and Heroes*, page 36. Giving the impression that Brereton only ordered the charge after the injured soldiers were brought in. When in fact, according to original statements by the officers of these troops they were brought in *BECAUSE* of the sabre charge not before. So Ludlow's statement was clearly made after this.

As Captain Gage of the 14th Dragoons confirms in his statement at the Court of inquiry.

"(The troop) which continued moving about as before until about 10 o'clock, when the mob not being dispersed. Lt Colonel

Brereton gave Captain Gage distinct orders to disperse by force. – The troop then drew swords and obeyed the order. – they were soon assaulted with bottles, stones, square pieces of iron (apparently cut for the occasion) and other missiles which wounded three of the men."

(Statement Captain Gage Court of Inquiry. PRO HO52/12)

Indeed Town Clerk Ludlow concedes this, for after giving his evidence at the Court of Inquiry which the chronological order of these events were based, he later stated that;

"His evidence given yesterday having been read over, he is desirous of saying that he has given the dates and times to the best of his recollection but cannot pledge himself to there strict accuracy in ever respect".

(Statement of Town Clerk, Sergeant Ludlow Court of Inquiry. HO52/12*)*

So one of the planks that were used to build a case against Colonel Brereton is based on a false recollection of times and events that do not tally with the soldiers accounts who were actually there.

However, already by this time, despite Ludlow's statement; who let's not forget had not left the Mansion House; most of the city was in fact cleared. So Colonel Brereton decided that it was now time the troops in Queens Square should be relieved, as men and horses were getting tired. As the fresh troops arrived however he heard that a section of the mob that he had driven from Queen Square were now attacking the Council House in Corn Street so he directed Captain Gage and his detachment of the 14th to go directly there and deal with the situation before retiring. As the troops arrived at the Council House, Captain Gage observed a large body of rioters and so immediately formed the troops into two divisions one under himself and one under Lt Lawson. He then ordered the charge and dispersed them. This was to the relief of Thomas Gerrard a 44-year-old Chamberlain of Bristol and his civil force of 35 men armed with cudgels who had been trying to repel the mob through a storm of missiles and broken glass. It was just as they were beginning to feel that they could not hold out much longer that the troops arrived and the mob fled with the troops in pursuit. Some rioters fled into Wine Street and a passage too narrow for the horses to enter and no lighting due to the gas pipes being vandalised. This situation just illustrated the weakness of a mounted force without any infantry back up in the confining space of narrow city streets, and the lack of the required Magistrate to instruct them and would lead directly to a further escalation of violence. For it was here that Captain Gage's half of the troop were again pelted with various missiles with impunity. On the second passing of this passage, Gage observed a man in light coloured dress rush out with a large stone or piece of metal, which he threw at him narrowly missing his head and rattling against the shutters on the other side of the road. In reply Gage drew his pistol and fired, but the gun flashed in the pan so a soldier immediately to his left fired and the man fell. This was despite not being authorised to use firearms by Colonel Brereton or the Mayor, despite a direct request by Gage himself. Nevertheless, the passage now fell silent, as did the Street and by 12.30am the whole City was now quiet. Colonel Brereton then directed half the detachment under Lt James Dawson to remain at the Council House, and Gage took the remaining troops back to their quarters to rest.

This use of firearms was a pivotal moment in the proceedings and was to lead directly to the later escalation of violence and disorder. For it was later claimed that the man shot was Stephen Bush, who had come up from his master's stables at the Pithay near Wine Street after hearing the disturbances. His curiosity was to cost him his life as he died within minutes with a large wound in his chest. He was just an innocent bystander. Another casualty was Daniel James who was walking home from work when he was slashed in the head by a sabre and died later in the infirmary.

Colonel Brereton and his remaining troops continuously rode through the square and surrounding streets to enforce and maintain the peace but the city remained perfectly quiet. On retuning to the Mansion House to reported this to the Mayor and other Magistrates, the Mayor asked Colonel Brereton to provide an escort to take the prisoners arrested earlier to the Gaol but the Colonel advised it would be better to do this in daylight and arranged an escort to be available when required.

Even Town Clerk, Sergeant Ludlow had to concede that Brereton had been right when he said that he would take the responsibility on himself and that if the last remaining protesters were left alone they would soon retire. For at the trial of Mayor Pinney when asked by the court;

"Did Colonel Brereton turn out to be right?"

Ludlow replied; "Yes, he certainly did"

(*The Trial of Charles Pinney.* Page 288.)

Ludlow himself stayed on until nearly 1am but after a Magistrate finally braved the streets to confirm the Colonels report and observed the streets were indeed all quiet. Therefore, he left along with Alderman John Savage the previous Mayor of Bristol in the latter's carriage as they both lived in Clifton two miles away.

(*The Trial of Charles Pinney.* Page 228.)

Also by 1am Sunday morning Major Mackworth who had stayed on in the Mansion House also looked out on the streets and thought it was all over. Nevertheless, he decided to stay on until 2 o'clock but with no further signs of trouble, he too left for Clifton and bed.

However, Colonel Brereton was not taking any chances and at 3am he placed a patrol of the 3rd Dragoon Guards at the Mansion House and a patrol of the 14th Light Dragoons at the Council House and ordered the remaining troops to their stables. However, as a precaution, he ordered half to remain armed and in readiness should they be needed. Later between 3am and 4am without any further incidents Brereton himself retired with them and with whom he remained throughout the night in readiness and was later to declare;

"It was certainly a satisfaction for me to know that the objects for which the troops were called upon to act had been effectively obtained without any material injury to the populace, who

sustained no damage beyond a few sabre cuts. The case of one man should be accepted who was killed in Wine Street by a shot from the 14th, which although I believe it was fired under strong provocation, was certainly without order from me. And it happened unfortunately that the individual, who was killed, was stated to have been in no way connected with the riotous proceedings of the mob."

(Lt Colonel Brereton's statement at the court of inquiry.
PRO HO52/12. Page 8)

Though in *Hotheads and Heroes* by Peter Macdonald, page 39, he writes that at this time;

"Others, like Brereton, were very worried men".

However, the fact is that Brereton was far from worried, as the above *original statement* confirms. Which is further proof that the fictional account of the riots by the Mayor has been added to and reinforced as time goes by until people now consider it factual.

Sunday 30 October 1831

The day dawned wet and misty in the town, it had been fairly quiet since about midnight, though the streets where littered with the debris of the night's protests and bearing witness to how violent it had been, leaving many hurt and some dead. Those poor souls never to wake up again, even on such a miserable day as this. The Mansion House had been guarded throughout the night by a small picket of the 3rd and another of the 14th, which had been changed regularly through out the night but they had not been needed as there had been no more sight of the rioters.

The Mayor and his Clerk, Burges and two Aldermen Gabriel Goldney and James George were the only dignitaries who had not left and had remained all-night. But without much sleep or food to eat, even if they had felt so inclined it would have been difficult with the noise of the carpenters banging away repairing the broken windows and doors. The Mayor had spent some time at 5am writing a letter to his sister Mrs Mary Anne Ames at 4 Cavendish Place, Bath to reassure her of his safety and to tell her of the events that had occurred;

"My dear Sister – I write a few hasty lines to say thank God we are all safe; fortunately I had the precaution to send off Fanny and her mother early to Clifton. At one time we were in great peril, the mob had knocked down every door and window and made a wreck of the lower part of the Mansion House – the Constables could not resist – and a truss of straw carried by some desperate villains into the dinning room covered with turpentine to set the house on fire when the Military arrived – two of the soldiers were brought in seriously bruised and I fear many of the Constables. I have forebore ordering the troops to fire – but men could not stand being knocked off their horses and in one place I fear a man

has been shot. The troops are now bivouacking in the square and Sir Charles has escaped over the roof and gone to London and the Assizes are of course necessary put off – I hope we shall not have a recurrence tomorrow – I was obliged in the end to read the Riot Act, one Constable knocked down by my side and two of the Aldermen struck, one stone lodged in my hat, but we are now taking much precautions that there can be no danger – write to my sister and my brother, for exaggerated accounts will reach them; I have been as you may suppose with the Magistrates up all night.

Your Affectionate, *Chas Pinney*

5 o'clock (A.M.)

Sunday morning, Mansion House"

(From the Pinney Archive, DM58, University of Bristol Library Special Collections.)

This letter was not intended for public scrutiny and was just a hastily scribbled and candid personal letter to his sister devoid of any political leanings, it was simply to calm any fears she may have harboured concerning her brothers safety. However, the line, "*I have forebore the Troops to fire*", is very illuminating, as Mayor Pinney and others were later to deny this and were to claim it was Colonel Brereton who refused to allow the troops to fire. So if this personal letter had not come to light (long after the trials and Court's Martial were concluded) we would be none the wiser to the true orders issued by the Mayor, and so at the time we were led to believe that it was Colonel Brereton who had himself issued this order.

While the Mayor was penning this letter, Colonel Brereton was sending his adjutant to Queen Square to report on the current situation there. He returned saying; that though there were a few people gathered there they just seemed to be curious as to what had happened the night before, with no inclination to riot. After receiving this information, Colonel Brereton proceeded to the Mansion House arriving at 6am to report to the Mayor and receive any further orders he had. However, as all was quiet there were none, so Colonel Brereton returned to his quarters thinking no doubt he could at last have some rest.

At the same time, the carpenters who had been working all-night repairing the damage finished their work, and as they left Alderman Gabriel Goldney and the Mayors clerk Daniel Burges decided, it was now safe to go home. Alderman George also decided it was time to go and left on foot, leaving around ten Constables in the building that they had spent so much time protecting. This weary apprehension was probably mirrored throughout the town as its shocked residents awoke and started to remember the night's terrors and wonder if it was all over. Some started to congregate in Queen Square and stood around in small groups discussing with each other their recollections and experiences of the nights dramas. No doubt, the main topic was the men killed last night by the 14th Dragoons.

At 7am Major Mackworth reappeared refreshed from his night's sleep in Clifton, and on entering Queen Square saw several small groups discussing the night's events. One saying in solemn tones as he finished his entreaty on the injustices of the military with a biblical quote;

"He that sheds men's blood, by men shall his blood be shed".

The Major entered the Mansion House and climbing the stairs soon found the Mayor and sat down with him to discuss what had happened the night before and gave him the benefit of his opinions on what should now be done. However, after about an hour, they became aware of an occasional rapping and tinkling sound, and then another, this sound was ominously familiar and so when the sound of rising voices from outside also joined in and became louder, it was time to investigate. On looking through the windows down into the square, it was immediately obvious that the crowd had increased dramatically.

Authors Note;

(In Geoffrey Amey's *City under Fire,* page 50 Pinney and Mackwork; *to their horror, realised the soldiers had vanished".*

However, it seems they were perfectly aware that the troops were no longer there as it was Major Mackworth who had suggested it during his chat with the Mayor and it was Pinney himself who gave permission.

In fact Pinney had done exactly the same yesterday evening when he had dismissed the troops followed by the Constables guarding the Mansion House and with exactly the same response from the mob, they had attacked it.

Major Mackworth in his *Narrative of the Bristol Riots* also confirms this;

"Sunday morning at 7o'clock I returned to the Mansion House, and found a small crowd re-assembled, and some of the Dragoons quietly parading up and down before it. It immediately struck me that their presence only served to attract a mob, and that it would be very desirable to send them away on that account, as well as because Men and Horses absolutely required rest!"
Mayor Pinney stated;

"The troops being much harassed, and everything then being quiet, I made no objection to the troops being withdrawn".

(Mayor Pinney's statement, Court of Inquiry (HO52/12))

So who exactly did ask for the troops to be removed? The Colonel does not mention any such request in his detailed statement to the Court of Inquiry. He mentions going to the Mansion House not long after daybreak and the Mayor having no further orders for him. Major Mackworth also confirms in his narrative that when he arrived an hour later the troops were still present. The Major admits it was he who advised the removal of the troops, which his statement confirms and the troops left shortly afterwards. However, what about the ten Constables who were there? No mention of them by the Mayor or the Major, is that because the Mayor sent them home at the same time just as he had on the Saturday? Major Mackworth continued talking with the Mayor and soon after the sound of breaking wood could be heard as the newly repaired doors and windows were smashed in and a shout of triumph arose as the first of the mob gained entry. Upstairs the petrified inhabitants looked to Major Mackworth for instructions who quickly decided that the only way open to them was escape across the roof without delay.

Therefore, for the second time in less than 24 hours the dignitaries of Bristol found it necessary to escape through a window.

This time it was the landing window above the first floor and out onto the roof. Next door at Leman and Sons Solicitors, the clerk, Mr George Humphries heard a noise from a nearby room used by the office cleaner. After going into the back kitchen, he heard someone calling for assistance, and observed the Mayor peering over the tiles. In almost a re-run of the previous evening escape yet another ladder was procured this time by Mr Humphreys to scale the wall down into the courtyard of the Solicitors office. The Mayor who seemed very agitated cried out for God's sake is there any escape route through the back without using the front door? Mr Humphreys then directed the Mayor and his party of four or five up the stairs and out through the garret window where they entered the loft and scrambled through into the Custom House, finally making their escape along a back street where they parted, leaving the Mayor heading for College Green.

It is at this point that in Peter McDonalds *Hotheads and Heroes* page 41;

"On College Green Pinney confronts Brereton and demanded to know why the troops had been withdrawn from the Mansion House"

However, as we have discovered this is yet more fantasy and did not happen.

In fact, Colonel Brereton did not hear from the Mayor until 9.00am, around three hours after he had left the Mansion House. Therefore, any rest he had planned was interrupted by an urgent message from the Mayor for the troops to attend as the Mansion House was now being attacked by the mob. After assembling the 3rd Dragoon Guards in College Green they were all ordered as usual to load their weapons and Brereton lead them at a trot with word for the 14th to join them as soon as they were ready. On crossing the Drawbridge, he saw the Mayor and Alderman Hillhouse and requested from them the immediate presence of a Magistrate to accompany the troops. The Mayor replied he would go, but only if Brereton would protect him. Therefore, Brereton instructed the Mayor to walk by his side and he placed another mounted Dragoon on the other side so the Mayor was protected from both sides. In this fashion they proceeded to Queen Square but on the way the Mayor disappeared and was nowhere to be seen until much later when he reappeared in the Council House at 11o'clock. This was to be a familiar pattern during the riots, the Mayor or Magistrates would seek assistance from the military or the citizens and lead them heroically towards the rioters, only to disappear in transit and reappear after all danger had passed.

On the troops arrival at about 9.30 in the square, they were again cheered and there was no sign of any mob violence but the Mansion House was all broken open. The 3rd Dragoons then cleared the square and formed up soon after, but on the 14th's arrival at around 10 o'clock the mood of the crowd changed suddenly and dramatically. News of the two deaths last night had passed around the town like wildfire and then it was pointed out that the 14th had also been involved in putting down the agricultural swing riots in Hampshire the year before and in Merthyr only recently. Later inside the Mansion House where citizens had gathered answering the Mayors plea, the talk amongst them was about the 14th as Benjamin Ralph related about his decision the night before;

"I heard the military had fired, and a great deal of disapprobation upon that principle; and when I found that they had fired without any person giving them orders, I thought it my duty to retire home, which I did."

(Benjamin Ralph, *The Trial of Charles Pinney.* Page 165.)

Outside as the tension mounted and shouts of; *"Bloody Blues who shot the man". "Who cut with their swords".*

Then as more missiles were thrown, one observer saw a soldier withdraw his pistol and aim at the mob but not fire. Another reported seeing Colonel Brereton knock the soldiers arm up to stop him firing, while the milling crowd cried; *"bring them down"* and *"The reds forever, down with the bloody blues we'll murder them"* while the furious protesters rushed at them and tried to bring their horses down. In response, Colonel Brereton ordered Sergeant Major John Martin of the 3rd Dragoons to clear the rear of the 14th from the protesters. While he rode into the crowd in an effort to calm the situation.

Corporal William Smith of the 3rd dragoons was there in the square with Colonel Brereton and saw him ride into the crowd and heard him say;

"For Gods sake, my good fellows, go home," and they replied *"we will not go home till you send away the 14th".*

"If I send the 14th out of town will you disperse?" said he.

"They returned, "Yes they would" And Then cried, "Hurrah for the King and reform".

(The Courts Martial of Colonel Brereton. Page 133. Thursdays Statement of Corporal William Smith the 3rd Dragoons Guards)

So by 10.30 Colonel Brereton rode up to the 14th, and with the escalating malice directed at them decided it would be prudent to send them back to their stables before the situation got completely out of control. On receiving the order Gage turned his troop around trotted out of the square leaving by the Excise Avenue with a swarm of rioters in pursuit throwing missiles at them as they left. As the troop reached the Hole-In-The-Wall public house a large crowd of 500 attacked the rear with stones and brick bats making the horses plunge. So the Sergeant rode up to the front to inform Captain Gage, who halted the troop and turned them to face their tormentors. He ordered them to draw swords, and three charged down to the bottom of Princes Street. However, on turning, one of the horses fell, and the mob surged forward to attack the Dragoon. A further three Dragoons charged to his assistance as he just managed to remount his horse. Having cleared the street the soldiers rejoined the main body and commenced their route back to their quarters along the Quay. However, after the troops passed Marsh Street, the mob ran down it through the lanes reaching the Steam Packet Office near the Drawbridge. This was ahead of the troops and they again pelted them with missiles, but the troops pushed on until they passed the end of the Drawbridge where the mob rushed them again at their rear, and Gage turned the rear rank around to face their tormentors they backed off and withdrew, just as they had during the night. Nevertheless, as soon as the troop started to trot away up St Augustine's Back, out came the rioters again with more missiles. Therefore, as they ran forward,

Gage ordered the Troops to load pistols as a dozen powerful men rushed one of the Dragoons seizing his horse and trying to bring him down. The soldiers fired around a dozen shots and one man dropped dead on the spot, and two others were hit, right outside the church door of St Augustine's. The morning worshipers looked on in shock as a stray bullet just missed the head of the Town Clerk, Ebenezer Ludlow who was on route to the Guildhall and embedded itself into the church door. The crowds here were much larger than normal, swelled by protesters who had come hoping to see Sir Charles going to church as was normal after his civic duties. For they had no idea he had already left the city the evening before, as no one had thought to inform them. The startled parishioners and would be protesters looked on in horror as they saw the man shot in front of their very eyes, and outside the Church of all places. Some complained bitterly to Ludlow about Sir Charles Wethrell, having the audacity to enter the city when so much malice was directed at him after his inflammatory pronouncements. Ludlow replied that Sir Charles had every right to his opinion, but at this they warned him to take care what he said, and that he had been seen at the Guildhall defending Wetherell and if he was not careful, people might think he was just as bad.

The Dragoons meanwhile continued their hazardous journey back to quarters but at the top of Unity Street, they were again attacked by the mob who had overtaken them by taking a short cut through Hanover Street and Denmark Street. The mob however were again driven back down Unity Street by an officer on horseback, who to their great astonishment rode his horse up the Grammar School steps dislodging a group who were pelting them from above. The troops were further attacked as they reached College Green where one of the Dragoons was severely injured as his comrades jumped the railings and iron hurdles driving away the mob. They then proceeded through College Green into College Street where they were yet again attacked and four or five people were wounded before they finally reached their quarters. It was now obvious at this stage that the mob were both infuriated by the 14th's behaviour the night before, but which was now increased by their further outrages on the Sunday. However now they knew exactly how small the total numbers of troops were available and they also realised that they had the upper hand. For even with the 14th freely using both sabres and pistols the mob was not daunted. In fact, the killing of their numbers only managed to inflame and infuriate them further and a quarter of an hour later a party tried to attack the stables but were driven back by a sentinel firing at them.

Back in the square, Colonel Brereton heard the all too familiar sound of carbines being discharged. He quickly mounted his horse and galloped towards College Green in the direction the troops had gone. As he passed over the Drawbridge, a large crowd met him with horrible expressions shouting out that the 14th had murdered another boy and wounded others. Brereton pushed his way through the teeming crowd until he reached his office in College Green where he quickly dispatched an orderly to find Captain Gage asking why they had fired, the answer soon arrived that they had fired in self-defence. The mob was now outraged in the extreme and vowing vengeance against the 14th threatening to burn down the stables with the troops inside. Colonel Brereton who had sent the 14th from the square in the first place in an effort to calm the situation was now facing an even more volatile one. For as news of yet more death and injury spread around the town the enraged populace was making their way to the stables to wreak vengeance on the cornered 14th. Leaving very little time for Brereton to consider what his options were, and with only 30 men of the 3rd Dragoons left to assist the beleaguered 14th. He realised that he had to act fast and although he could put down the mob for the time being, with no civil force to support him how could he maintain it day and night? They would soon be overwhelmed. He could not guarantee the safety of his men who would not be able to protect themselves constantly against an infuriated enlarged mob who were threatening to roast them alive in their stables. Moreover, once the only barrier against the mob was removed they would run riot through the whole city and attack the banks and the shipping, both of which they had threatened. Therefore, he decided to send them a distance from the town away from the mobs fury to calm the situation. While at the same time sending out requests for fresh reinforcements.

The Mayor later conceded this fact, when he stated in his letter to the Attorney general dated 4 Nov 1831 that;

"The Colonel said it would be better to keep the mob in temper, until the next morning, when a reinforcement of troops might be expected".

Colonel Brereton and Captain Warrington then left for the Guildhall to seek permission from the Magistrates to implement this measure. On arrival, the Colonel quickly announced his proposal and spoke of the dangers of delay and so the Magistrates unanimously agreed. The Magistrates had come to the same decision only yesterday regarding Sir Charles Wetherell when they had also advised him to leave to calm the situation. However, on this occasion Town Clerk, Sergeant Ludlow voiced his unease about the decision and then said he did not agreed. After which the Mayor, who was uncomfortable without a majority decision joined him as well. So now, the familiar pattern of indecision that had plagued this whole affair raised its head once more. Ludlow realised that they didn't have enough troops as it was, and had said to the Sheriffs the night before that the Posse Comitatus should be called out to supplement them, and when Mr Taunton suggested it as well Ludlow replied;

"I think so too, and I said so last night."

(*Trial of Charles Pinney.* Page 298.)

Yet now Ludlow said rather contradictorily;

"I thought those troops would have been sufficient to have done anything required of them".

But Colonel Brereton replied;

"You may rely on it they are not".

"All we can do, is temporize and keep the mob in good humour until the reinforcements come".

Ludlow protested that the troops had been sent for their protection. To which the Colonel replied that their numbers were too small to achieve this and that he; *"would not have the soldiers lives sacrificed".*

Ludlow replied; *"Good God! Is that a soldier's reason?"*

To which the Colonel replied; *"Soldiers lives are not to be sacrificed unnecessarily"*.

(*The Trial of Charles Pinney*. Page 299.)

The Colonel then told them;

"I had so far done my duty. The Mayor shall be responsible for the consequences."

The Mayor and Sergeant Ludlow who along with the other Magistrates had spent the whole time trying to avoid any responsibilities were now aghast that the Colonel had pointed out where it lied. So now feeling the weight of that responsibility resting on them, they retired to another room for further secret discussions. Eventually Colonel Brereton and Captain Warrington who was also present, were summoned in to hear their decision.

"When entering I was told that the Magistrates didn't like to take the responsibility of removing the troops. I told them it was a measure and a responsibility I could nor would not take upon myself".

"Captain Warrington heard me object in such strong terms against taking upon myself the responsibility of removing the 14th".

"I state this to prove my decided objection to take upon myself the responsibility of removing the 14th without the sanction of the Mayor and Magistrates, of which I do solemnly declare, was the case before I left the room".

(Colonel Brereton's Statement, Court of Inquiry.
Page 12 (PRO HO52/12)

The Colonel obviously knew that it was his duty to obey the orders of the Magistrates but it was also his duty to advise them on military matters. His advice on this occasion was that for the safety of the 14th Dragoons they should be sent out of harms way to defuse the malice directed at them until a larger force was available. When they could then return and combined with the reinforcements, he could deal with the situation successfully. Also lets not forget that Brereton had seen this malice directed towards 14th first hand, where as the Magistrates had only heard about it.

Several arguments then took place between the magistrates when at last they reverted to their original decision and it was agreed to remove the 14th. Though Town Clerk Ludlow again later contradicted this when he stated;

"Colonel Brereton could have no doubt that if the removal of these troops did take place it must be on his own single responsibly".

(*Trial Charles Pinney*. Page 289.)

Several places were then mentioned as suitable before Brislington was agreed, but then it was announced that there was no suitable stabling there so in the end it was decided to leave these arrangements to Colonel Brereton.

Many concerned citizens were also arriving to see what was going on and a few to offer their help and assistance, amongst these were Major General Pearson who lived locally at Clifton. He was a very distinguished and experienced soldier who had served in the French Revolutionary Wars and Napoleonic War and in the War of 1812 against the United States of America. Indeed, in the Napoleonic war he had served under Sir William Beckwith in the West Indies alongside the then Major Brereton in the taking of Martinique from the French in 1809. Born in Somerset a year before Brereton, he received his commission two years earlier, though unlike Brereton's his was by purchase, promoted to Major in 1804 at the age of 24, Brereton had to wait until he was 27 to attain the same rank. He had also served as an "Inspecting Field Officer "in North America in 1812. Therefore, in some respects his military career had been similar to Brereton's, which gave him an insight into the difficulties he was now facing.

Known as a strict disciplinarian he stood no nonsense. When he was Commanding officer in Canada he was known as *"Tartar Pearson"*. When a soldier there applied to go on leave, Pearson replied bluntly, *"Go to hell!"*

"Yes sir, your honour," the soldier replied; *"and has your honour any orders for the devil?"*

Pearson was amused and impressed by the plucky answer, so in response doubled the man's leave and gave him a pound.

Pearson was a consummate professional soldier who was just as tough on his fellow officers if he felt they were not up to scratch. He complained to the authorities about Canadian part time Militia officers who, *"irreparably injured the service by their imbecility."*

(*Fix Bayonets,* by Donald E. Graves.)

It is not recorded whether he noticed any of that imbecility when he entered the room at the Guildhall, but after hearing the heated exchange he came down firmly on Brereton's side, telling the Magistrates that he too agreed with Colonel Brereton, and that with the excited state of the mob the removal of the 14th was indispensable. Therefore, if he did notice any, it was evident by his declaration it was not coming from the Colonel.

MAJOR GENERAL PEARSON 1781–1847

Courtesy of the trustees of the Royal Welch Fusiliers Museum, Caernarfon.

After receiving the Magistrates approval, Colonel Brereton left immediately from the Guildhall and now accompanied by Major General Pearson, rode straight to the stables at Fishers arriving around 12pm to inform Captain Musgrove the decision of the Magistrates. Musgrove asked him what for?

Brereton replied; *"Through killing that poor unfortunate at the top of The Pithay"*.

Musgrove then asked on whose orders they were to leave and the Colonel replied it was by order of the Mayor and Magistrates. At this point Captain Gage returned and was told to take his troops out of town as quick as possible before they were all murdered and go to Brislington or if nowhere could be found there, to Keynsham. Nevertheless, to keep their horses saddled, and to be in readiness to return when reinforcements arrived. Brereton advised them to take the road by Gloucester House to avoid the mob. Then with the crowds outside gathering, Gage and his troop accompanied by Major General Pearson left at a trot only to be spotted by the baying mob outside who pursed them up Limekiln Lane. Yet again, the 14th fired at the mob who tried to attack a trooper who fell with his horse, another victim of the wet cobbled street. It seems at this time though, that the mob was in such numbers and so enraged that even with the troops firing upon them it did nothing to discourage them, only to enrage them further. Therefore, it would seem that Colonel Brereton was right in sending them out of harms way until reinforcements arrived, and then when he had sufficient numbers then be able to force the Mob into obedience.

"In walking through the streets on Sunday afternoon, I heard many respectable persons say, the peace of the city would never be restored till the 14th were sent away. I cannot help thinking Colonel Brereton exercised a sound judgement in sending them out of the city".

(J.T. Manchee *The Bristol Riots*. Page 29.)

General Pearson rode with them through the Hotwells until he came to a road that lead to Clifton at which point he wished them good luck saying, he would visit them that evening or tomorrow morning before he left them and departed for home.

At the Guildhall the Mayor was busy drafting and sending urgent requests to the nearest Yeomanry and regular troops from Bath, 11 miles away, Tetbury some 23 miles away, and Gloucester the depot of the 14th dragoons 30 miles, away and Cardiff, Wales. 43 miles away. Mr James Bush was given a letter to deliver to 26-year-old Captain Codrington, heir to Sir Christopher Codrington at Doddington Park. Doddington Park was some 15 miles away and had been owned by the Codrington family since the 16th century.

After the 14th Dragoons had left the city with Major General Pearson, Colonel Brereton had returned to Queen Square to check the latest developments. The crowd there had done as they had promised and were now calm and not engaged in any mischief. Nevertheless, the Colonel decided to leave a party of the 3rd Dragoons guarding the Mansion House. While he paraded another detachment on the gravel drive opposite, in an effort to prevent any assemblage of the mob and to dissuade them from committing any further outrages. This seemed to work, for though the square was occupied by a number of drunks the only thing of note to transpire was when one of them climbed upon the statue of King William and waved a tri-coloured cap on a pole declaring out aloud;

"The cap of liberty".

This one act was to later cause much consternation and alarm to the Government fearing the dreaded revolution was now planted on English soil.

The Mayor finally put up a poster informing the crowd that Sir Charles Wetherell had indeed left the city. However, in their haste they had put the wrong year which only led to further confusion. Nevertheless, an old Quaker gentlemen present pleaded with the crowd, telling them that the poster was correct and Sir Charles had indeed left the city. Several of the ringleaders who listened to this then declared that the Quaker would never lie and deceive them and therefore if this was the case there was nothing left to do there.

But instead of leaving for their homes one spoke up saying;

"Then, if Sir Charles is gone, we have nothing more to do here; we'll now go to Bridewell and liberate the prisoners taken up

last night, and afterwards we'll go and release the prisoners in the Gaol, whom he came to try".

After being informed of this, one of the Aldermen is reported to have thrown up his arms and said;
"Poh! Stone walls are strong enough".

(*The Bristol Riots* by W.H. Somerton. Page 20.)

As they reached the Bridewell House of Correction, the Governor Thomas Evans and his wife were having their Sunday dinner. Alarmed by a sound of hammers pounding the prison gate, the Governor armed himself with a sword, as did Taskmaster Boyse and the Jailer called Stone and rushed out to defend the gate. During which Governor Evan received a nasty gash on his forehead, as the mob now redoubled their efforts pounding away and as their number swelled the gate could stand no more and finally gave way. The rioters now stormed their way in, pulling the broken gate off its hinges and throwing it into the river Throme.

Governor Evan's wife and staff escaped over the roof while he remained, but he could not stop the rioters releasing all the prisoners and watched helplessly as they set fire to the prison chapel and other buildings in the complex.

Now realising how powerless he was and the danger he was in if he stayed, he reluctantly made his escape just as the mob stormed his house looting and ransacking it before setting it on fire. A body of fire fighters arrived to extinguish the fire but were not allowed to perform their duty and could only look on as the fire raged through the buildings.

The mob their work done marched out of the broken gateway as a pall of smoke and flames rose behind them into the damp autumnal air. Exhilarated by their success the 600 or so looters now marched down the road to their next target, the New Gaol so called because it was only 11 years old having been built at much expense.

At about the same time the Governor of the New Gaol on hearing of the mobs intentions arrived at the Guildhall looking for the Magistrates and found two Alderman, Mr Hillhouse and

Mr Savage the former Mayor who collected up around thirty Citizens and Constables and headed to the Gaol a mile or more away. On circumventing the high prison wall they came around to the door only to be confronted by a crowd of over 15,000 strong and were straight away assaulted by missiles, severely injuring some of their party and as they tried to withdraw a Mr Little was badly hurt by a sledge hammer blow to his back.

Charles Grisley was present and saw the men being beaten back and was instructed by the Alderman to run quickly to the Horse Bazaar and seek Military assistance. On his arrival he spoke to a sergeant who took him to Reeves Hotel where he delivered the Magistrates message to the exhausted Captain Warrington who complained of being on continuous duty since Saturday, he was also suffering from the effects of Flu due to being constantly wet during this long period of duty. Nevertheless, he immediately ordered the sergeant back to the Horse Bazaar and to ready 10 men and turning to Cornet Kelson ordered him to take charge and report to Colonel Brereton at College Green and ask for orders. It was now around 3.30pm when the Colonel now back at his office received information that the New Gaol was being attacked and so ordered Kelson to join up with Sergeant Major Martin in Queen Square, making a total of 21 men, who then proceeded together to the Gaol. Sometime later Cornet Kelson returned saying countless thousands were assembled and with his small force and no sign of any Magistrates or a civil force to assist them it was impossible to act.

Not long after this, Colonel Brereton wrote a report to Major General Lord Fitzroy Somerset. In which he emphasised the need for reinforcements;

"Allow me to say, in the present state of the city, a strong military force does appear to be highly necessary"

(PRO HO 40/28)

At this same time, 200 worried citizens answering the Mayor's call for assistance were gathering at the Guildhall to hear his proposals, amongst these was Mr Isaac Cooke a solicitor who arrived on

time with his eldest son. He first saw some Magistrates but not the Mayor who arrived a little later and sat down at the head of the table to update those present on the state of the city and the fact that the mob were attacking the Bridewell. The Mayor told them that the mob were armed with sledge hammers, crowbars and other weapons and expressed his fear that they could make their way afterwards to the very building they had gathered in to destroy it too. On hearing this, Mr Cooke asked the Mayor what plan he had to propose to the meeting, but the Mayor replied; "*None*".
To which Mr Cooke replied;

"*I thought it a very extraordinary circumstance, that he, as the chief Magistrate of the city, in whom the preservation of the peace of the city, in a most peculiar manner was reposed, should suffer the mob to prevail so long in the city, and then to call the citizens together, and to inform them that he had no plan of operation to submit to their consideration.*"

This also shocked those gathered there. But Mr Cooke then asked if the Mayor could instruct the 8 or 10 soldiers outside to accompany them they would endeavour to quell the riot themselves to which the Mayor replied rather strangely that he had no power over the military. Mr Cooke then asked, and then who does?

"*The Military Commander, of course;*" the Mayor replied

(*The Trial of Charles Pinney.* Page 108.)

Mr Cooke expressed his surprise that such an essential person should be omitted from the meeting in which case the Mayor said he would send for him immediately. However, as it has already been revealed the Mayor had omitted Colonel Brereton from all such meetings.

In answer to this summons, Colonel Brereton arrived at the Guildhall around 4.30 and was taken into the Magistrates room, which had been cleared of the citizens, who like the Colonel previously, had to wait outside the door while the discussion took place. The Magistrates called on him to allow the troops to act.
Mr Benjamin Holder Green stated on Colonel Brereton's entrance;

"*he was ushered into the hall, and he mounted upon the table, and advanced towards the bench; He said, his men had been on duty for upwards of thirty hours, and were so exhausted, together with their horses, with fatigue, that the horses were scarcely able to pick up their heels from the ground, and that the men must have refreshment."*

(W.H. Somerton, *Trial of Charles Pinney.* Page 139.)

But Mr Willam Protheroe who was also there stated that he:

"Heard Colonel Brereton say that his men were ready to act, but the horses were too fatigued".

(W.H. Somerton, *Trial of Charles Pinney*. Page 22).

The Magistrates then asked if the Dragoons could not act on foot. The Colonel replied that measure was out of character for that service.

Authors note;

(Though Dragoons could of course fight on foot when necessary, the whole point of cavalry is that on horseback a soldier, (even a small one) is much more intimidating and can cover more ground. To dismount would render these advantages redundant. The Dragoons Guards only numbered around 30 so they needed all the advantages they could get in front of a Mob of countless thousands.)

As the Duke of Wellington himself expressed when he said;

"It is much more desirable to employ cavalry for the purpose of police than infantry; for this reason, cavalry inspires more terror at the same time that it does less mischief."

(C.M. Clode. *Military Forces of the Crown*,
London, John Murray, 1869. Vol.1, P302.)

Therefore, they then offered to get fresh horses for the troops and asked if the troops could then act. The Colonel replied that men need much less time for refreshment than their horses do, so if horses could be procured he felt that then the men could act. There now was a very noisy discussion where many offered of horses were promised and that they could deliver them to Fishers Stables.

As the Colonel left the Mayor and Magistrates decided to retire to the Council House ,which they felt would be easier to defend and because also valuable civic artefacts were stored there. But the men gathered at the Guildhall received no further instructions from the Mayor or Magistrates and so some decided to take the only advice that had been offered to them and so went home to try and defend their families and property as best they could. Nevertheless, some others decided to follow the Mayor to the Council House to see what could be done there and soon a large body of men arrived. So many in fact, they occupied the whole staircase from top to bottom and all the avenues leading to and from, but there was no sign of the Mayor or indeed any Magistrates.

Yet with the city in peril and the citizens seeking guidance the Mayor was reported to have gone to bed around this time;

"I believe he was in bed some part of Sunday. I believe he was in bed in The White Lion in Broad Street. The chambermaid informed me so the day before I left Bristol. She told me he went to bed for two hours".

(Statement of James Townsend,
Trial of Charles Pinney. Page 85.)

With the lack of civil leadership, there was a very great confusion, but no plan. A noisy discussion then ensued amongst the gentlemen gathered there about the Magistrates not offering them the protection they felt was their duty to do. Therefore, by 6pm Mr Cooke and others had had enough and left to go to the city to see for themselves if anything could be done. Colonel Brereton had already left, riding over to Reeves Hotel the quarters of Captain Warrington where he told him of the offer of fresh horses. Captain Warrington however was less enthusiastic saying it was impossible.

"as he could not suffer his men to act upon untrained horses".

So now tired and hungry, the Colonel retired to his Adjutants house to eat for the first time since Saturday morning. In any case no horses arrived and despite their promises, Colonel Brereton felt that the Magistrates had made no effort to obtain any. The discussion at the Council House had continued but had come to no conclusion. Someone mentioned the Posse Comitatus and Major Mackworth who had arrived replied that;

"if the Posse Comitatus would meet in College Green at six in the morning, I would come down and organise them, as well as I could".

But this was also rejected and so the Major increasingly annoyed by their indecision told them that they would only be motivated into doing something when their private houses were attacked as it seemed only that would rouse them into action when they were confronted by a sense of their common danger. So the Major much disgusted left to retire to Clifton;

"I retired to rest, resolved to do nothing until the following morning; 'ere which I was convinced some scenes must occur, as would really rouse the public feeling, and render our small military force tolerable effective";

(*A Personal Narrative* Major Mackworth.)

Later the Mayor and five or six gentlemen arrived at Colonel Brereton's office in College Green appearing very wet and agitated it had been raining most of the day but now it fell in torrents. Staff Sergeant William Platt who was on duty told them that Colonel Brereton was not there, but at the Adjutants across the green having his meal but had left orders to send for him if any one enquired.

"The Mayor forbade him saying[1] *'No, no, we do not want him, we will do without him'."*

He then asked for paper and ink and dictated a letter to Lord Melbourne while Town clerk Ludlow also wrote a note to his family warning them that he had heard that his house might be a target for the mob.

The Sergeant left to carry out the Mayor's request but while out also informed Colonel Brereton who had scarcely sat down when the Sergeant arrived to tell him that the Mayor and Magistrates were at his office. He quickly made his way there only to be told by the Mayor that;

"He didn't require my presence or indeed wish it to be known that he, or the Magistrates were there, but which they considered the only place of safety for them under existing circumstances[2]*"*.

At 8pm, Sergeant Dinnage returned to the recruiting office after delivering a message to under Sherriff Hare and noticed that the Mayor was upstairs in conversation with Colonel Brereton. The Mayor and Town Clerk Ludlow had arrived to inform the Colonel of the Mobs intentions to fire their shipping in the Docks and to see what he could do for them to prevent this happening. However, Colonel Brereton had already sent Sergeant Dinnage out to find the Mob to determine what their strength and intentions were. On returning from this task he reported to the Colonel and told him in the presence of the Mayor that the Mob were approaching and were intending to attack the Bishops Palace not the Shipping. On hearing this news the Colonel ordered him to go to the stables and fetch his horse and with orders for the 3rd Dragoons Guards to mount and get under arms as quickly as possible. Within less than 20minutes, Colonel Brereton led a party of 20 Dragoons Guards into the Palace courtyard and dispersed the Mob driving them all away.

In his statement in *The Trial of Mayor Pinney* Town Clerk Ludlow states that he never heard any discussion of escaping or heard any talk of personal fear made to Sergeant Dinnage. In fact he further stated that because:

"The mob were understood at that time to be at Lawford's Gate, in the county of Gloucester."

So was then asked; *"Bristol at this time was relieved of them?"* and replied, *"Yes it was"*.

[1](Statement of Staff Sergeant William Platt at the Trial of Charles Pinney)

[2] (Colonel Brereton's Statement at the court of inquiry)

2 (PRO HO52/12)

Yet he admitted that he had heard, *"something about the Bishop's Palace"* and did recollect hearing Colonel Brereton say; *"We must not rest any longer – we must turn the troops out and see what we can do".*

Therefore, Ludlow's statements are contradictory.

While this was going on the Mayor and Ludlow left, but instead of going to the Bishops Palace to assist and instruct the Colonel, they retired to Ludlow's room at the Council House in an effort to escape any confrontation. However, there they discovered around 700 residents still assembled waiting to hear the Mayor's plans for the defence of the city. Unfortunately, they were again disappointed to hear that the Mayor still had none. However, while they were gathered there, Alderman Camplin came out of the Magistrates room and standing at the top of the stairs called out to the people gathered below,

"shall we proceed to the Mansion House, which is on fire, or to the Bishop's Palace which is not on fire".

Hearing at last talk of some positive action a cry of "*The Bishop's Palace*" went up and then a request that the Mayor should also accompany them. The Mayor on hearing this from Town Clerk Ludlow's room then asked him; "*What shall we do about this?*" Ludlow replied that, "*as the people wish you to go, you had better go*". So the Mayor replied ,"*very well*" *but* "*will you go with me*". So the two men left "*arm in arm*" and on the way Ludlow asked others in the street to join in and assist the Mayor but none would.

This statement however does not comply with that of Mr William Protheroe, who was the person who went to tell the Mayor that the people waiting on the stairs and below wanted him to lead them to the Bishops Palace. Though he confirms that after a short discussion with Town Clerk Ludlow the Mayor and Ludlow left the room and started to ascended the stairs to loud cheers from the waiting men bellow but;

"When Mr Protheroe got to the bottom of the stairs he turned to look back and saw the Mayor and Sergeant Ludlow returning up the stairs".

(W.H. Somerton. *The Trial of Charles Pinney.* Page 21)

Mr James Jenkins who was there at the time tells a similar story;

After seeing Alderman Camplin at the top of the stairs asking those assembled to accompany him to the Bishop's Palace to defend it and a cry went up from those there that indeed, they would go with him but they wanted the Mayor to go too. The Mayor then appeared at the top of the stairs to a loud cheer from those assembled;

"we immediately, upon his commencing to descend the stairs, left the hall of the Council House, to proceed to the Bishop's Palace." But on route the Mayor was no longer with them? "No, I did not see him afterwards."

(Statement of Mr James Jenkins.
The trial of Charles Pinney. Page 143.)

The Mayor was later to claim he had only gone back for his hat and had indeed gone to the Palace but that he was prevented from passing into the courtyard by the military who had blocked the passage leading to the courtyard. Therefore, he retired to Colonel Brereton's office were he watched events from the safety of the back window.

However, no one saw him after he and Town Clerk Ludlow turned on the stairs and returned to the direction from which they had come. He wasn't seen again until he appeared at Colonel Brereton's office where he was seen by Sergeant Samuel Dinnage, who showed him to the back room where he could observe the Palace from a safe vantage point.

A similar story is told about the conduct of Alderman Camplin;

Mr Henry Bulgin a bookseller confirms this when he states that when he left the Council House with the group led by Alderman Camplin. He only saw the Alderman as far as the Palace gate but when they went through and entered the courtyard he was no longer with them and he didn't see the Mayor at all and though the Military was there they offered no impediment to their entering the Palace.

In fact when asked if he saw any of the Aldermen or the Mayor at the Palace he replied;

"Not any at all".

This was also confirmed by another in the party who left with Alderman Camplin, William Protheroe who stated referring to Camplin;

"I did not see him at the Palace. I saw him as far as the Green."

(*Trial of Charles Pinney.* Page 148.)

This seemed to be the modus operandi of the Mayor and Magistrates, who would rally the people to follow them here or there, only to disappear on route and retire to somewhere safe, leaving the people to fend for themselves. This was commented on by many people, and even the military complained of the same procedure.

While this was all going on, the Colonel and his troops had cleared the Mob from the Palace courtyard. Colonel Brereton was then informed that a number of looters were inside the Palace just as several fellows arrived, so the Colonel ordered them into the Palace to clear the plunderers, which they did, arresting three men who were imprisoned in the Palace vaults. Meanwhile the Colonel had received a report that the Mansion House was on fire and so he ordered the Constables to protect the Palace while he with the troops went over to see what could be done to save the Mansion House.

Before leaving the Colonel spoke to the Constables saying;

"I then told the Constables that their numbers, between 30 and 40, were quite sufficient to protect the Palace, if they would but do their duty, particularly as we had dispersed the mob."

(Colonel Brereton's statement to the Court of Inquiry. Page 16.)
(PRO HO 52/12)

One of the men who had gone inside to secure the building was a Mr Bulgin along with small group who searched the rooms to check they were secure, but when they came downstairs, they were shocked to see that the main body of defenders had disappeared along with all the Constables and the rioters were now coming back. Therefore, they had to escape out of a back window to avoid them and reach safety. He also confirmed that the military had also gone, but independently agreed with what the Colonel had said that to secure the building all that was needed was;

"20 or 30 resolute men would have done it".

(*Trial of Charles Pinney.* Page133.)

"exclusive of the military – without the military"

(*Trial of Charles Pinney.* Page 134.)

However, just as the Mayor and Town Clerk Ludlow did not manage to make it into the Palace yard let alone the actual Palace, Alderman Camplin strangely did not either.

(Also Town Clerk Ludlow's statement is rather contradictory as he states that Bristol was not in danger when he and the Mayor left to go the Council House, yet also stated that they went to the Recruiting office in the first place because they heard that the mob were intending to attack their shipping. He also admits to hearing Colonel Brereton saying that the Palace was being attacked and he was going to protect it.

Town Clerk Ludlow made his escape alone, but once in the street met again with Mr Burges and retired to his house and after a while left for his own house in Clifton where he had sent the message earlier from Colonel Brereton's office. It was around this time that the Mayor and Mr Henry Daniels, a surgeon arrived at the house of Mr Sherriff Lax at 52 Park Street. The door was opened by Mr Townsend, who had helped the Mayor escape earlier and was now looking after the house, as his master had left the city earlier in the day. On seeing the Mayor, Mr Townsend asked him if he remembered him from the morning, and the Mayor said that he didn't. Mr Daniels then said that he knew Mr Townsend very well and that he could be trusted with knowing where the Mayor was going and not telling anyone. However, the Mayor seemed disinclined to trust him until Daniels again reassured him and they then told him that the Mayor would be at

Mr Daniel Fripp's in Berkley Square but that he was not to tell anyone except from the Corporation. Several people did call that night but Mr Townsend did as instructed and told no one except Under Sherriff Hare.

Unfortunately, this was all happening just as Yeomanry reinforcements were arriving and were fruitlessly searching for them.

On the Colonel's arrival at the Mansion House, they found it already in flames, and there was nothing they could do. The horses were very much unsettled by ferocity of the fire, which illuminated the area so completely that you could see a pin on the ground. But alas, not any Constables or Magistrates, who as usual were nowhere to be seen. The Colonel left a party of the 3rd Dragoons nearby, to prevent, as far as possible any further outrages, and then made his way back to his office in College Green to see if the Mayor or any Magistrates were still there. However, there was no sign of them or any messages to instruct him or intimate where they could be found. It was now 10pm and in another part of town the 58 much needed reinforcements of Yeoman Cavalry under Captain Codrington were arriving at the Council House answering the Mayors request. As they halted outside the Exchange Building they were seen by Mr Jarman and Mr J.T. Manchee who were elated to see them. Mr Jarman offered to go and find a Magistrate for them but as he was gone for such a long time, Mr Manchee also offered to go and found the Chamberlain and together they went to the Council House and then the Guildhall but the Mayor and the Magistrates however were nowhere to be found. So they returned to the troops and Mr Manchee introduced Captain Coddrington to the Chamberlain who told the Captain that the Riot Act had been read and he could get the authority of the Under Sherriff to act. Nevertheless, the Captain insisted that he needed to see a Magistrate or hear the Riot act read himself, so the Chamberlain left and went in a further search for a Magistrate. Not wishing to waste any more time Mr Manchee suggested that they go to College Green as he thought that as the Bishop's Palace was on fire a Magistrate might be found there and if not certainly Colonel Brereton whose headquarters was close by. After a little while the Captain consulted his other officers and it was agreed that Mr Manchee would show them the way. On arriving there, they were informed that Colonel Brereton was not there so Captain Coddrington dismounted and followed Mr Manchee through the arch in search of a Magistrate and while engaged in this they were approached by someone who told them that the Colonel had arrived and so took them over to him.

The Captain on finally finding someone said how he; "*was very glad to hear of some authority*" and asked him the whereabouts of a Magistrate. The Colonel informed him of the near impossible task of finding Magistrates as they had all long since disappeared and had left no instructions as to where they could be found. However, he suggested that if he could borrow a horse he could take the Captain over to Park Street where he was sure the Under Sherriff lived. On arrival in Park Street however despite a desperate search they could not find the Under Sheriff, so Brereton advised that they should go to Fisher's stables where he could offer them quarters to refresh while he would continue to search for a Magistrate. As part of this endeavour, he sent Lieutenant A.H. Mcleath of the 38th Regiment in an effort to accomplish this, and who later stated;

"*I proceeded to the Council Chamber, and delivered your request that a magistrate should attend at the district office, for the purpose of authorising the Yeomanry to act. I was answered that no City Magistrate was there, nor could I learn where one could be found. A County Magistrate then said he would accompany me, which he did for about 15 paces, but returned, saying he would meet me at the district office in College Green in five minutes. I went there, remained some time but did not see him, and the sergeant informs me that no Magistrate came there at any time*".

(Statement of Lieutenant A.H. Mcleath 38th Regiment. dated 4 November 1832 Bristol.) (PRO HO52/12)

Therefore, Captain Codrington and his troop accompanied the Colonel to the gate of Fisher's stables in College Street. While the Captain was forming up his troop, the Colonel spoke to Mr John Fisher who told the Colonel that he was ready to accommodate them but that they would have to double up in the stalls as the 14th had done previously. The Colonel asked if someone could go and find Mr Hare the Under Sheriff but was told that they could not leave the stables, and anyway no one knew where to find him. In that case said the Colonel, turning to Captain Codrington, take your troop into the stables for the time being, while I go and try and locate a Magistrate myself. He then gave further orders before going down the side of the Stables to make sure the stables were lit up and it was all clear for the troops to enter. However, after the Colonel had left, the young inexperienced Captain claimed he spoke to a man near the gate. (He doesn't remember who this man was, or indeed if he was even connected to the stables) and asked if there was room for them, and the man replied; *"No there is not room for half a dozen horses much less for your troop". On hearing this, the Captain turned to his lieutenant and said;*

"This is too bad; I will not be humbugged in this manner any longer";

The time was now about 12.30am and they decided they would not wait, but ride back the way the Colonel had brought them, in the hope that they might see a Magistrate. Nevertheless, there was no sign of any, but neither did they stop to inquire as they passed the Council House, instead they left Bristol and did not stop until they dismounted at Downend, four miles from Bristol. Here they waited about two hours for orders, but no orders were received because no one knew they were there, as they had neglected to tell any one they were leaving, let alone where they were going.

Unfortunately they were not the only troops who had responded but not been utilised. A small detachment of the Bedminster Yeomanry Cavalry under Captain Henry Shute had also been waiting armed and ready for most of the day, in Portwall Lane less than a quarter of a mile away from Queen Square. At Colonel Brereton's Courts Martial Alderman Hillhouse claimed he didn't know that Captain Shute and the Bedminster Yeomanry were under arms and waiting at the Riding school in Portwall Lane the accustomed place of muster. But Captain Shute confirms that at about noon he sent a letter to the Mayor telling him such and that they were waiting for orders from the Civil authority and after some delay he actually received a message from a City Magistrate telling him that he should remain where he was, so he waited but received no further instructions. He further stated that he does not know if Alderman Hillhouse or Colonel Brereton were informed but the City Magistrates certainly were.

This confirmation is from the details of a letter from Captain Shute written to the Editor of the *Bristol Mirror* and published after Colonel Brereton's death on Saturday 14 January 1832

Colonel Brereton meanwhile on returning to usher the soldiers into their temporarily accommodation was astonished to find that it was no longer needed as every one of them had left, leaving no message, or indication as to where they had gone. Exasperated, he went back to College green to see if they were there or had left any message at his office, but finding no sign of any troops, and no messages from them or the Magistrates, he finally decided to retire to his Adjutants to get some rest arriving at 1am.

Monday 31st

They Flew as Leaves would Fly Before the Wind

As the Colonel arrived at his quarters, he reflected on the day's events and the options available to him to resolve them.

For though his force was small he felt that if he and the small number of tired troops could refresh then they would be far more effective and he could then also recall the 14th and together with the further military aid expected later this morning (Monday) he would then be in a position to use them with advantage. Therefore, with this in mind he went to his room and sat down to write his report after telling Captain Warrington to expect him at 6am. Unfortunately, this was not to be, for not long after, he was delivered a letter by the Adjutant from the Mayor and some instructions for billeting the Doddington Yeomanry.

The Mayor of Bristol desires Colonel Brereton to consider himself fully authorised to take whatever steps and give whatever orders he, as the Military Commander of this City, may think fit to restore and preserve, as far as possible, the public peace. The Riot Act has been read three times today. Colonel Brereton will have the goodness to consider this order to apply not only to the troops at present under his command, but to any which may subsequently arrive in the City.

Mr Daniel Fripp's, No 30 Berkeley Square,

Sunday night, 12 o'clock, 30 October, 1831

So Colonel Brereton now had the authority of the Magistrates to command the Yeomanry, but all too late, as they had already left. These letters had been sent just as the Colonel and Captain Codrington had been searching for a representative of the civil power. However, the Mayor himself was hiding away telling all not to disclose his whereabouts to anyone but members of the municipality but not the military.

Francis Tuckett a 29-year-old who had signed up as a Special Constable observed as much when he also wrote a letter, not to the military but in his case to his fiancé Mariana Fox but at exactly the same time, (12 o'clock);

"There is not a magistrate in the city, everyone having shamefully deserted his post. The chamberlain is the only public man at his post at the Council House where he, with a few constables, are awaiting an attack. There are three companies of the 14th Light Dragoons in the town but the Commanding Officer (Colonel Brereton) has refused to act, I suppose from the inadequacy of his force. Should reinforcements arrive there is no magistrate to warrant their acting and I very much doubt if the troops can be depended on, which in the abstract I should be thankful in believing to be the case."

(*Eyewitness! Letters of Francis Tuckett* Published by the Frenchay Tuckett Society. Page 5.)

I doubt if Mr Tuckett knew how prophetic his observation was, for just as he was writing it, in another part of town those much needed troops had indeed arrived and had, just as he had feared, searched in vain for a Magistrate and had left, because; *"everyone having shamefully deserted his post."*

So by the time the Colonel received this letter from the Mayor, it was all too late, the Doddington Yeomanry had all ready left without saying where, so what could he do? His available troops were all now exhausted and it was now 1am with no sign of a Magistrate to accompany them despite an exhaustive search.

In any case, the city was now fairly quiet, so the best course of action was to get some rest and return to the fray later that morning at 6 o'clock when the rioters could be expected to have;

"Became so fatigued by their diabolical exertions and lastly broken by drunkenness."

(Colonel Brereton's Statement to the Court of Inquiry PRO HO 52/12)

Also regarding the Mayors letter;

Town Clerk, Sergeant Ludlow recollected that after he had returned from Clifton about 10pm in the evening he had gone to Mr Fripp's house later with Mr Burges to obtain billets for the Doddington Yeomanry.

Asked in court later about the time the note was written he said;

"Before the note was sealed, somebody looked at his watch to ascertain the time, and the time was put in the note."

(*The Trial of Charles Pinney.* Page 297)

These billets were in response to Mr James Bush whom you may remember was sent by the Mayor to summon the Yeomanry and after he had done this he returned to Bristol and had spent most of the evening trying to find a Magistrate to inform them of The Doddington Yeomanry's approach. Unfortunately, by the time, he had located them and the letters and billets were written and delivered, these much-needed troops had already arrived, searched, and then left the city.

After these billets were signed;

"Town Clerk, Sergeant Ludlow then conceived that he could be of no further service, proceeded on horseback to his own residence Down House, about two miles from the city, where he arrived about 1 o'clock am/"

(Court of Inquiry PRO HO/5212)

Ludlow was not to return to the City until 10am on Monday morning.

Alderman Abraham Hillhouse was also making his way home stating;

"When he retired to his own house on the Sunday morning about 1 o'clock, he thought the mob had all gone quietly away."

(Court of Inquiry PRO HO52/12)

However, an hour later at 2am a Surgeon, Mr Samuel Oviatt Goldney and Mr Wintour Harris both residents of Queen Square were becoming worried about the safety of their properties after seeing a small rabble entering the square. Therefore, as so many had before them, decided to search for the Mayor and Magistrates, going first to the Council House and inquired of the Chamberlain Mr Gerrard where the Magistrates were. However, there were informed they were not there and so after a fruitless search where no sign or indication as to where the Magistrates could be located, they decided to seek the military instead, so proceeding to Leigh's Livery Stables where they saw Cornet Kelson and the troops by their horses and asked if they could go to Queen Square. Cornet Kelson said he was ready, but could not act without authority, so Mr Goldney left with Mr Harris to procure some. Mr Goldney had heard a rumour that the Mayor might be at Daniel Fripp's house in Berkeley Square so the two decided to take a gamble and see if indeed he was. After knocking at the door the head of Mr Fripp appeared from an upstairs window and asked *"Who is there?"*

"I want to see the Mayor," replied Mr Goldney. Mr Fripp came downstairs and talking through the closed door asked who he was. After giving his name the door was opened and Mr Goldney inquired if the Mayor was there. Mr Fripp hesitated and so Mr Goldney said tersely, *"Sir, is he here or is he not?"*

"He is," was the reply. Then, *"I wish to see him,"* replied Mr Goldney. *"What do you want of him?"* said Fripp, Mr Goldney told him about the state of the city, and the rabble he had seen intent on mischief and how he felt it could be put down by a small organised force. However, he needed an order from the Mayor or a Magistrate to instruct the troops. After listening to his request, Mr Fripp led the two gentlemen into his parlour to wait, while he went back upstairs. After about a quarter of an hour he returned without the Mayor but a note from him addressed to "Colonel Brereton or the Commanding Officer of the troops in Bristol. "Mr Fripp on passing the note to Goldney said, *"Here is what you want; And you are particularly requested not to say where the Mayor is."*

Without answering, Mr Goldney and Mr Harris took the note and left the house running all the way to the stables arriving at

3am where they found Sergeant Deane and ask them for the Commanding Officer, who thought they meant Captain Warrington and so directed them to the stable were the Captain could be found. They then handed the letter to Captain Warrington, who under the light of a lantern noticed it was not addressed to him, but to Colonel Brereton. This is not for me exclaimed the Captain but Colonel Brereton, you should take it to him instead. You can find him at the office or at number 2 Unity Street. However, they said that they had been looking for him for three quarters of an hour or more, and could not find him. After which he was repeatedly urged to open it by Mr Goldney, but he still hesitated in breaking the seal. Until Mr Goldney offered to take the responsibly upon himself, he then did so, and on reading it out loud in front of the two gentlemen. He replied that he was perfectly willing to act but that it was Kings Regulations that a Magistrate should accompany any troops going out, or that he should have the authority of his Commanding Officer. He then asked the two men if they were Magistrates themselves, to which they replied they were not. Captain Warrington then again reiterated that he was willing to do everything within his power but that he could not act without a Magistrate to accompany him every inch of the road, but Mr Goldney didn't know of the whereabouts of any Magistrates except the Mayor and he had expressly requested him not to tell any one. Captain Warrington also expressed his regret that the Doddington Yeomanry had already left Bristol as they would have been of great service as he only had 25 men and their horses were so tired, they were scarcely able to carry them, announcing there; *"was a great screw lose somewhere, but where he did not know"*.

During the course of Sunday alone, the small number of troops had been called out around 50 separate times according to Sergeant Major Martin so no wonder they were so tired. The Captain now assured that no one knew the whereabouts of any Magistrates, so instead, again urged the gentlemen to inform Colonel Brereton to get his authority, and instructed them as to exactly where he could be found. In anticipation of the imminent arrival of this order he turned to Sergeant Deane and instructed him to bridle up the remaining horses and assemble them altogether in readiness. On hearing this, Mr Goldney and Harris left. Captain Warrington believed they had gone to inform the Colonel and so waited patiently for their return, but he was to regret not taking any measures himself because they had not. After some time waiting, he turned to Sergeant Deane and said;

"My God! What a time those gentlemen are away!"

(Court Martial of Captain Warrington. Page 81.)

Earlier Alderman Camplin had been watching from the safety of Mr Edgehill's house the attack on the Bishop's Palace while the mob fed the flames with many priceless books. He stayed there until 2.30am until it was much quieter before he felt safe to venture out again and made his way to the Butts where he noticed a mob now starting to set fire to private houses in Queen Square. The sight of private property being destroyed finally had the desired effect, just as Major Mackworth had predicted earlier and at last induced Camplin to seek some means to stop it. Nevertheless, with no one else available he went straight over to inform the military and seek their assistance. On his way through College Green he met up with another worried property owner Frederick Danson a barrister and together the two men made their way the short distance to Leigh's Horse Bazaar to call out the troops. On entering the stables, they found Captain Warrington still waiting for the return of the previous gentlemen.

And so when Alderman Camplin announced that he had come for the troops. Warrington said, "*Very well, Sir; they are ready.*" thinking that there visit was related to the earlier one. Warrington again declared that he was ready to act but needed a Magistrate to accompany him, but Camplin hesitated for some time, and then asked if that was according to regulations, Captain Warrington replied; "*yes it was, or an order signed by two Magistrates.*"

This point had been cleared previously by the Law Officers who had stated;

"The authority of a Magistrate was absolutely necessary because military would not be assisting the civil power unless a

*representative of the civil power was actually present and needed their assistance"**

(**A History of English Criminal Law*. 1956 by Leon Radzinowicz. Vol 4 page 146–7.)

Mr Danson then had a quiet word with Camplin before saying out loud; *"Of course, the Alderman will go down; he will go as a Magistrate to direct the troops."* Reassured, Captain Warrington then remarked about the Mayors letter he had received and Alderman Camplin said, *"That confirms what we have come about"*.

(Court Martial of Captain Warrington. Pages 81-82.)
(This statement is further collaborated by Sergeant Major Martin also on page 82 and Mr Danson on page 64.)

Camplin then said, as he was a Magistrate, if there was need to fire, you will of course fire. To which Warrington replied, *"NO, my orders are not to fire.."* "I suppose these orders are from Colonel Brereton?" replied Camplin, in which case they asked the Captain to accompany them to the Colonels lodgings at no 2 Unity Street. (We now know of course that the orders *Not to fire*, came directly from the Mayor not the Colonel.)

The difficulties experienced between an Officer in Command of troops and the civil authority when engaged to suppress a riot can be judged by this insight on the Burdett riots of 1810

"I heard a Magistrate saying to an Officer of the Guards at Burdett's riots, 'Sir, you must disperse the rioters.' 'Yes Sir,' answered the Guardsman. 'Soldiers, prime and load.' 'Stop Sir,' said the magistrate, you must not fire! 'What are you about?' 'Shall I charge with the bayonet then Sir?' asked the officer.' 'Oh no! You must disperse the rioters.' 'But how am I to disperse them if I neither fire nor charge?" Oh, that is your business not mine do as you like, only you must not fire or use your bayonets'."

(Lieutenant-General Sir Charles Napier, Remarks on Military law and the punishment of flogging. (1837) Page 47.)

Captain Warrington then left with Alderman Camplin and Mr Danson and on route were joined by several other concerned citizens also looking for help. They all walked together the 200 yards to Unity Street where they rang the bell and two ladies opened an upstairs window and asked what they wanted. When they asked to see the Colonel, the door was opened and within five minutes they were ushered into the Parlour where the Colonel who had still not retired entered fully dressed but wearing his slippers.

Despite all the claimed obdurateness of both Captain Warrington and later by Colonel Brereton, they in fact only spent fifteen minutes in and about the Colonels quarters before the troops were called out. In total it had only been half an hour since Mr Danson had first met Alderman Camplin in College Green and the troops were already mounted and heading for Queen Square, which seems fairly quick and efficient.

Based on the statement of Frederick Danson
(a barrister and resident of Queen Square.)

PRO HO 52/12 (Captain Warrington's Court Martial. Page 64.)

Captain Warrington also stated he never refused to fire but merely reminded Camplin before they left the Bazaar that the Magistrate who authorises firing must remain with the troops when they performed this task.

(Court Martial; of Captain Warrington. Page 62.)

But Alderman Camplin states that;

"Ringing violently at the bell, two females, looked out of the central window of the drawing room upstairs, of whom he enquired whether Lt Colonel Brereton was there – they replied he was not, – Alderman Camplin then enquired if Captain or Mr Francis lived there – the females said yes, – they were desired to tell him that Alderman Camplin must see him instantly – in about eight or 10 minutes the street door was opened when he the

Alderman saw Colonel Brereton in the hall in his slippers but in other respects dressed."

(Statement of Alderman Camplin Court of Inquiry (HO52/12))

However Frederick Danson the Barrister who had accompanied Camplin there states;

"I heard no denial of the Colonel being there."

(Statement of Frederick Damson Court of Inquiry (HO52/12))

Camplin also stated that Captain Warrington told him he didn't know where Colonel Brereton was. Which seems a rather remarkable thing to say, for unlike the Mayor and magistrates, it was common knowledge where the Colonel could be found at all hours. Also the Captain was reported as telling Mr Goldney and Mr Harris when they had called earlier, and Warrington had consistently informed anyone who asked where the Colonel could be found. Even Camplin himself asked Captain Warrington to accompany them to the Colonel's residence at 2 Unity Street, so it seems everyone *did* know where he was?

Frederick Danson also states he never heard Captain Warrington complain of the state of the horses or men alluded to by Alderman Camplin.

(Court Martial of Captain Warrington. Pages 63 and 64.)

Authors note;

The statements are similar but Camplin's which only the relevant section has been quoted, differs in such that it is more critical of the military, with many details that seem to suggest that the military was less cooperative than the statement made by Mr Danson *and* the others present. The time that they arrived at the Colonels lodgings was around 4am* in a quiet side street where one would of imagined you could hear a pin drop, yet Frederick Danson heard no denial of the Colonel being there. This all seems curiously very similar to the actual events when Mr Goldney and Mr Harris called at Daniel Fripp's house in Berkeley Square looking for the Mayor earlier and was perhaps repeated by Camplin, but inserting the Colonel's name in place of the Mayor to discredit him.

However, there seems to be far too many of these instances to be just down to mere coincidence. It appears far more likely that the Magistrates are purposefully attempting to sully the reputation of the military and Colonel Brereton in particular.

* PRO HO 52/12
(Statement of Colonel Brereton to the Court inquiry. Page 17.)

Mr Danson does not remember if Captain Warrington gave the Colonel the letter he had received earlier from the Mayor but thought he remembered them discussing it. However, Colonel Brereton states he was never given the letter.

The Colonel then turned to Captain Warrington and ordered him to get as many men as were fit for duty under arms immediately and assemble in College Green.

When they left at around 4.15 am Charles Bissett Esq, a Merchant walked with the Colonel down to College Green and according to Mr Bissett the Colonel showed none of the reluctance to act complained of by Alderman Camplin in fact the Colonel told him that;

"He should be most happy to accompany the troops to the square, and that he should be on his horse in three or four minutes."

(W.H .Somerton. Page 134.)

On the Colonels arrival in the Green he instructed Captain Warrington, (who still wasn't looking very well) to wait in reserve with 12 troops,

Leaving Cornet Kelson in command of the main body of the troop of around 20 in number and led them at a trot to the Drawbridge, where he found Alderman Camplin wrapped in a black cloak waiting with the small civil party of about four people. They proceeded to Queen Square with the civil party following behind, and on entering Princes Street they saw a large crowd of 600–700 people opposite a burning house.

Colonel Brereton then formed up his troops and led them at a charge and cleared the street, to the cheers of the crowd, who called out, *"do your duty soldiers cut them down"*.

At the top of Princes Street they turned into Queen Square by the furthest avenue, they could see two sides of the square in flames with a mob of 700 outside the last house to be fired.

Mr Benjamin Holder-Green an accountant had stayed up all night in Queen Square and watched as upwards of 12,000 people were plundering and looting. But by 5.30 am;

"They dropped off in the morning very considerably; their physical strength for destruction appeared to me to be consumed in a very great degree".

Nevertheless, those left, around 700 were moving to the third side of the square where he had been stationed all night when he saw the troops make their entrance. At the sight of the troops the mob fled;

"They flew as leaves would fly before the wind".

Mr Holder-Green, then thought it prudent to also depart at this point.

(*Trial of Charles Pinney.* Page 140.)

The troops divided into two and at a gallop cleared the square and formed up outside number 42, Mr Claxton's house, on the far side of the square under Colonel Brereton's personal command. Where Robert Hopton, Claxton's negro servant was defending his master house throwing the rioters out and extinguished the flames as the rioters fled, the troops could not help but cut some with their sabres, but according to Troop Sergeant John Martin of the Third;

"The Colonel immediately ordered that no violence should be used"

But Cornet Kelson states that;

"The edge of the swords was then applied for the first time in earnest. Lt Colonel Brereton did not then seem to mind."

PRO HO 52/12

Perhaps the Colonel didn't mind because he now had the Mayors written permission, and which stated he was;

"fully authorised to take whatever steps and give whatever orders he, as the military commander of the troops in this city, may think fit to restore and preserve, as far as possible the public peace."

(The Mayors letter to Brereton, dated 12 o'clock Sunday night)

Several parties of the rioters reassembled in different parts of the square and the detachments again moved against them in two divisions dispersing the mob. It was at this time that the Colonel ordered Cornet Kelson to send Dragoon Llewellin to Captain Warrington and the 12 reserve troops to attend. Captain Warrington arrived by 7am taking over the command from Cornet Kelson and continually charged the mob wherever they tried to reassemble. After about an hour the square was clear of the mob without the aid of any Magistrates or Constables who were no where to be seen. It was only after this that true to form Alderman Camplin reappeared;

"I do not recollect seeing him until we had the square nearly cleared, and free from further attempts to fire the houses."

(Colonel Brereton's statement to the Court of Inquiry. Page 18)

It was during this time that Major Mackworth reappeared from his night's rest in Clifton and joining in, and was later to claim;

"It was no time to consider numbers or to await Magistrates' orders. I called out 'Colonel Brereton, we must instantly charge' and without waiting for his answer-he could not but approve – I called out, 'Charge men and charge home'. The troops charged with much alacrity, Colonel Brereton charging with much spirit at their head; and I trust in God every man there injured was actually engaged in plunder or in burning and that not a single innocent person there fell beneath our sabres. Numbers were cut down and ridden over; some driven into the burning houses, out of which they were never seen to return, and our dragoons, after sabering all they could come at in the square, collected and formed and

then charged down Princes Street and again returned to the square, riding at the miserable mob in all directions; about 120 or 130 of the incendiaries were killed and wounded here."

(Major Digby Mackwoth, *A personal narrative* a 16 page pamphlet published by the Major after the riots)

Not everyone agreed with the Majors account however;

"Subsequently, at about half past six in the morning, about 50 of the mob manifested a desire to renew violence, but they were quickly dispersed by the soldiers, under the direction of Colonel Brereton, the men, with but few exceptions, sticking with the flats of their swords. The whole credit for this service has been claimed by Major Mackworth. Our information, however, goes to prove that this statement is overcharged; that none were killed; none driven into the burning houses; and but few wounded."

(W.H. Somerton, *Narrative of the Bristol Riots.* Page 29.)

Also;

"As, in my subsequent observations, I may have occasion to refer to Major Mackworth's narrative, it may be necessary to state the degree of credit to which it may be considered entitled. No doubt the style is extremely objectionable and egotistical; but his foolish vanity must not be allowed to discredit his statement of facts, particularly where it is corroborated by the representations of the Magistrates. There are two very extraordinary circumstances, which require some explanation; one of which tends so immediately to destroy the reputation of Colonel Brereton that we can no longer view the Major as his apologist, and therefore I think the Colonel fully entitled to all the benefits of any incidental admissions in his favour. The first is, that an officer of inferior rank, in plain cloths, should presume to issue a command to the soldiers in the presence of that officer, and that the soldiers should obey him!"

(T.J. Manchee, member of the committee of inquiry. *Riots of Bristol.* Page 26.)

This was corroborated by the statement of another witness to this event, Barrister Frederick Danson Esq who replied in answer to the Courts of inquiry question;

"Do you attribute this check to the operation of the mob, and to the destruction of property, to the measures taken by Lt Colonel Brereton previous to Major Mackworth's arrival?"

Mr Danson replied, *"Certainly"*

As did Dr Carpenter who arrived after the Colonel had cleared the mob and saw the Colonel and Dragoons quietly observing when Major Mackworth arrived, (who possibly misread the situation and instigated a charge).

Dr Carpenter stating it;

"was in my judgement next to useless; and sudden, and without notice, As it was, did not do credit to the discretion of the individual who caused it. Major Mackworth an officer, who was on a visit to the neighbourhood, who after having spent the night at a distance, came down to the square about the time I did myself, urged and even directed the troops to charge home and though I believe all riot was now over."

(*The Monthly Repository.* Vol 5. Page 850.)

A retired Officer writing to *The Times* made a similar point, wanting to know on whose authority Major Mackworth was there and;

"by what authority he presumed to take upon himself the command of any of the troops."

and that while in civilian cloths he gave orders;

"To charge, and charge home upon the people". "If this be consistent with either the Articles of War, military regulations, or any of the military codes upon which the discipline of the army has been established, it is quite novel to me, the narrator even goes so far as to say that he actually took the command of a senior officer, Colonel Brereton, and directed him to charge with the troops. In my days in the army, both at home and abroad, we were always amenable to superior officers, and we never could act with troops unless we were in uniform. The narrator was determined, although

a step below him in rank to be Major Domo upon this grand occasion. I knew a time– -and there is no alteration in the rules of the service upon this point since then, – when, if an officer appeared in coloured cloths to give orders to, or command troops, he would have been placed in arrest and brought to a Court Martial for doing so; and I am sure the crime is tenfold, when an officer does so where the lives of his fellow creatures are sacrificed, however glorious the narrator might have fancied the achievement."

*(*Letter to the editor of *The Times*. London. 24 Nov 1831.*)*

This opinion is given further credence in another letter to the *Bristol Mirror* dated Saturday 3 December 1831 from a writer calling himself FAIR PLAY who says;

"In what situation Major Mackworth stood at the time he ventured to order to 'charge and charge home' he being then in plain cloths and holding no official situation at Bristol, Lt Colonel Brereton, of sixteen years standing, (sic) being at that crucial moment by his side, and having been appointed by Government the inspecting field officer of the district, and consequentially having the command of all regiments quartered therein. I wish to learn, did Major Mackworth act as a Magistrate of the county of Gloucester, or as a Major in the Army, and belonging to the staff of Lord Hill, if in the former case, why did he not, instead of going to bed on Sunday night, leaving the city to be sacked and then burned, give that aid to Lt Colonel Brereton, by his advice as a Magistrate, which it has been said was much needed on that occasion? But on the other hand, if he acted as a military man, could he be so bold, after the severe punishment, which Mr Editor, you, with many of your readers, cannot have lost sight of, namely, the case of General Sir Robert Wilson, who, when the funeral possession of our late Queen, was being escorted by the Life Guards, Major Oaks having the command, ventured to take command upon himself, and for doing which was dismissed from the service.

"If, therefore, Mr Editor, a General could not take upon himself such a responsibility, how is it a Major does so when a Lt Colonel is in Command? And not only does so with impunity,

but is eulogised at the head of all the troops in Bristol, by the Commander-in-Chief, for committing what here to-for , has been considered a breach of the Articles of War."

(*Bristol Mirror.* 25 November 1831.)

So even at the time, many people thought that Major Mackworth's participation was both dubious and somewhat suspicious, also how did his account which was supposed to be just a military report to Lord Hill, end up being published, and under whose authority? The publication of an internal army report in itself was surely a chargeable offence, yet again Lord Hill the Commander-in-Chief said nothing about this either. So It would seem that Mackworth's participation was sanctioned and authorised by Lord Hill himself and that Mackworth's claim to be just "*visiting friends*" in the neighbourhood was just a cover, nothing else explains the Majors lack of censure for his actions.

In addition, his account was somewhat overblown as he was only in the square for a short time arriving sometime around 6.30am. Mr Bissett said he left with the Colonel at 4am a full two and half hours before and Mackworth was already gone on Colonel Brereton's orders to return the 14th Dragoons before Captain Warrington's arrival with the 3rd Dragoons at 7am, so he was probably there for only half an hour and certainly less than an hour, and what is more curious, on who's authority did he take such steps while "*visiting friends in the neighbourhood*"?

Therefore, it seems that though we shouldn't ignore all that the Major said, especially when it can be corroborated by others, but we should treat it with a little caution, particularly when he talks in such glowing terms about his own actions. For it seems that Mackworth has some form in writing overblown accounts of his own endeavours.

As Captain Digby Mackworth he served as a junior Aide-de-camp to Lord Hill at the Battle of Waterloo in 1815 and his account of his actions there were also published as his diary of events. But later when Captain Siborne wrote his famous two volume set, *History of the War in France and Belgium, in 1815.*

Siborne questioned Mackworth's account of his part in the attack and defeat of the French Imperial Guard on 18 June. Writing in the United Service magazine saying;

"No officer of either Adams or Maitland's brigade will confirm Sir Digby Mackworth's statement, which is inconsistent not only with the evidence of other officers of both higher and lower rank, but also of military reasoning."

(*United Service Magazine.* 1845 Volume 48. Page 423.)

Which also seems to ring true of Mackworth's *A Personal narrative* reporting the Bristol riots which is also, *"inconsistent not only with the evidence of other officers of both higher and lower rank,"* but also those of the public that also witnessed events.

Was it as George Orwell later stated in *Politics and the English Language* (1946) when he said that political prose was formed;

"to make lies sound truthful and murder respectable, and to give an appearance of solidity to pure wind."

Three things had changed since Sunday and were making a marked difference, and had given the small military presence a decisive advantage;

Firstly, the mob who had been tolerated and even encouraged in their destruction of civil and Church property were to lose that tacit support of the populous when early Monday morning they changed tactics and started to loot and burn private property. This alone caused the good citizens of Bristol to rise up and to actively engage and support any measures to terminate the destruction just as Mackworth had been anticipated on the Sunday evening;

"I retired to rest, resolved to do nothing until the following morning; 'ere which I was convinced some scenes must occur, as would really rouse the public feeling, and render our small Military force tolerable effective;

(*A personal narrative.* Major Digby Mackworth.)

Secondly, the mob had now entered the third day of rioting and looting and with little rest they were starting to run out of steam.

Thirdly, a large number of them had consumed large quantities of alcohol and were now entering the hangover period and its debilitating effects. This had been predicted of course by Colonel Brereton, who had planned to take advantage of this fact later this morning. When he and the troops had rested and when he could recall the 14th and both could act with advantage. However, after the mob started to attack private property the citizens awoke from their torpor and he was required a couple of hours earlier than he had planned. But his assumption was right and the small military force was now much more effective as the rioters had indeed;

"Became so fatigued by their diabolical exertions and lastly broken by drunkenness."

(Colonel Brereton's letter to Lord Hill. 3 November.)

"the greater proportion, indeed almost the whole of the rioters, had gone to their miserable homes and hiding places."

(W.H. Somerton *The Bristol Riots*. Page 32.)

Special Constable Francis Tuckett also wrote describing the scene on the Monday morning further confirming this by saying;

"Many of the incendiaries are lying in the grass in Queen Square in the most brutal state of intoxication. I believe many more are smothered and burnt in the ruins of the houses which they have fired."

(Letter of Francis Tuckett. Page 6. *Eyewitness*, published by the Frenchay Tuckett Society.)

The troops continued to keep the square and adjoining streets clear but by 8am, two thirds were able to retire to the stables leaving Sergeant Dean and the remaining 10 troops as a token force to maintain the peace. Also belatedly, a large number of citizens had started to answer the Mayors call to sign up as Specials. A number of whom had arrived to assist and keep the square clear. One such Special was a half pay army officer Captain John

Crosley Lewis, who had been a Special since January 1830 as all half pay officers and had been ordered to act under the orders of the Magistrates as serious rioting had been expected even then. Captain Lewis had returned to Bristol from Devon to perform this duty on the day that Sir Charles Wetherell entered the city in anticipation that there could be trouble. On the Sunday morning, he had seen the 14th dragoons attacked while he was on his way to the Cathedral for divine service, so changed his plans and went to the Guildhall instead. After witnessing the attacks on the Bridewell, New Gaol, Bishops Palace and Queen Square, by about 2am in the morning he had tried to stop some ruffians entering the Customs House and was brutally attacked and knocked to the ground. So on this occasion he had asked Alderman Hillhouse if the Constables could arm themselves and the Alderman replied that they should defend themselves with arms or anything else in the performance of their duty as Constables. Therefore, with his beating at the hands of the rioters fresh in his mind he decided to follow these instructions and arm himself with two pistols. On entering the square after the troops had charged and cleared it. He saw the place littered with bodies, some dead some stupefied with drink. At about 8:30am with a group of his fellow Constables he tried to drive out a small group of men who were lingering. One of these men refused to go shouting, "*Why don't you go home yourself?*" while he grabbed hold of him with both hands demanding to know who he was. Fearing for his safety the Captain drew his pistol and as he did so he was struck by one of his assailants and the pistol went off and an innocent 12-year-old boy called Thomas Morris fell to the ground fifteen yards away with a mortal wound in his stomach .

Reinforcement Arrive

Earlier in another part of town at around 7.30am, Major Beckwith of the 14th Light Dragoons had arrived in plain clothes with his Adjutant in a post chaise. He went straight to the Council House looking for a Magistrate he was lucky enough to find not only the Mayor but three other Magistrates together with the Town Clerk, Sergeant Ludlow, who he said;

"Appeared to him bewildered and stupefied with terror".

(Major Beckwith's statement at the Court Martial of Captain Warrington. Page 88.)

He requested that one of them might accompany him on horseback to deal with the rioting, but all the Magistrates refused, even though they were strongly urged to do so. One referring to his house, another to his shipping, each one offering another reason as to why they could not comply, even saying that none could ride, except they pointed out a tall gentleman Mr Alderman Hillhouse but he declared he hadn't ridden a horse in 18 years and would hold any responsible if they repeated it . Therefore, the Major then said if they would not accompany him they must supply him with a written authority to act, which was given to him before they urged him to report to Colonel Brereton.

They then complained bitterly about Colonel Brereton not supporting them and that they had no authority whatsoever and the mob had complete control of the city. However, if any of them had been brave or courageous enough to go out into the streets they would have known that this was already not the case. But now armed with the Mayors authority, Major Beckwith was now empowered to do much as he pleased, and would later exploit it to its fullest extent when any opportunity arose.

"The Magistrates, it is to be presumed, ignorant alike as to the state of the city and of the description of persons composing

the majority of the multitude assembled in the square, thought proper to issue an order for the cavalry to charge through the streets."

(W.H. Somerton. *The Bristol Riots*. Page 33.)

In order to exploit this authority Beckwith asked where the 14th Dragoons were and was told that the Colonel had sent them out of Bristol the day before. However, they informed him that the Colonel had already sent for them to return, and the Mayor then suggested that he should go and report to Colonel Brereton in Queen Square. On reporting to the Colonel in the square, he asked again about the 14th and was told that they had been sent temporarily to Keynsham, but would be returning shortly. The Major expressed his astonishment at what had happened and the Colonel told him that with only a small body of troops and totally unaided by the Magistrates who would not authorise the use of force made it very difficult to act decisively. Major Beckwith replied that the General Orders of the Army made it imperative for him to act without a Magistrate if one was not present. However, the Colonel disagreed, and in any case replied, that it was impossible with the small over-stretched force available, and so he had to wait until the reinforcements he had requested arrived.

Authors note;

The situation regarding the troops acting without a Magistrate as quoted by Major Beckwith was in fact not as clear cut or defined as he claimed. As stated earlier the Government itself had asked for clarification on this point and was told by the Law Officers that without the presence of a Magistrate how could the army offer them support? Although contradictory to this at the Court Martial of Captain Warrington a few months after the riot, Major Beckwith's opinion seemed to be confirmed when Major General Dalbiac stated;

"*The court rejected the contention that an Army officer could refuse to act against civilians unless he had the sanction of a Magistrate. Such doctrine, it said would enable every officer, when placed in command of His Majesty's troops for the suppression of tumult, to place the inertness of the civil power between himself and the personal responsibility of his station, and under the protection of such inertness, to shelter himself from blame and disgrace."*

But only a month later at the House of Commons this was challenged by Sir Henry Hardinge former Secretary of War probably as a result of Colonel Brereton's difficulties when he said;

"He strongly objected to the calling out of the military in any part of the kingdom; without the authority and presence of a Magistrate to sanction the proceedings. It was placing the Officer in Command in a most painful situation".

(Parliamentary Debates, 3rd series. Vol. 10 1832 Page 968.)

Yet at Charles Pinney's trial later that year Mr Justice Littledale in his summing up stated a some what confusing view;

"The military Officer may act without any Magistrate, but no prudent military man would do so, because his acting may be attended by a loss of life, but if the Magistrate gives him an order to act that is all that is required."

Nevertheless, even with this *"order to act"* it did not protect the soldier from prosecution, as Captain Lewis was to find out after the Bristol riots when he was charged with manslaughter. He could also not rely on any support from the civil authorities either after Alderman Hillhouse said he had not the slightest recollection of sanctioning the Captain's use of pistols, even though the Captain maintained that he had.

As lieutenant General Sir Charles Napier was to point out in *Remarks on Military Law and the Punishment of Flogging,* London 1837. Page 47;

"The soldier has all the responsibility, while at the same time no precise power is confided in him, no line of conduct defined for his guidance... His thoughts dwell upon (to him) most interesting questions, shall I be shot for my forbearances by a Court Martial, or hanged for over zeal by a jury?"

Only a couple of years later in 1835 and probably as a result of all this confusion highlighted by the Bristol riots the War Office issued the following confidential orders;

"No officer is to set out with troops in the suppression of riot, the maintenance of the public peace, or the execution of the law, except upon the requisition of a magistrate in writing," The magistrate was also to accompany the troops, and the Officer was "not to give the word of command to fire unless distinctly required to do so by the Magistrate."

On the accession of Queen Victoria to the throne in 1837 these were embodied in the Queen's Regulations for the Army. Therefore again, Colonel Brereton was indeed right!

Moreover, his interpretation would have been the prudent line to have followed at the time of the riots and in keeping with the ultimate clarification of this order in due course as well. He was not alone in this, as it also seems to have been the interpretation of all the officers involved from Colonel Brereton down to Captain Coddrington, who all sought out a Magistrate to seek their authority and presence before they would act. In the Bristol Bridge riots of 1789 the Magistrates had marched along with the troops as they had done recently in Merthyr, The Forest of Dean and Nottingham and so this must have been fresh in the minds of all concerned. Indeed, even Major Beckwith whose interpretation after the event seemed to differ to everyone else's, did himself seek a Magistrate's authority and presence, as his first act on entering Bristol, even though he was curiously later to state it was not necessary.

It was now around 8am and with the mob dispersed and the streets quiet again the Colonel ordered two thirds of the 3rd Dragoons to their stables to rest leaving Sergeant Dean and the remaining half a troop to maintain the peace. The Colonel also took this opportunity to retire to his lodgings to refresh himself and put on some clean clothes in readiness for the imminent arrival of fresh troops. Before the Colonel left he ordered Major Beckwith to meet him at the Recruiting Office in an hour. A little later the refreshed 14th Dragoons arrived in Queen Square and relieved the tired half a troop of 3rd Dragoon Guards, who then continued patrolling for three-quarters of an hour until they too were ordered to returned to their quarters as there was no reason for them to remain. Major Beckwith meanwhile was arriving at the Recruiting Office for his appointment with the Colonel, but the Colonel had not yet arrived, so the Major decided to go to his lodgings where he found the Colonel dressing in his room. The Colonel told him to go and wait downstairs in the parlour while he dressed. The Major did this, but returned impatiently asking for permission to retire to his quarters at the Bress Inn as he himself was still not in uniform.

It was also at this meeting that the Magistrates finally came to a decision and decided at last to call out the Posse Comitatus. They also made an application to Mr Herepath for the assistance of the Bristol Political Union who was invested by the Magistracy with the same power as that of the Under-Sherriff. So rather belatedly, a large body of men were assembled to police the streets and maintain the peace.

Joseph Fry the chocolate manufacturer writing to his sister on Monday the 31st referred to this decision and the previous meeting when he wrote;

"I suppose nothing has been known in England like it since the riots in London in 1780 and this arose from the same cause, hesitation and indecision in the Magistrates and especially the Mayor. He yesterday requested the advice of the principle inhabitants: some of whom accordingly met him to adopt what is today adopted, to call out the posse-commitatus. If this had been done yesterday all the mischief would in all probability, have been avoided, but he thought it unnecessary and said people must protect themselves."

(*Eyewitness!* Page 15. Reproduced by kind permission of the Frenchay Tuckett Society.)

Joseph Fry is referring to the Gordon riots of 1780 when the Lord Mayor of the City of London, Brackley Kennet, refused to call out the military or read the Riot Act saying;

"I have orders to employ the military if necessary, but I must be cautious what I do lest I bring the mob to my house".

Also just like the Mayor of Bristol he refused to give any orders to the military when they asked for them. Later in March

1781 Kennett was charged with criminal neglect of duty, and was fined £1,000 but died less than a year later.

(*Oxford Dictionary of National Biography*, Kennett, Brackley (*c.*1713–1782))

Later at 10am the new Squadron of the 14th Dragoons, together with soldiers of the Bedminster Yeomanry Cavalry arrived.

Joseph Fry reported this fact in the postscript to a letter, writing;

"I am just informed that 200 soldiers are arrived but without officers. The Magistrates are so dispersed that there is no knowing how to act, so when and how it will end no one can tell. Do not feel anxious about us, I believe we shall be preserved."

(*Eyewitness!* Page 13. Reproduced by kind permission of the Frenchay Tuckett Society.)

Their arrival was also dramatically witnessed by a young girl who's father was Head of the Watchmen, her younger sister latter wrote a dramatic account of what had been witnessed;

"On the Monday morning, mother told my eldest sister to go up to Stokes Croft and try to find out if the city was quiet. When she reached the top of the Croft, where the turnpike gate then stood and where the weighbridge was after, there were the soldiers just come down from Gloucester. The turnpike gates were shut and the soldiers were waiting the word to enter. My sister ran over to some houses which stood at the left hand side of Stokes Croft with small gardens in front and iron railings, and got into one of these gardens. When the word of command was given the gates were opened and the soldiers rushed in with drawn sabres, cutting right and left. There were a great many people there who had nothing to do with the riots, men going to work and women and children come out to see the soldiers. Numbers were wounded and some said children were killed in their mother's arms. My sister lay down under the low wall of the garden and for a long time was afraid to move. When the place seemed quiet she crept

out and ran back to us, but the riots were over and there was no more trouble or burning after that."

(*Eyewitness!* Page 22. A hand written manuscript. Frenchay Tucket Society.)

These fresh troops of the 14th Dragoons made their way into the city and reported to the Colonel who assembled them at College Green, but Major Beckwith still had not arrived after retuning to his quarters at the Bress Inn. The Colonel sent an orderly to inform him that they were waiting for him after which the Major soon arrived. However, after the recent rout of the mob, there were none to be seen and no riotous behaviour was witnessed, so all the troops were ordered to their stables.

Some time later however, a report was received that the Bishop's cellar was being plundered for wine. Brereton immediately went in person to Fisher's Stables and ordered Major Beckwith to get a troop of the 14th under arms. They then proceeded to the Bishop's Palace where the looters were dispersed. Brereton then lead the charge through College Green, the Square and several streets and part of the environs towards the New Gaol, dispersing any number of people assembled in their way. It was during these manoeuvres that the Colonel noticed yet again the unruly nature of the 14th Dragoons, and was later to record:

"I rather fear a large number were severely sabered by the troops."

(Colonel Brereton's statement to the Court of Inquiry. Page18.)

With this in mind and the streets now cleared the Colonel ordered the troops back to their quarters, while further reinforcements arrived literally by the hour. At 11am the North Somerset Yeomanry arrived, at 12 midday the Tetbury troop and before dark the North Wilts troop together with 5,000 citizens now belatedly swelling the ranks of the Special Constables patrolling the streets and so there was no further outrages by the mob.

Authors note;

Major Beckwith in his statement to the court of inquiry makes no mention of Brereton's calling out the troops and plays down his involvement saying;

"Lt Colonel Brereton occasionally fell in with the troops during these movements but assumed no command."

Also after Colonel Brereton's death and at the Court Martial of Captain Warrington he claimed;

"Colonel Brereton was the senior officer, but I gave all the material orders; about 10 o'clock Monday morning recommended Capt Warrington of the third Dragoons guards what to do. About 12 o'clock, Col Brereton gave me authority to give orders to the 3rd Dragoon Guards, if I deemed it necessary."

But this was hotly denied by Colonel Brereton in his statement to the Court Of Inquiry when he stated;

"From the moment his reporting himself to me on Monday morning until the arrival of Major General Sir Pin Jackson, Major Beckwith was acting in every respect under my orders as his Commanding officer."

(HO52/12 Colonel Brereton's statement to the
Court of Inquiry. Page 19.)

It is not the job of a Commanding Officer, nor is it possible for him personally to ride out with all the troops under his command on every occasion. That is why he has subordinate officers like Major Beckwith to carry out his orders. The fact that Beckwith states he ignored those orders and issued his own instead, just as his subordinate officer Captain Gage had done earlier says more about the lack of discipline in the 14th Dragoons than any failings on Colonel Brereton's part.

This is illustrated later when at 2pm while in the Council House with the Magistrates to arrange the dispersal of the newly arriving troops, Brereton was astonished to see the 14th go thundering past. Major Mackworth who was also there, commented that; *"the 14th were very wild"*. Brereton determined he must follow them to see where they were going, and not having his horse on hand Major Mackworth offered him his. Brereton caught up with them at the top of Old Market Place and inquired of Major Beckwith where they were going. Major Beckwith told him that they were responding to a report that the mob were committing some depredations in that direction so Colonel Brereton rode with them for some considerable distance towards Fishponds but they found no mob and the report appeared without any foundation.

W.H. Somerton in his narrative of the Bristol riots makes a similar point;

The Magistrates; "*thought proper to issue an order for the cavalry to charge through the streets. This order was fulfilled to the letter by a party of the troops (The 14th Dragoons) which had experienced some rough treatment, and had in consequence fired upon the people the previous day. The sight of this useless piece of duty – this act of cruelty, it may be justly called – was particularly distressing: On every side were to be seen unoffending women and children, running and screaming; while several men, apparently on their way to work, were deliberately cut at, several seriously injured, and some killed. It is impossible to particularise the number of victims who suffered in this affair; as it is well known many were materially hurt who never applied for assistance at the public institutions. At the top of the High Street, one man nearly had his head severed from his body; and near Peter's Street, another was mortally wounded in the throat. The troops cut at every one they met with indiscriminately; in some cases they rode their horses upon the pavement and aimed at terrified individuals who had sought refuge in some corner; and this was the case, not only in the streets adjacent to the square, but in every part of the city: one person had his arm nearly severed from his body near the New Church, Lawford's Gate. This unnecessary charge, it must not be forgotten, was executed without the least intimation being given to the public, if we accept a notice which had been issued the day previous, that the riot act had been read.*"

What Somerton was referring to in this last point was that the Magistrates did not notify the populace until later in the day and so there was no opportunity for them to avoid this onslaught, even members of the newly enlisted civil force were in danger.

So in response to this they were instructed to wear white cloths tied around their forearms.

The city now appeared as under siege as the continuingly swelling numbers of military appeared, augmented by 500 Specials Constables and the Posse Comitatus. Two hundred and fifty naval and military pensioners were also called out and other bodies of men patrolling the smouldering ruins and guarding all parts of the city. All normal life of this normally bustling city was put on hold. Shops remained shut and business ceased while the frightened populace cowered in their homes.

It was around this time and after the charge of the 14th that the Mayor belatedly issued this notice;

COUNCIL HOUSE, BRISTOL, 31 0CT 1831

The Posse Comitatus of this City and County, having been called out to act in conjunction with the Military to endeavour to restore the peace of the City and, as the most severe measures must be adopted to accomplish that objective, the Magistrates earnestly caution all persons not engaged in official duties as Constables to keep within their respective dwellings as they otherwise be exposed to the most imminent peril.

C. PINNEY MAYOR.

After riding with Major Beckwith and his troop for some time but finding no sign of any further outrages the Colonel ordered Major Beckwith and the troops back.

(Remember Beckwith claimed he was in charge from 10 o'clock this very morning yet here we have Colonel Brereton issuing orders and Beckwith obeying them.)

Nevertheless, the city was now calm, and with fresh soldiers continually arriving there was now no longer any danger.

On his return, the Colonel continued the arrangements he had started with Major Mackworth concerning the distribution of these newly arriving troops around the city and arranging with the Major the disposal of the 11th Foot that were imminently expected from Cardiff. The Colonel then rode off on patrol and found them arriving at the end of Park Street under the Command of Colonel Love , so he directed the district Sergeant Major who was with him, to show the Colonel the way to Queen Square where Major Mackworth was waiting to take them to their quarters for the night. On satisfying himself that the city was indeed quiet, Colonel Brereton returned to the square and found a picket of the 11th Foot stationed there as had been arranged. Having finally had the manpower to clear the streets and with new Troops arriving hourly the city was now safe.

Therefore, the Colonel retired to his lodgings at the Adjutants house in Unity Street. Where he wrote his latest report to Lord Fitzroy Somerset, updating him on the destruction of the Gaols, and property around Queen Square. He also reported the arrival and swift departure of Captain Codrington the night before, but also that he had recalled the 14th and cleared the streets of rioters. Now with such a formidable supply of troops in the city the night passed without incident and the Colonel could benefit at last from an uninterrupted sleep.

The mayor also sent his own letter to Lord Fitzroy-Somerset;

Lord Fitzroy- Somerset Monday 31 Oct 1831

My Lord,

I had the honour to address your Lordship twice yesterday after the unfortunate state of this city imploring your further aid since which the riot has increased and a considerable portion of the largest square destroyed by fire nearly 40 houses as well as the Bishop's Palace the business suspended and the shops closed and the inhabitants in the greatest alarm our application to our neighbourhood has furnished us with a reinforcement of yeomanry the people have assembled in large numbers in the immediate vicinity and we have every reason to think we shall have a repetition of last nights occurrences if so the sacrifice of lives will be considerable should the perpetrators of the civil force supported by the military form adequate for the preservation of the peace we fear the neighbourhood will be the object of attack, no doubt you have received the fullest information from the Commanding Officer of the district but I can safely afford your Lordship the aspect of the affair has been most serious and alarming the plans of operation will organize and carried to affect in the most comfortable manner to the destruction of property to a very large amount including the Mansion House, Custom House, and Excise Office

I have the honour to be your Lordships most humble obedient servant.

Charles Pinney (Mayor)

PRO HO 40/28

Captain Codrington of the Dodington Yeomanry also sent his report in an effort to explain his sudden departure from Bristol.

My Lord,

I have the honour to represent to your lordship that in consequence of a requisition from the Mayor of Bristol, between two and three o'clock yesterday, I collected my troop of Yeomanry with as little loss of time as was practicable. When your Lordship considers that I had to send some miles in different directions, you will, I think, admit the alacrity of my men when I state that we were enabled to march from hence (Dodington), with scarce a man missing, by seven o'clock. Having, however, fifteen miles to go, and the night being very dark, we could not reach Bristol till after nine, when, I lament to say, we found the city on fire in many places, the gaols emptied, and the town in the greatest confusion. Having paraded through the principal parts of the city for more than two hours without being able to find a Magistrate – hearing that they had, in fact, left the town, after withdrawing both his Majesty's troops and the police – finding ourselves thus unsupported, and without a hope of being in any way serviceable – the city being actually in the uncontrolled power of the populace, I had no alternative but that of withdrawing also my men, and we returned home about five o'clock this morning.

Feeling it my duty to make this statement to your Lordship, I should ill perform it towards the brave men I am proud to have the honour of commanding, if I did not further state that no men could have come forward with more alacrity; and, although they might not have acted with the discipline of his Majesty's regular troops, they would not have been exceeded by them in zeal, loyalty, or a determination to have done their duty; and had they had an opportunity of acting, they would have shown themselves not undeserving of his majesty's approbation.

I have the honour to be, my Lord, your Lordship's obedient servant,

C.W. CODRINGTON,

Captain of the Dodington and Marshfield Yeomanry Cavalry.
Dodington,

31 October

PRO HO 40/28

Later the Posse Comitatus was organised and patrolled the empty streets in groups of 60 to 100 and as darkness descended lights were lit in homes and Churches in compliance with the Mayors instructions. Also precautions were taken to protect the shipping particularly the *Earl of Liverpool,* that had been threatened the night before. Through the night the church bells rang, and guns on board the shipping would take it in turn to fire throughout to signify readiness in case of attack, but none came and for the first time in three days the city populous was quiet, unnaturally so.

Butcher on Horseback

Early in the morning of Tuesday 1 November Colonel Brereton returned to Queen Square to check on the troops and rode through the streets with Major Mackworth but all was well, there had been no more protests and the streets remained quiet. After some time an orderly rode up with a note from Major General Sir Robert Jackson who had recently arrived and requested to see him at the White Lion Inn. Colonel Brereton immediately rode over to the Inn and gave over the command of the troops to the Major General.

The city was now much better served with military personnel, not just Calvary supplemented by a fresh detachment, but a proper effective and supported force comprising of the 170-strong detachment of 11th Foot soldiers that Colonel Love had marched into town yesterday at around six in the evening. Together with various troops of Yeomanry, let alone all the Specials and the Posse Comitatus. If a fraction of these had been available from the start and organised properly there would have been no rioting in the first place. You could blame this on Lord Melbourne whose policy was to let things get a little out of hand before responding but perhaps he now regretted this after hearing of all the destruction, but with all the various disturbances around the country numbers were limited. In addition, it was the Mayor and Magistrates whose duty it was to police their own city not the militaries. You may remember that Melbourne had previously sent a circular to all Magistrates to remind them of this. Extra forces were available in Bristol like the Posse Comitatus which had been suggested to the Mayor from the start, but which he had rejected. The next day Tuesday 2 November Major Beckwith wrote a letter to Major General Lord Fitzroy-James Henry Somerset the Military Secretary at Horse Guards, in which he arrogantly wrote;

"It is no use in the world sending more troops, there being no cause of any further riot at Bristol. In fact there was from the

beginning plenty of troops here to have prevented what happened had they been properly employed, as was very well proved on Monday morning when the same squadron that had been ordered out of Bristol and being unable to protect itself from the mob without any assistance from the Third even left in their quarters, in about an hour so completely destroyed and intimidated the mob that I am certain, had no further force arrived, it would never had made head again."

Authors note;

As has already been said, when Major Beckwith arrived on Monday the rioters that had numbered up to 20,000 at its height was already broken, both by drunkenness and fatigue, so it was a fairly easy task for Colonel Brereton to quell the 700 or so exhausted remnants of the rioters with just the 30 or so 3rd Dragoon guards that he had available.

Nevertheless, shortly after he had crushed them, not only did the 14th Dragoons return but a further squadron followed Beckwith into the city later. The effectiveness of Colonel Brereton's destruction of the mob can be gauged by the fact that when the returned 14th were united with their newly arrived comrades under the immediate command of their Commanding Officer Major Beckwith they were not needed, and after parading at College Green Colonel Brereton ordered them to their stables.

Only later when a report reached Colonel Brereton of a minor pillaging the Bishop's cellar, were Beckwith and the 14th used and it was during this sortie that a number of people were severely sabered. However, this relatively small outbreak was completely crushed and the troops returned to their stables. Major Beckwith made no mention of Colonel Brereton's command of this operation and claimed all credit for himself. It is also worth mentioning that at this point and at the same time as the mob was greatly reduced by drunkenness and general fatigue, the troops were in much larger numbers than they had been at any time during the riots with two whole squadrons of the 14th Dragoons totalling 120 men plus the 3rd Dragoon guards so there were 150 Dragoons in total plus the Bedminster Yeomanry Calvary and 5,000 citizens who had at last answered the call to service and also the Posse

Comitatus where 250 were organised to guard the burnt out ruins of the New Gaol.

The Political Union was also sworn in to help police the streets and groups were organised to guard the Bishop's Palace and other ruined buildings to prevent any further pillaging. Therefore, there was a formidable force patrolling the streets of Bristol all at a time when the mob had been crushed and yet more troops were arriving by the hour. So how can Major Beckwith say, *"there was from the beginning plenty of troops here,"* when he had no experience at all of the riot, only the tail end of a rabble that was easily crushed by a greatly augmented force. Major Beckwith was anxious however to prove his own and his Dragoons worth, and even though resistance had ceased he still rode through the streets cutting and sabering any one he came across regardless of sex, age, or indeed guilt. This was after all Monday morning, in the second City of the Kingdom and despite the rioting its people would still be anxious to continue their trade. But Beckwith soon ran out of people in the Bristol streets to terrorise and so rode out of town in pursuit of more prey boasting;

"On Monday morning, everything was done at the gallop and with the sword and, in consequence, for one that was killed a hundred were wounded. The greater number of our opponents did not belong to Bristol as was evident from the number of broken heads that were to be seen on almost every road leading from the town"

PRO HO 40/28

Remember we are talking about unarmed civilians here and how did Beckwith know that his "opponents" had no business in Bristol? He certainly did not ask anyone, before or after he sabered them. It is fair to say *some* may very well have been up to no good, but how many were, and how many were not. We shall never know, the dead cannot complain.

A letter from a Bristol resident J. Barnett Kingston is yet another who complains about the Magistrates refusal to accompany Major Beckwith and see for themselves that the rioting was over. But instead issued him with written permission to act as he pleased, instead of accompanying him to instruct and control his movements as was their duty;

"I had previously visited the scene of the fires, and I found none there, with the solitary exception of one poor wretch dead drunk upon the ground; for rioting had then ceased, the citizens had come forward to restore tranquillity, and the engines of the various insurance companies were employed upon the flames. But the Magistrates knew nothing of the restoration of order; they refused to place themselves in a position acquainted with it; they let the soldiery loose upon the people in the blindness of their ignorance."

(Letter from J. Barnett Kingston published in *The Morning Chronicle*. 9 April 1836.)

The behaviour of the 14th Dragoons was realised and admonished at the time as this report in the *North Devon Journal* 24 Nov 1831 reported that during his address to the troops General Jackson read out the order of the day from the Commander in Chief ;

"Severely reproving the 14th for their conduct during the late outrages, and cautioning the other troops practising similar excesses."

The Rev J. Jackson also wrote in a letter at the time that:

"This morning an actual slaughter has taken place; it is supposed, though of course nothing precise can be known at present, that about seventy persons have been killed, besides a large number who have been wounded. The military charged through some of the principal streets, cutting right and left."

Though Charles Greville a clerk to the Privy Council noted in his journal;

"The details are ample, and to be met with everywhere; nothing could exceed the ferocity of the populace, the imbecility of the Magistracy, or the good conduct of the troops. More punishment was inflicted by them than has been generally known, and some hundreds were killed or severely wounded by the sabre. One body of Dragoons pursued a rabble of colliers into the country, and covered the fields and roads with the bodies of wounded wretches, making a severe example of them."

As the military and civic forces took control of the city and law and order returned about 40 of the released prisoners were either recaptured or felt it was in their interest to surrender themselves. It was not until Wednesday that the fires were finally extinguished and it was only then that the true account of damage could be ascertained. It was an awesome sight to behold in the second city of the greatest empire the world had ever known, with the smouldering wreckage of one of England's most spacious squares, where precarious walls were knocked down before they fell and the great clear up could begin. The stench of rotting flesh was evident to all, as three bodies were found under rubble outside the Custom House and pulled onto the grass where they remained for some time in full view.

During the height of the riots the flames could be seen over 40 miles away and the fuel that fed those flames was mostly civic and church property although in the last phase of the riots some 50 private houses were also consumed and a further number damaged. The costs of this destruction was estimated at the time to be almost half a million pounds. The official number of casualties that were reported seemed surprisingly low in the circumstances with only 12 dead and 94 injured but these were only referring to those who had been taken to the infirmary and for obvious reasons not all had reported there, so the real figures were much higher.

The Rev John Eagles estimated the number of dead alone to be 500. However, Major Mackworth in a second letter to Fitzroy-Somerset had to update his original figure of 400 killed and injured by the Dragoons to 800. When you read the truly blood curdling way in which Major Beckwith and his troops hacked their way through the streets of Bristol, showing no quarter to anybody with complete disregard for age, sex, innocence, or guilt, it makes the higher figures seem all the more believable yet this butcher on a horseback was praised as a hero after the riots. The man who arrived after the worse was over, and after only two hours in the saddle attacking unarmed civilians managed to be elevated to the hero of the riots by the Magistrates, as a useful tool in their effort to discredit Colonel Brereton and distance themselves from the blame that rightly was theirs.

Nevertheless, whatever the figures were, one thing is certain there were far more killed in Bristol than at the infamous Peterloo Massacre at St Peter's Fields Manchester on the 16 August 1819, where 12 innocent people were killed. Yet it is the great destruction of property in Bristol that is remembered, not the far greater loss of life. Perhaps because those killed were not regarded as innocent and so it has gone down in history not as the Bristol Massacre but the Bristol Riots.

The Storm Clouds Gather

In London, as news of the rioting reached the King and his Government there was outrage and a fear that the long anticipated revolution had finally spread to England. Especially after hearing a report that the tricolour and cap of liberty were flown on the statue of King William in Queen Square. Was this a further sign that the rioting that had spread all around the country and particularly the dramatic events in Bristol were all indications that the overthrow of the ruling classes had begun? Many thought so at the time, even the Russian Ambassadors wife wrote home to her brother saying; *"We... in England are just on the brink of a revolution"*[1].

[1]*A British Revolution in the 19th Century.* Professor Eric Evans.

Something that Charles Cavendish Fulke Greville, Clerk to the Privy Council also confirms when he recalls seeing the Tory, Colonel Lord Wharncliffe last night who said; *"he thinks there is a strong revolutionary spirit abroad"*.

(The Greville Memoirs for 14 November 1831; A journal of the reigns of King George IV and King William IV.)

Therefore, Lord Melbourne felt he had to act quickly and decisively just as he did in Merthyr and the Forest of Dean in order to make an example. For it was Melbourne's opinion that rioter should be dealt with, *"in the most exemplary and speedy manner"*.

(Letter to Grey, 29 October 1831. Durham University archives. Grey mss folio 40.)

Unfortunately however, justice is diminished if it is sacrificed to speed, just as it was recently in Merthyr Tydfil and the Forest of Dean. Melbourne was more interested in stopping any rioting escalating into revolution and threatening the position of the ruling classes than exercising any justice. Therefore, in reality vengeance and a terrible example needed to be set to stop further outrages rather than justice.

In addition, though a Whig politician Melbourne was, as has been stated in all other respects a Tory and against reform. Whereas Bristol though it had many Tories in prominent positions the population was pro-reform and even Colonel Brereton was reported to be pro-reform. Bristol had also just elected two pro-reform Whig MP's and a pro-reform Whig Mayor Charles Pinney, even though interestingly, he would himself later become a Tory. Therefore, even at the time some thought it highly probable that Melbourne supplied insufficient troop numbers in an effort to punish the Bristol Reformers and put them in a bad light. However, he never dreamt that the result of this decision would lead to such destruction and loss of life.

In fact as a result of Bristol he seems to have been woken from his procrastinating torpor after fearing a repeat could happen in London so he;

"was frightened to death at the Bristol affair, gave Lord Hill and Fitzroy Somerset carte blanche, and they made such a provision of military force in addition to the civil power that the malcontents were paralyzed."

(Page 19. *The Greville Memoirs* for November 11th; A journal of the reigns of King George IV. and King William IV.)

Nevertheless, in Bristol though the population was pro-reform most of the Magistrates were Tory and anti-reform and so perhaps this explains to some extent their lack of action:

"Most of our magistrates are anti-reformers and there is no doubt would not have disliked a moderate row, but this is, I think, too much even for Wetherell and his fellows. The Mayor is a reformer and better things were expected of him, but I think him a hollow reformer, and most West-Indian people are."

(*Eyewitness!* Page 15. Frenchey Tuckett Society.)

Perhaps Mayor Pinney's later moves to become a Tory are indicative of his true feelings and confirm this opinion of him as just *"a hollow reformer"*.

In Bristol, in fact many citizens held the Mayor and magistrates responsible. Therefore, when peace did return it was not unnatural for the citizens to start to think back on what had befallen them and seek punishment for those they held responsible. Public outrage was such that a meeting was arranged and at this meeting, it was decided to reconvene the next day when more citizens could attend and a proposal could be drafted to Lord Melbourne to investigate the reasons why such calamitous events had gone unchecked in their city.

So the next day 3rd November in the Commercial Rooms an even larger number of citizens arrived and debated on the points needed to be made and on the general wording of this letter and in the end the following was agreed on;

"We, the undersigned, Merchants, Bankers, Traders and other inhabitants of the City of Bristol, deeply lamenting the riotous and disgraceful proceedings that have recently occurred in this city, and the sad destruction of property resulting there from, bearing in mind that the lives and fortunes of the citizens were for a considerable period entirely at the mercy of a desperate mob, and firmly convinced that all this might have been prevented if proper precautions had been adopted, do earnestly require your Lordship will be pleased to cause an investigation to be instituted, as the only course that will satisfy the minds of the public and restore confidence in future."

Francis Tuckett a Special Constable referred to this meeting in a letter the day after on Thursday 4th November expressing the widely head opinion of the populace as to who they blamed and wanted punished;

"A memorial addressed to the Secretary of State is now in course of signatures, requesting an immediate enquiry into the conduct of the magistrates. There appears but one opinion amongst all parties as to their inefficiency, and I think they must be superseded."

Just as the badly served populace were meeting to make sure those that had brought disaster to this great city were brought to justice, the Magistrates were well advanced in their plot to shift all the blame onto Colonel Brereton. The Mayor had made sure to criticize him in all his letters to Lord Melbourne and Lord Hill thereby planting the seeds of blame at an early stage in an effort to distance themselves from the almost universal recriminations.

In fact the Mayor's sister, in a letter to Mrs John Frederick Pinney revealed the Mayor's intentions when she informed him that his brother Charles, the Mayor, had told her "as a secret" that the magistrates were sending a report to the Government and urging that an inquiry should take place into Brereton's conduct, and that he had accused Colonel Brereton of being "either a traitor or a coward". She finished by saying "you must not let a word of this drop".

(From the Pinney Archive, DM58, University of Bristol Library Special Collections.)

Calling any officer of his majesty's troops, "a traitor or a coward" is reprehensible, especial coming for an individual who spent most of his comfortable life amassing a fortune from slavery and shamefully spent the riots neglecting his duties and hiding away, while the officer whom he criticizes was active in trying to restore order unaided. This fact was known to the citizens themselves and even Special Constable Francis Tucket knew where the blame lied when writing to his fiancé on Thursday 4 November wrote;

"We now have an immense Posse Comitatus in regular operation night and day and the military force is very strong and has been increasing daily, but I hope they will not be called into action again and they need not have been at all had our magistrates acted like men."

(*Eyewitness!* Page 7. Frenchay Tuckett Society.)

However, Charles Pinney was a member of various influential West India societies and would later be chairman of the powerful Merchant Adventurers and the West India Association. The chairman of the WIA was Alderman Thomas Daniel who was also a former Mayor of Bristol. He lived in Berkeley Square in Clifton and was one of the biggest sugar merchants, so rich and powerful he was known as "the King of Bristol". You may remember the Mayor had hidden away in Mr Daniel Fripp's house also in Berkeley Square.

The records show he owned 8,970 slaves in 1833, and received a staggering £257,032 in compensation when they were freed after Abolition, or £22 million in today's money.

He was chosen as an Alderman in Bristol in 1798 and became incredibly powerful within the city. Alderman Daniels was also the chairman of the Tory campaign committee that helped Lord Edward Somerset in his campaign in Gloucester in 1831.

(*Bristol and Its Municipal Government,* 1820–51.
By Graham William Arthur Bush. Page 40.)

(University College London;
Profile of Thomas Daniels, Legacies of British Slave-ownership.)

The Powerful West India Committee also had around 48 MPs according to their secretary and agent for Jamaica, Stephen Fuller a contemporary source in early 1781. The members included William Manning, a West India Merchant and a Director of the Bank of England and a Lt Colonel in the Westminster Light Horse.

Richard Pennant was the chairman of the West India Planters and Merchants also Sir William Codrington, whose son Captain Coddrington had lead his Yeomanry troops in and out of Bristol rather rapidly during the riots. Sir William was a plantation owner who followed its fortunes in minute detail and helped to orchestrate parliamentary opposition to the abolitionists. An alternative definition by Richard Sheridan discovered 70 who sat in the commons between 1730–75 but a still broader definition might also include the parliamentary friends of those with West India interests like merchant bankers, extended family, ex governors, patent office holders, military and naval officers who served on the islands. So the West India merchants were a powerful group who wielded political influence as well as trade and financial.

When John Pinney died in 1818, aged nearly eighty, he gave his Bristol house to his son Charles and his assets were valued at £340,000 about £17 million today. Charles increased his wealth further after his father's death and later claimed about £36,000 about £1,800,000 today, as compensation after the banning of slave ownership in 1833. Therefore, he was a very rich and powerful man and his brother-in-law was the Bristol MP James Evans Baillie. So Pinney was used to getting what he wanted and his character was described as;

"a hypocrite... cold hearted and pious."

(*Hotheads and Heroes,* by P. Macdonald. Page 20.)

In an effort to undermine the anti-slavery campaign of William Wilberforce he even had the arrogance to ask for the hand of his daughter Elizabeth. Wilberforce of course turned him down; he probably did not want a slave trader who branded his slaves like cattle in the family. Nevertheless, the arrogant Pinney, *"saw him self as the wronged partner and sent a petulant and ungracious letter, to Wilberforce."*

In her book *Slavery Obscured*, Madge Dresser believes that Pinney's motivation regarding Elizabeth was just cynical self-interest. As he was a member of the West India Association, so if he married Elizabeth it would further their attempts to undermine her father's anti-slavery campaign.

(From, *Slavery Obscured*: *The Social History of Slavery in an English Provincial Port.* Continuum, 2001)

This just illustrates the lengths Pinney would go to in order to achieve what he wanted and with so much influence and an unwavering determination to achieve his goals Colonel Brereton was in a very difficult situation.

Pinney together with the other; *"merchants of Georgian Bristol had a reputation for boorishness and greed and for being as rough mannered as their sailors."* Many of these merchants not only influenced Bristol political life they also influenced national politics.

(Slavery Obscured: The Social History of Slavery in an English Provincial Port. Continuum, 2001. Page 116)

So whose version of events would be believed, Brereton's or the powerful influential Pinney's?

In an effort to counter all this misinformation, Brereton in his report on 3 November to Fizroy Somerset at Horse guards sent a long explanation of his actions and motivations;

District Office Bristol, 3 November 1831

My Lord.

I hope I shall stand excused, if under the feelings excited by your Lordships letter of the 31st instance.

I again intrude myself upon your notice respecting that paragraph which conveys the disapprobation of Lord Melbourne after my sending of the 14th Dragoons as a temporary removal to Keynsham, permit me to say my intention was a peculiarly distressing one. Between an overflowing infuriating mob and a Magistracy from which no effective aid could be procured, I was left in a very unenviable condition.

With all the sense of a soldier's duty in my mind it became necessary to weigh well the steps I should take. Nor did I think it prescient to rest upon my personal opinion only but called for the sentiments of others to guide and fix my own. To have attempted anything against the mob at that moment, could have been putting too much to hazard, supposing we had shot any one of them and dispersed them for the instant they would have reassembled with considerable augmented numbers which I could not have prevented, for I had not force, to occupy the many outlets to this large city, men and horses would have been exhausted and so exasperated were the mob previously, that they had determined to attack all the houses for arms to destroy the defence forces in their quarters, when they went to refresh, would it have been right under such circumstances to hazard the troops being repulsed, for if they had possession of the whole city and firing the shipping of this intention they made no secret, nor of their plan to attack the banks, and then throw all the surrounding country side into confusion at the same time they very cheerfully and with the greatest earnestness promised to turn to peaceful conduct if the 14th were removed, now at this moment I had also a confusion after my mind. That as I might reasonable expect a further military force would be ordered to this station it would be judicious to use every means that might abate their fury until the further aid was obtained on the morning of the Monday, they had became so fatigued by their diabolical exertions and lastly broken by drunkenness that I could then use the 14th with advantage.

And the Magistracy having then commenced what they should have done originally the city was placed in safety. It is necessary also I should observe I did not remove the 14th without the concurrence of the Mayor. I also beg leave to assure his Lordship of my constant endeavours during this calamitous proceeding as can be sufficiently proved by respectable persons not suffering under it, or connected in any way to bias their opinions. For I was continually, day and night exerting myself in every direction for the public welfare and the best execution of the duties committed to my charge.

Signed Thomas Brereton

PRO HO 40/28

Despite what Col Brereton was saying in this report, it seems that other influential players were also becoming involved and telling a particular version of events in Bristol. For just after the rioting Lord Granville Charles Henry Somerset the Tory MP and his father the Sixth Duke of Beaufort arrived on the scene. The Duke was the elder brother of General Lord Charles Henry Somerset, Governor of South Africa, Colonel Brereton's former superior. He was also the father of Henry Somerset, the future 7th Duke of Beaufort who had been a Lieutenant in the 14th Dragoons and married twice to the daughters of Wellington's sister Lady Anne Wellesley.

The Duke like his son was also a former Bristol MP and like Mayor Pinney voted against the abolition of slavery and it is likely the two had other connections. He certainly knew Alderman Daniels who was also the Chairman of the Bristol Tory campaign committee and 13 of the corporation helped Lord Edward Somerset in his campaign in Gloucester in 1831. Lord Edward Somerset was the younger brother to the Sixth Duke. Goldney, Fripp and Hillhouse were other members of the Tory group in Bristol who had all played leading roles alongside Pinney during the riots and Pinney himself would later join them in the Tory party.

(Bristol and its Municipal Government, 1820–51,
by Graham William Arthur Bush. Page 40.)

Both the Sixth Duke and his son Lord Granville had already played prominent and unexplained roles related to the rioting in the Forest of Dean only months previously. Was this just another coincidence like Major Mackworth who also "*just happened to be around at the right time*", or is there some more sinister roll behind all their involvements? They were all anti-reformers and were busy writing reports of their incriminating version of events to their relative the Duke of Wellington the head of the anti-reformers. Lord Granville sent his one sided report written on the same day as the Colonel's, but repeating all what had been said by his friends the Mayor and the civil power. However, not one mention of the more widely held opinion castigating the same Mayor and the civil powers. Lord Granville of course was the nephew of Lord Fitzroy James Henry Somerset, the Military Secretary at Horseguards. And now we find them both here in Bristol, together with the ever present Major Mackworth just a few months later, all sending damning letters to the Duke of Wellington and even repeating the claims of another manipulator of facts Major Beckwith, saying that;

"*he obtained the necessary authority from the Mayor and Magistrates of the city, the former giving it with great reluctance, and having made the necessary dispositions with that single squadron and receiving no assistance whatever from Lieutenant*

Colonel Brereton or the Dragoon Guards, the former shewing no alacrity whatever to co-operate, he dispersed the rioters then at the height of their triumph and within two hours the city was completely reduced to the authority of the civil power."

"The quiet of the city is certainly, according to all accounts which I have heard, due to the resolution of Major Beckwith and his small squadron."

(WP1/1201/6 The Wellington Papers Southampton University)

Whose were, *"all accounts which I have heard,"* seemingly only the Mayor and civil powers? Together no doubt with the boastful Major Beckwith, but even at the time many took exception to their accounts, so why didn't the honourable Lord represent their accounts as well ?

(*Bristol and its Municipal Government, 1820–51*, by Graham William Arthur Bush. Page 40.)

(*Profile of Thomas Daniels, Legacies of British Slave-ownership.* University College London.)

The next day the 4th, a further six company of troops arrived direct from Portsmouth after arriving there from their duties in America. These troops from the 52nd were to replace the outgoing 11th Infantry of Foot together with field artillery and guns and over 1,5000 rounds of ammunition. Despatches had also been sent to army garrisons throughout the country to ready further troops while warships from the Royal Navy patrolled the Bristol Channel. All this was in marked contrast to the meagre supply of less than a hundred cavalry soldiers only a few days before.

In London after reading the Mayor's letter The Home Secretary, Lord Melbourne replied by return of post asking how it was possible that the heavily fortified jails were not defended?

With all this criticism levelled at his handling of the affair, the Mayor who had already implicated Colonel Brereton in the eyes of the Government and the Army's Commander-in-Chief in

London, now moved to phase two of his *"secret plan"* by releasing all these letters to the local press. This was all in a further effort to place all the blame on Colonel Brereton in the eyes of the local inhabitants as well. And in doing so to admonish himself and the civil authorities of any blame whatsoever.

All this double-dealing paid off, because on 15 November Major General Jackson after parading his troops in Queen Square, read out a communiqué from Lord Hill the Commander-in-Chief, where he praised the conduct of the 3rd Dragoon Guards and the 14th Light Dragoons and the admirable conduct of Captain Gage and Cornet Kelson and also his A.D.C. Major Mackworth for assisting the Magistrates with his advice and help. He now also told Major Beckwith that although he had only arrived on Monday morning his services were also appreciated and were, *"by no means less important"*. The two officers notable by their absence in these praises were Lt Colonel Thomas Brereton and Captain Warrington.

Fitzroy Somerset had previously told Jackson that he sincerely wished he could include Colonel Brereton in the commendations but was, *"precluded from doing so by circumstances which imperiously call for early and minute investigation"* for after reading the accounts of Mayor Pinney of his alleged conduct he said he was left with no alternative but to comply with Pinney's request. Therefore, it became Major General Jackson's distasteful task to tell a fellow officer that there would be a Military Court of Inquiry into his behaviour during the riots, opening in just two days time at the Merchants Hall in Bristol. This must have been a dreadful blow to the Colonel's self-esteem, for as the Governor of Senegal and the Commander in South Africa it had been he who had convened Courts of Inquiries and indeed Courts Martial and now he was to be in the dock himself and in the full glare of the press and public scrutiny.

But the fact that the Mayor had already undermined Colonel Brereton's defence was at least not lost on Lord Hill, the Army Commander-in-Chief who wrote to Lord Melbourne denouncing the Mayor on the very day of the Court of Inquiry commenced;

Horse Guards 17 November 1831

To Lord Melbourne

My Lord,

I can't avoid drawing your Lordships attention to the fact that the Mayor of Bristol has thought fit to publish the report which he addressed to your Lordship and myself of the occurrences at Bristol on the three October days of the last month. As each of these reports contain serious matter of charges against Lt Colonel Brereton and as the natural consequence of such communication was the institution of an inquiry into the conduct of that officer, I cannot but lament and even reprobate a proceeding, which will have the effect of magnifying the question and of inducing the public to form a view of it unfavourable to Lt Colonel Brereton without his having an opportunity of stating anything in vindication.

It may be said that the Mayor had not been informed that an inquiry had been determined afore.

This is certainly an omission on my part, but it had for many days been a matter of notoriety that such a recommendation was in contemplation and on the other hand nothing had transpired to cause Mr Pinney to believe that his representation would be unheeded.

I have the honour to be your Lordships most humble servant Lord Hill (Commander in chief)

PRO HO 40/28

Of course it was also the Mayor who had requested a Court of Inquiry in the first place and by constantly complaining about the Colonel he had not only achieved his goal but he had also already prejudiced the Colonel's case, by publishing all his criticism in the local press when it was sub judice. Thus committing <u>contempt of court under Common Law</u>:

For any material published with the intention to prejudice or undermine criminal proceedings that are pending or imminent, is deemed contempt. Also there is a clear definition between calling for a prosecution of an individual, which is acceptable, and trying to influence public opinion and perception of that individual before prosecution, which is forbidden.

This contempt was not by just any body either, it was from the Chief Magistrate himself, (The Mayor) and his fellow Magistrates, who all should have known better. Despite this, the Mayor received surprisingly, no public admonishment. The only criticism was in the letter by Lord Hill to Lord Melbourne but nothing was done and the trial went ahead regardless.

Unfortunately this wasn't the only publication prejudicial to Colonel Brereton's case which found it's way into the papers, for the *"Army report"* that Major Mackworth had written for Lord Hill the Commander-in-Chief of the Army had also strangely found its way into publication giving his highly contentious version of events.

Also following the Mayor's example, Captain Codrington of the Doddington Yeomanry who had left the city to the mercy of the mob, arrogantly wrote to the papers explaining his excuses for leaving the town to its peril without informing anyone.

All this was very prejudicial to the Colonel's case and left him at a terrible disadvantage, needless to say as an honourable and honest man, none of his official reports or private letters made there way into publication.

Another disadvantage for the Colonel was cited in the *North Devon Journal,* 24 November 1831 regarding the Court Of Inquiry;

"But, Strange to say, this court, if my information is correct, is to be a closed one I consider it to be a case of exceeding cruelty and injustice to Colonel Brereton to debar the press for the exercise of its usual privilege in a matter in which the whole people are deeply concerned."

Nevertheless, a closed Inquiry did go ahead;

The Court of Inquiry

The court assembled at 11am on Thursday 17 November 1831 by the command of General Lord Hill. Colonel Brereton attends the opening of the Court but is too ill to attend most of the dates and so his friend Major Ellard attends in his place. Though the Colonel was not well during the rioting, I can see no evidence it affected the performance of his duty. However, the strain it put on his health together with this Court Of Inquiry obviously manifested itself afterwards, when he finally took his doctors advice and rested.

The President of the Court was Major General Sir Charles Dalbiac who was the Inspector General of Calvary, responsible for the very troops Brereton had lead. Indeed he had inspected the 14th Dragoons fairly recently and would no doubt be anxious to remove any stain on their reputation.

The preamble is read to Colonel Brereton but his request for legal representation is denied and he is also told that he must not promulgate or make known any parts of the court proceeding until authorised. Which is a really ironic request, when you consider that this is exactly what the Mayor and indeed Major Mackworth had already done. Another blow was the fact that Captain Warrington would not be allowed to testify as the court felt he also had charges to answer of his own. This of course would also deny the Colonel the testimony of an important witness.

The Colonel is then shown various letter and asked to confirm whether he had received them or not. Amongst these letters is one from the Mayor dated 12pm Sunday night, which the Colonel admits receiving at 1am and another dated 3am, which the Colonel states to have never received.

The first letter is interesting in that it was delivered with some billets for the Doddington Yeomanry and states;

The Mayor of Bristol desires Colonel Brereton to consider himself fully authorised to take whatever steps and give whatever orders he, as the military Commander of this city, may think fit to restore and preserve, as far as possible, the public peace. The Riot Act has been read three times today. Colonel Brereton will have the goodness to consider this order to apply not only to the troops at present under his command, but to any which may subsequently arrive in the city.

Mr Daniel Fripp, No 30 Berkeley Square,

Sunday night, 12 o'clock, 30 October, 1831

The Colonel confirmed he had received this letter at 1am after returning to his temporary quarters and after spending hours looking for the Mayor and the Magistrates. However, as it took so long for these letters to be delivered events had now moved on and these letters were now out of date. It would have been little point in going out again and continuing that fruitless search, especially as the city was now quiet, which was confirmed by the deliverer of the letter (Town Clerk, Sergeant Ludlow) who left the city straight after to retire to his own house. As did Alderman Abraham Hillhouse who had also retired to his house about the same time, saying;

"he thought the mob had all gone quietly away."

In addition, the letter says *"The Mayor of Bristol desires"* but it's not signed by him. In fact it ends with Daniel Fripp's name and address, so is the Colonel supposed to conclude that this is from the Mayor or Mr Fripp?

Also these troops *"which may subsequently arrive"* had not only arrived but because they could not find the Mayor or any Magistrates, had already left so there instructions were superseded by events.

Later it was claimed that there were two letters delivered at this time together, the other letter giving the Mayor's location and reading;

The Mayor begs to inform Colonel Brereton that if he should have occasion for the orders of a Magistrate, either the Mayor or some other magistrate will be found at No 30 Berkeley Square, Mr Daniel Fripp's, the second house on the right-hand on turning into the square from Park Street.

Berkeley square 12 o'clock Sunday night.

Nevertheless, all references previously are to *"a" "letter and some billets"* not two letters. Even later at the Court Martial of Captain Warrington, Sergeant- Major William McCloud in his evidence states that:

"Sergeant Dennenge and Platt were with him excepting for a short period, when they went over to lieutenant Colonel Brereton's quarters about billets and A letter "

Which was confirmed by Sergeant Platt, when he states:

"Upon the second occasion, between twelve and one o'clock, he left in company with Sergeant Dennenge, to carry A letter and a blank precept for billets, to Colonel Brereton in Unity Street."

(The Court Martial of Captain Warrington.)(My underlining)

The Court was curious as to why two similar letters were sent and both dated with 12am? The Mayor explanation of this at Captain Warrington's Court Martial was;

"The Copy of the Letter that witness (Mayor Pinney) had given into the court, as the purport of a letter addressed to the officer commanding the troops on the 31st of October, witness wrote three or four days ago, from the copy of the original taken at the time."

This *"copy"* turned up as evidence later, was this letter written after the event in an effort to convince people that the Mayors whereabouts were not a secret and were known by the military? The Mayor maintains that the two letters were delivered together and the second letter was written after closing the first without his location being mentioned. Yet when a third letter was written to the Colonel but delivered to Capt Warrington a whole three hours later no mention of the Mayor and no address was included;

31 October 1831

Bristol, 3 o'clock, Monday Morning

Sir, I direct you, as commanding officer of His Majesties troops, to take the most vigorous, effective and decisive means in your power to quell the existing riot and prevent further destruction of property.

Per Mr Goldney

Mr W. Harris, Jun

And strangely the deliverers of the letter Mr Goldney and Mr Harris were still being told the Mayors location was secret and not to tell anyone. If it was no longer a secret and the Colonel already knew where the Mayor was, why were they still being instructed not to reveal it? In fact they delivered the letter to Captain Warrington and when he asked for a Magistrate to accompany the troops they complied with the Mayor's request and told him they didn't know where any were, not even the Chief Magistrate, the Mayor himself! They were also asked by the Captain to deliver the letter to the addressee, the Colonel, but they didn't.

Next to attend is Major Mackworth who confirms he wrote *"A Personal Narrative"*, this and letters dated 31 October and 3 November to Lord Fizroy Somerset which are used as his evidence and he was not asked any questions.

The Mayor of Bristol Charles Pinney is the first to give evidence, and is asked to confirm various letters addressed to the Secretary of State that he had published in the *Bristol Mercury*. Together with another letter addressed to the editor from him and published on the 15th in the same newspaper criticising Colonel Brereton's conduct on the arrival of the Doddington Yeomanry. Along with several other letters or papers written by him and published with his authority. These documents are also placed in the hands of the Colonel so that he may have the time to read and refute any allegations there contained. The Mayor answers question until the court adjourns at 5 o'clock but he is also requested to return the next day Friday the 18th.

Captain Warrington was summoned from Trowbridge in order to give his evidence but because he was to face charges himself at another time, he was not allowed to give any and so the Colonel lost a valuable witness.

On 24 November the Court assembles at 11 o'clock for the 7th and last day of the proceedings, that amounted to some

23 individuals over seven days mostly from the civil authority of Bristol all giving a critical picture of Brereton's conduct during the riots.

Colonel Brereton had been informed that on this, the last day of the proceedings, the Court would be ready to hear anything in refutation or explanation of the evidence advanced against him. The Colonel attends the court for the first time for some days but offers no witnesses or evidence in his support, but instead in typical military fashion, hands over a written report. In the military, it is the normal procedure to write a report at the end of a campaign or operation as Major Mackworth had also done. But this was a Court of Inquiry and it would have been much more advantageous to the Colonel's case if he had taken the time to refute all the major points advanced against him and answer them one by one and where necessary called witnesses to back him up. Nevertheless, the prosecution had six days to mount their case and the Colonel had only one. Unfortunately, the Colonel had also been unwell and so perhaps was not up to this task and as he had not been allowed to have a legal counsel, it was all down to whatever effort he could muster. That amounted to a 23-page report which he handed over to the Court. Though it has many good points I feel personally that it does not go far enough and does not make the best of his case. That is why legal representation would have made all the difference. A legal brain would have scanned all the detail and made a watertight case for him using all the corroborated facts freely available.

After Lt Colonel's Brereton presents his Statement to the Court, it is read and included into the Court proceedings. But after taking so many day's with the prosecutions' evidence it seems that the Colonel's evidence was given scant reference before the Court formed an unanimous opinion that;

1. *"That Lt Colonel Brereton ordered the detachment of the 14th Dragoons from Bristol to Keynsham, on Sunday 30 October, against the wishes and opinion of the civil authorities of the city."*
2. *"That Colonel Brereton was not justified, by existing circumstances, in ordering that movement."*

Authors note;

I find it strange that the court "unanimously " agreed that the Colonel was wrong on both points and just took the magistrates version over the Colonels and the two other officers who were there at the time, Captain Warrington and Major General Pearson. Both these officers could have confirmed Colonel Brereton's claim that the Magistrates had agreed to his proposal

If a Captain, a Colonel and a Major General *ALL* thought this was right at the time of the rioting how come not even *ONE* of the officers at the court agreed too? Even after the very experienced and distinguished Major General Pearson had had time to reflect on this decision he still, wholeheartedly endorsed it. In fact he had written two letters to Brereton which the Colonel had presented to the court in his evidence the first as follows:

1 November 1831

My Dear Colonel,

With respect to the temporary removal of the squadron of the 14th Light Dragoons from Bristol on Sunday last, I have no hesitation in saying, that from the infuriated state of the mob, and the overpowering and constantly augmenting numbers of the countless thousands everywhere assembled, the continued presents of that small force, who had brought on themselves the furry of the populace, by having killed one man and wounded others, would have endangered the safety of this small body, whose weak numbers were too small to enable them to act with any effect against the excited population independent of which, there is no doubt but, by their continuance on the spot at the moment, the loss of private property would have been much greater than it unfortunately was, and could not have been prevented by their longer continuance, on the contrary, from the almost exhausted state of the horses this squadron at the time of being withdrawn, required both rest and feeding, to render them again efficient for service.

Signed; Major General T. Pearson

(Let's not forget Pearson was actually there at the time and could judge the state of the crowd and the troops in Queen Square and as he rode with them out of the town followed by the baying mob. In fact a couple of day's latter after further consideration the Major General wrote another letter reaffirming his opinion in even stronger terms in Brereton's favour.)

(PRO HO 52/12 Court of Inquiry)

(From Major General Pearson to Lt Colonel Brereton received 3 November 1831.)

Mr Dear Colonel,

On reassessing your correspondence, I am led to think you have omitted some circumstances which will bear you out in the temporary removal 14th. In the first place, independent of the fury and excitement occasioned by their having injuriously fired on some person WITHOUT YOUR ORDERS, *and without the presence or any* AUTHORITY *of the* CIVIL POWER, *by which they made themselves so obnoxious. It must be observed that had the rioters been defeated in their object of attack and plundered in Queen Square, It was their determination to assail and plunder the banks, by which all this part of the country, as well as the city generally would have suffered. Was it not therefore an object to prevent their disaster at all events; for had the fires been lighted in that part of the city, whence would they have stopped, and what would the loss have been in comparison with what did occur.*

Your force, under any circumstances, unaided by the civil authorities, and without any constabulary force, would not have protected both, and when the multitude of the rioters and their determined and avowed object, the destruction of property, are taken into consideration, it certainly was prudent to try the effects of conciliation, grounded on the solemn observation of the mob, that order and peace would be instantly restored, if the causes of discontent were removed.

The truce was made – the banks were saved – and thousands saved from ruin, which would have followed if that part of the city had been fired, which would have been the case had the

OSTENSIBLE cause of the riots not been removed. The more I consider the circumstance in all its bearing the more I am inclined to justify the measure. Had you but possessed the means of securing the communication by the Bridges much good would have been affected; but your military force did not allow you to take this necessary precaution.

State these observations in your letter of the day.

Yours truly T. Pearson

(Court of Inquiry PRO HO 52/12)

No doubt, the head of the inquiry, Major General Sir Charles Dalbiac, who was of course also head of Cavalry would not have liked to hear the condemnation of these troops under his command and moreover supported the case of Colonel Brereton. All by such an experienced and distinguished officer as Major General Thomas Pearson, who of course like Brereton were both Infantry officers.

(Captain Warrington who was also with the Colonel at the Guildhall, stated that he too *"was convinced it was then the best measure for the safety of the city"*. As did Major Mackworth, who though not there at the time this decision was made having left the town after escaping with the Mayor over the roofs early Sunday morning but later wrote :

"I must pass lightly over the events on Sunday, having had little to do with them. Of the deployment of the Third Dragoon Guards and the sending of the 14th Dragoons to Keynsham I knew nothing. I can only say, in answer to many things which I have since heard on the subject that the troops were in absolute need of some rest. They might have executed a few charges, and cleared the streets again and again, but unless supported by some other description of force, they could have done no permanent good, and would soon have been so exhausted as to have left the city wholly defenceless."

(A personal narrative)

So these four officers, who were there at the time of the riots and three of them who were there when the crowds attacked the 14th, all agree it was right to send them out of town to calm the situation. The only officer who disagreed was an officer of the very same 14th Dragoons and the least experienced, Major Beckwith. Yet Beckwith was not there at the time, only arriving after the event and also seemed to take it as a slight to both his personal honour and that of his Dragoons.

The Court findings Continued with:

> 3. *That Lt Colonel Brereton, as Commanding Officer of the Troops assembled at Bristol in aid of the civil authorities, did not display that degree of judgment, activity, or firmness, which the circumstances under which he was placed, on the 29th, 30th and 31st Ultimo required.*
>
> *The court having thus reported its opinion, upon the three points to which their attention was more particularly directed (by the adjutant general letter)12 November 1831. It cannot close it's proceedings without adverting to the conduct of the local Magistrates, who when apprehensive of disturbances (as proved by their application for military assistance) appear to have neglected to take sufficient measures for the organisation of a civil force, to co operate effectively with the military at their disposal, for the suppression of disorder and the protection of property.*
>
> *Under such circumstances, (of which Lt Colonel Brereton must have been fully aware) The Court is of decided opinion, that it was the imperative duty of the Commanding Officer of the troops, to have checked, under authority of the local Magistrates, by the most prompt and determined measures, the first attempts on the part of the mob, which endangered the security of property or the safety of individuals.*
>
> *It appears that Lt Colonel Brereton was fully authorised and frequently required, by the competent civil authorities, to disperse the mob on the Saturday evening; by any adequate forceful means which,*

he had under his orders and the Court cannot but mainly attribute the outrages, the devastation, and the destruction of property which took place during the following day and night, to the disinclination and the refusal on the part of Lt Colonel Brereton, to allow the troops to act with due rigour and decision in dispersing the mob which first attacked the Mansion House, as well as his expressed disapprobation of the conduct of the 14th Dragoons, who only acted in self-defence, and to their consequences removed from the city, by his order, in opposition to the publically declared wishes and opinions of the civil authorities of the city.

The Court avails itself of the present opportunity, of expressing their decided opinion of the mischievous and dangerous affect of bringing troops into contact with a lawless and infuriated mob, without permitting them to act even in self defence; – thus proceeding on the minds of the people a feeling of confidence and security in the perpetration of outrage, and on the soldiers a consciousness of degradation, the forerunner of a disregard of discipline and good order.

It is the painful duty of the court to invite the attention of Lord Hill to the fact, that on the Sunday night, whilst many parts of the city (in which he was the Military Commandant) was in flames, Lt Colonel Brereton undressed and went to bed for several hours together, neglecting to attend to the requisition from the Mayor, dated 12 o'clock that night, which was delivered to him in due course, or to take any steps for the suppression of the extraordinary outrages which continued to be perpetrated without opposition.

Yet in fact, the Colonel had indeed dispersed the mob on the Saturday evening and returned the city to tranquillity, so why do they say he had not ?

Also on the Sunday night the Colonel retired to his quarters at 1am and was still in uniform when he was called out again at 4am so I am unsure how they can claim he *"undressed and went to bed for several hours"*. The Court (led by Dalbiac, the Head of Cavalry) then went on unsurprisingly to praise the conduct of the very same Cavalry, by praising the 14th Dragoons and made a special mention of Major Beckwith in suppressing the rioting, even though the facts don't support this.

They summed this up by saying;

> *The Court abstains from making any observations on the evidence which, in its opinion, effects the conduct of Captain Warrington, as that has already formed the subject of a special report; But the Court cannot refrain from availing itself of the opportunity, to express it's highest admiration of the conduct of the Officers, Non-commissioned Officers, and men, of the 14th Dragoons, throughout the disturbances which took place in the City of Bristol during the 29th 30th and 31st October, and of the general good discipline maintained by the squadron of that Regiment, under circumstances of most peculiar trial.*
>
> *The Court maintains a confident hope that, upon a perusal of the Courts proceedings, General Lord Hill will be disposed to consider, that to the soldier like and steady conduct of Captains Gage and Musgrove in the command of their respective troops, and to the prompt, the judicious, and energetic measures adapted by Major Beckwith, in repairing to Bristol (from Gloucester) without the slightest delay, and in obtaining, at a most critical moment the command of his own men, is to be ascribed that a much larger portion of the city of Bristol was not reduced to ashes, and that His Majesty's service did not receive a stain, which no suppression or want of co operation on the part of the Civil Authorities could possibly have wiped away.*
>
> *Signed;*
>
> *Major General Sir James Charles Dalbiac.*
>
> *Colonel Sir Edward Miles, 89th Regt.*
>
> *Colonel J. Ferguson, 52nd Regt.*

Lt Colonel Lord Loughborough 9th Lancers.

Major Edmund Yeamans, Walcott Royal Horse Artillery.

BRISTOL 24 NOVEMBER 1831

(PRO HO 52/12 Court of Inquiry)

This conclusion together with a separate report on Captain Warrington was forwarded to Lord Hill and as a consequence, Major General Jackson for the second time in a couple of weeks had yet another difficult message to convey to Lt Colonel Brereton. He was now to be Court Martialled on Monday 9 January 1832 at the Merchants' Hall and meanwhile would have to consider himself under arrest and report daily to Major George Cawley, who would take charge of the Recruiting Office for the time being. Captain Warrington was similarly advised.

Lord Hill had expressed *"earnest regret"* in having to adopt *"this course towards so old an officer"* but after reading the report, it was *"utterly impossible"* to reach any other conclusion.

The Dark Road to Oblivion

The dark nights of November soon turned into December and a cheerless Christmas came and went. It must have been hard for the Colonel to take his mind of the forthcoming Court Martial as he tried to put it behind him for the time being, to enjoy the festivities with his two young daughters. Nevertheless, January 1832 came soon enough with the melancholy second anniversary of his wife's death further heightened by the impending trial.

The Colonel was not the only one waiting for judgement in the New Year; there were also over a hundred suspected rioters who were to be tried by a Special Commission set by the Government. Excluded from this Commission was Sir Charles Wetherell, the Mayor and the corporation of Bristol. Sir Charles stood up in Parliament to complain of their exclusion citing the Bristol Political Unions criticism of them as being the cause. However, the Union was far from alone in their condemnation as it was a fairly widespread sentiment.

So it was on Monday 2 January 1832 Sir Nicholas Tindal accompanied by Justice's Taunton and Bosanquet made their ceremonial way to 6 Park Street to change into their ceremonial robes before heading to the Cathedral for Devine Service. After asking for God's Devine wisdom, they made their way to the Guildhall and by 2 o'clock the grand jury were sworn in and Chief Justice Tindal spoke at length about a citizen's duty under Common law to suppress or disperse any unlawful assemble. In fact he continued a citizen was empowered to act even without a Magistrates authority and this included soldiers who are also citizens and were both obligated to act to preserve the King's peace and further more any reasonable measures taken would be upheld under Common Law.

These fine words made the course of action seem very clear but as we have seen the case was not as clear cut as Chief Justice Tindal made it sound. For if you took this course of action you could very easily find yourself on the wrong side of the law.

The proceedings lasted until 14 January and during that time 21 were acquitted and 81 found guilty. Of these 31 were sentenced to death, but in the end 27 were reprieved and of these, 20 were transported for life to Van Dieman's Land or New South Wales. The remaining seven were imprisoned and given hard labour. William Clarke a well-built publican's son from Bedminster in his thirties who was considered a ringleader was charged along with five others of riotous assemble and destroying the Prison and the Governor's House. Two teenagers were the only ones out of the multitude convicted of burning down the Bishop's Palace, yet there were obviously many more that were responsible but who escaped conviction. Another notable case was Christopher Davis a supporter of reform who was aged 49 and had independent means of £300 per annum. He was well known and would take any opportunity available to berate the Corporation and the Bishops and any other anti-reformers. Because of this and his social standing it was felt by the Attorney General that he must be a ring leader and so he was accused of instigating the attack on the New Gaol and of stirring up the mob to commit other outrages even though not being directly involved himself. He was seen by various people at most of the sites of devastation swinging an umbrella and shouting loudly for reform while railing against the Bishops and Magistrates. It seems that Davis was not the ring leader he was being accused of, in fact even some prosecution witnesses played down his part in an effort not to incriminate him too badly. However, as Davis had previously said himself; *"There is one thing against me, it is what I said."* Unfortunately he was right, despite many testifying to his honesty, generosity and benevolent nature, his own views, drunkenly proclaimed to any one who would listen had sealed his fate. After an hour of deliberating at 9 o'clock on Wednesday 11January he too was pronounced GUILTY!

The next morning Davis was brought back to Court for sentencing trembling and crying out, *"Oh my Lord, I am innocent, I meant no harm,"* as he sank down into a chair resting his head and numbed by his pending fate. Others also found guilty were screaming their innocence and calling out to their wives and children. Those witnessing this sorry spectacle sat in silent remorse, brushing away the tears from their eyes and even the judges themselves were visibly affected.

After a long address to each man in turn there was a deathly silence as Chief Justice Tindal looked solemnly into the court and placed his black cap over his wig and delivered the final sentence;

"Every one of you will be taken hence to the place of execution, where you will be severally hanged by the neck until you are dead and may the Lord, in his infinite goodness, have mercy on your guilty souls."

Davis who until then had remained shocked into silence suddenly cried out;

"Oh my Lord, I hope you will have mercy. I never was in any depredation, I never meddled with any one thing; I never meddled with fires; I never threw a stone or nail; I was never in a gaol before."

At this point his voice trailed off into a whisper as his face twitched and contorted with uncontrolled emotion.

However, all to no avail for even a petition later signed by 10,000 fellow citizens and sent to the King asking for clemency received no positive outcome just as the petition of 11,000 in Merthyr had previously.

The newspapers expressed what a lot of people were thinking.

The Morning Herald;

"We do not say enough, but too much, blood has been shed already in consequence of the Bristol riots. Many perished in the fires – many have been slaughtered by military execution and many more maimed for life. The judicial destruction of five more human beings in cold blood will not be of the least advantage to the interests of society."

The Sun wrote a similar piece;

"If the Bristol rioters are guilty, the Bristol magistracy was double so; if the one party had a right to stand at the bar of justice, the other had an equal right to stand there beside them; nor do we know any earthly reason why the brave military and the misguided populace should have been made the victims of a slothful, chicken-hearted Magistry."

It was to this back drop that Colonel Brereton had a few days previously, on Monday 9 January attended the Merchants' Hall in King's Street to attend his Court Martial to answer the charges brought against him instigated by the very same;

"slothful, chicken-hearted Magistry."

The head Magistrate was of course Charles Pinney who was also a member of the influential Merchant Venturers and destined to become its president. The Merchant Venturers had actually built this very hall, so Brereton was very much in enemy territory. Although outside he was greeted by cheers from the populace as he alighted from his carriage, all waiting to see if they could gain admittance but there was only limited space inside although many chairs had been arranged to accommodate those lucky enough to gain access. The press were issued with tickets for admission by the deputy Judge Advocate and inside it soon filled up.

The court opened at 11 o'clock under the presidency of Lieutenant General Sir Henry Fane who sat at the head of a long table which ran down the centre of a large room seating fourteen officers of varying ranks all in bright red military uniforms. On the defence table situated to the right sat Lt Colonel Brereton who at last had some legal representation in the person of his counsel Sir William Earl of the Western Circuit and his solicitor Mr Evans. The Prosecution table was again headed by Major-General Sir Charles Dalbiac, who had also officiated as the President at the Court of inquiry only six weeks previously. The large grand room with high ceilings was now very crowded, particularly with women who seemed to take a great interest in the events unfolding before them. Amongst them was the artist Rolinda Sharples who was there sketching the participants and would eight years later display her famous painting which certainly conveys the atmosphere of the proceedings,

The Trial of Colonel Brereton by Bristol artist Rolinda Sharples. (Courtesy of the City of Bristol Museum and Art Gallery).

Adjacent is a Keyplan of this painting indication the position of the participants. Col Brereton can be see on the right with folded arms (No; 4) with his friend Major Ellard kneeling behind him. The diminutive figure of Mayor Pinney who must have felt quite at home here, can be seen just to the left of the middle of the table looking between two officers to the left. (No; 21)

1. Lieut.-General Sir Henry Fane (President).
2. Captain Arnold Thompson (81st Regiment), (Deputy-Judge-Advocate).
3. General Sir John Charles Dalbiac (Prosecutor).
4. Lieut.-Colonel Brereton (Defendant).
5. Mr. Erle (Defendant's Counsel).
6. Mr. T. M. Evans (Defendant's Solicitor).
7. Major-General Lord Burghersh.
8. Major-General R. Ellice.
9. Major-General Sir John Ross.
10. Major-General Sir Charles Br.
11. Colonel Lygon (2nd Life Guards).
12. Colonel Warburton (8th Foot).
13. Colonel Duffy (Unattached).
14. Colonel Lambert (Grenadier Guards).
15. Colonel Arnold (Engineers).
16. Colonel Forster (Artillery).
17. Lieut.-Colonel Keyt (84th Foot).
18. Lieut.-Colonel Grey (2nd Dragoon Guards).
19. Lieut.-Colonel Chatterton (4th Dragoon Guards).
20. Lieut.-Colonel Clarke (6th Dragoon Guards).
21. The Mayor of Bristol (Mr. Charles Pinney).
22. Sir John Smyth, Bart.
23. Mr. (Sir) John K. Haberfield.
24. The Rajah Ram Mohun Roy.
25. The Duchess of Roxburghe and Son.
26. Rev. Sydney Smith.
27. Dr. J. Harrison.
28. Colonel Faunce and Daughters.
29. Lieut. Hunter.
30. Miss Bunbury (afterwards Mrs. Hunter).
31. Mrs. Arnold Thompson.
32. Mrs. Bunbury.
33. Mr. Castle.
34. Miss Castle.
35. Charles Bowles Hare.
36. Thomas Colston.
37. Mrs. Bridges (*née* Colston).
38. Mr. George Powell (*Bristol Mercury*).
39. Mrs. Sharples (Mother of the Artist).
40. Miss Rolinda Sharples (the Artist).
41. Mrs. Rowlands.
Alderman Fripp.
Alderman Hilhouse.
Mr. Sergeant Ludlow (Town Clerk)
Mr. Hare (Under-Sheriff).
Major Mackworth (the hero of Stanley Weyman's *Chippinge*, Arthur Vaughan).

Rolinda Sharples was born in Bath in 1793 dying in Bristol in 1838. She came from a family of artists, her father James painted a famous portrait of the American President George Washington.

After the officers of the court had been sworn in, the President rose and instructed them in the modus operandi he would like them to take. After this, eleven separate charges were read out to the Colonel and to each one he pleaded;

"NOT GUILTY."

A list of witnesses for both sides is then read out by the Judge Advocate, and they are then instructed to vacate the Court, until they are called to give evidence.

General Sir Charles Dalbiac then rose and addressed the court declaring that some of the charges brought against Colonel Brereton, some of which on the face of it, carried an *"appearance of culpability unprecedented in the character of a British officer"*. Though there had been much discussion as to who was to blame some saying the civil authority others the military. The depth of this discussion had generated an interest that could scarcely be remembered in a case before a military tribunal and yet never were the facts less perfectly known or less perfectly understood and thus demanded the most vigorous scrutiny. Nevertheless, he also wished the Court to know that Colonel Brereton was completely unknown to him before the Court Of Inquiry on 17 November last.

He had scrupulously excluded from his mind any detrimental conversation or printed material that had emerged (obviously a reference to the Mayors and other publications in the local press). Instead, he confined himself to the evidence produced before the Court of Inquiry. He further hoped that the Colonel would remember that in the examination of the most important witnesses, (meaning the Mayor and Civil Authority who had instigated the trial in the first place) that he had taken pains to ascertain whether the Colonel had received their full co-operation during the most trying times of the riots.

Before presenting a number of letters to and from the Colonel, which he asked him to verify.

He then referred to the method of arranging the evidence before the Court and called his first witness.

Town Clerk, Sergeant Ludlow; who after confessing he had never met Colonel Brereton before the afternoon of 29 October

1831. When asked if any Magistrates had accompanied the troops in the suppression of the rioting, he replied; *"I have no personal knowledge of that fact."* And then went on to say that he left himself later when the square was mostly cleared.

The Colonel was not perturbed by Ludlow's testimony for as the court closed for the day, and he made his way home his footman James Wilson noticed his apparent cheerfulness. It could have been this very evening that he penned a letter outlining the Magistrates plans to implicate him that is mentioned below. Although the charges were very serious he also knew them to be false, and that the Magistrates had concocted them in an effort to defend their own actions. So with the cheers of the populace still ringing in his ears he was feeling confident of his acquittal once the true facts were known. As on 21 January *Farley's Bristol Journal* and the London newspaper *The Town* reported;

"We have been favoured with the perusal of a letter, written by Colonel Brereton shortly after the commencement of the trial, in which he expresses a great confidence of acquittal, and describes the means resorted to by the Corporation to acquit themselves at the expense of his character,"

No doubt, the Colonel wanted to counter the Mayor's damning letters that had been published prior to his court of inquiry appearance, but though these papers mention his letter none seemed to have published it.

On Tuesday morning when the Court reassembled at 10 o'clock, Ludlow was cross examined and admitted that the Colonel had frequently said he was ready to obey the Magistrates orders including to fire, provided those orders were explicit. When it was suggested that the Magistrates had avoided giving any explicit orders, he had to admit he never heard any such explicit orders issued and also that he had no personal knowledge of the Magistrates accompanying Colonel Brereton or the troops to direct them in the suppression of the rioters.

Mayor Charles Pinney was them sworn in and asked;

If the rioting increased after the troops were called out on the Saturday night? He replied that in his opinion they did increase but then admitted he didn't leave his room so; *"perhaps could not form so good a judgement, as those outside."*

(No doubt meaning the military, as no civic dignitaries left the safety of the Mansion House until they felt safe to do so after the mob was cleared).

He was then asked about the charge made by the troops that evening, but again said; *"I understood that there was but I did not see it."*

When asked if he felt the riot had increased in the evening because of the Colonel's lack of vigour replied; he couldn't tell, but felt the Colonel's familiarity with them must have given them confidence; for *"he certainly neglected to clear the square"*.

But again, had to admit that no Magistrates were in the street as they were all in the Mansion House and there they remained and that none left to direct the troops. He also stated that when he had ordered the Colonel to clear the streets he had implied he was to use any force that was necessary and believed the Colonel understood this to be his meaning.

Alderman Abraham Hillhouse was sworn and examined;

He stated that he had originally gone to fetch the military on foot and that in his opinion the rioting did increase during the night after the military under Lt Colonel Brereton arrived but decreased after 11 o'clock after the charge was instigated which he attributed to the strong remonstration from the Magistrates but then had to admit that he too didn't see the charge but had only heard about it.

Captain Gage of the 14th Dragoons was then sworn in;

The Captain confirmed that a troop was ordered to load by Colonel Brereton which it did, before going to the Mansion House and was then ordered to clear the streets without using violence. He then confirmed that there *Was* an increase in violence in Queen Square that night after the arrival of the troops, but only *After* Colonel Brereton ordered them to clear the streets by force at 10 o'clock;

The Court reassembled again on Wednesday and Lieutenant Jas Dawson of the 14th Dragoons stated that he saw no riot in the square from when he arrived with the troop at 7 o'clock to when he left at 10 o'clock only an immense crowd.

There then followed a number of witnesses that confirmed what had been stated before.

William Harmer a solicitor then recounted that he had seen the Colonel shaking hands with the crowd and waving his hat declaring he was for reform and saying as well as he could recollect; *"I am as well as you my boys"*.

Before admitting that he could not remember whether the officer he saw was wearing a blue or a red coat. Nevertheless, said he now recognised Colonel Brereton to be the man he saw in command of the troops.

Sergeant Edward Dean of the 3rd Dragoon Guards then stated that he had been in the square that evening and saw some rioters take hold of the Colonels hand and shake it and also heard him on several occasions address the crowd and say that if they did not go home, he would have to resort to violence. In response to questions put by the prisoner that no acts of violence were taking place while Colonel Brereton was acting in the way described and with respect to shaking hands with the rioters, he always supposed was against the Colonel's consent.

Sir Charles Dalbiac then rose and announced that the evidence was closed on the part of the prosecution in support of the first charge. He also felt that it would be proper to blend charges 2, 3and 4 as they were so similar in respect of facts.

Mayor Charles Pinney is then re examined regarding these three charges and is then asked if he considered the troops under the immediate command of Lt Colonel Brereton to be under his (The Mayor's) control? The Mayor replied that;

"No Magistrate was competent to say how troops should act."

Authors note;

Yet Lord Melbourne had sent a circular reminding Magistrates that this was indeed the case. Troops could only act under the presence and authority of a Magistrate and were there only to assist and reinforce the civil authority, but if the civil authority was not present how could the military assist them? Mr Alderman Abraham Hillhouse was then examined in relation to the three charges;

Regarding the Sunday morning when the troops were recalled to the Mansion House after it had been again broken into, he was asked if he or any other Magistrate gave orders for the troops to fire, to which he replied; I cannot swear that I did, but after I read the Riot Act I did tell the mob that the troops would fire.

(Even if this is true, it is unlikely that the crowd heard what he said in the noise of protest let alone Colonel Brereton and in any case threatening to use violence and authorising its use are two completely different things.)

The Colonel then asked him if he had not asked for permission to use firearms in Queen Square on that Sunday morning in the presents of Robert Marshall, but he had refused. Alderman Hillhouse then replied that he never heard the request nor did he refuse.

He than asked why he was not told that the Bedminster Yeomanry was in the city the whole of Sunday even though the Mayor knew of their presence. Alderman Hillhouse again replied he did not know they were in Bristol.

(The first point could surely be proved by just by asking Robert Marshall to testify. Perhaps he was one of the 32 witnesses that Brereton would later list in his defence. In addition, if Colonel Brereton had no intention of firing his arms why did he continually ask his men to load up when he called them out. So were they not used because as he stated here, he was refused permission?

As to the second point, the Bedminster Yeomanry had certainly been in the city the whole of Sunday, and had indeed sent a message to the Mayor giving their location. Moreover, they had even received a reply to wait, which they did for some time, but after receiving no further orders they retired from the city. This was confirmed after the Colonel's death by the officer commanding the Yeomanry in a letter published in the local press, but not at the time of this court martial.

The Court adjourned;

On Thursday 12 January the court reassembled and Cornet Kelson was then re-examined on how he was sent by Captain Warrington with 11 men to the Gaol on the Sunday at 3.30pm as he passed through College Green Colonel Brereton ordered him to the Gaol together with another nine, making 20 men in total. When Kelson asked what he should do there, he reported that the Colonel had said, "*That he could give no orders to act; he could find no Magistrate to give him any orders; I was to use no violence but to go there and return.*"

"*On my arrival at the gaol I saw an immense mob collected together. I marched the men up to the gaol door. Saw a great number inside the gaol, they were knocking some things to pieces. I don't know exactly what. I put the men threes about, and took them back to college Green. I reported my arrival in College Green to Lt Colonel Brereton in person. He asked me what I had done at the Gaol. I said I had done what he had told me – nothing.*

(There was laughter in the court at this statement)

He told me he heard I had shot men there. I told him I had done nothing of the sort. He told me I had acted perfectly right. It was then about four or quarter past four"

This version of events didn't fit the Colonels recollections, who reminded Cornet Kelson that when he returned from the Gaol he had told him that he had found 10,000 rioters there, and could do nothing against them, and neither could he find a Magistrate, or civil authority?

Kelson replied that he remembered telling him that he saw an immense mob destroying the Gaol and had done nothing to check them, but could not recollect saying anything about Magistrates.

At the start of the trial on Monday, Brereton had felt sure that once the truth was out he was certain of acquittal; he was even cheered as he alighted from his carriage outside the court. However, that assured mood of Monday was gradually replaced, as day by day a relentless stream of eager souls ready to discredit not only his actions and motives during the rioting but also his good name and character. Before the Court adjourned Brereton's barrister announced that an additional 32 defence witnesses were waiting to be called, to which request the Court granted permission. Nevertheless, Brereton who had sat impassive during the proceedings was now visibly shocked by the day's proceedings and with Kelson's statement in particular, not helped by the ripple of laughter that punctuated it. Sadly none of these 32 witnesses would ever be called.

"It is better to be stabbed in the heart by an enemy than in the back by a comrade."

End of an Honourable Man

The Colonel was a man who throughout his life had always been in control, but now he was losing that control. In the past, he had presided over Courts of Inquiry and Courts Martial yet now he was the subject of one. So he desperately needed to reaffirm some control of his life and destiny

As he made his way out into the street at around 5 o'clock, he retired to Reeves Hotel with his counsel William Earle, Dr Augustus Loinsworth and his friend Major Ellard. During the course of the evening, Dr Loinsworth noticed the Colonel's behaviour was rather strange and out of character. He observed him do and say the most inconsistent things, something he had noticed increasingly since the riots. He made proposal to his counsel William Earle to put before the Court that, *"as a military man, or any man in his senses, must have known would not be acceded to."*

Dr Loinsworth was probably referring to the end of the evening when the Colonel arranged for Mr Earle to attend at 18 The Mall, Clifton, where the deputy Judge Advocate Captain Thompson was staying for the duration of the trial. Arriving around 11o'clock he put before him the Colonel's proposals.

Captain Thomson was told the Colonel had been very hurt by the turn that the evidence had taken that day. The Colonel also felt it was hopeless in trying to contradict it, and so wanted his opinion as to whether the court would accept a proposal, that if he pleaded guilty to the remainder of the charges and just confining his defence to a few points, whether he could be excused from the humiliation of any further court appearances and no more evidence would be brought against him.

Captain Thompson expressed no personal opinion but referred Mr Earle to the Army Regulations, which state that when a prisoner pleads guilty;

"It is the duty of the Court Martial not withstanding to receive, and report in their proceedings, such evidence as may

afford a full knowledge of the circumstances, it being essential that the facts and particulars should be known to those whose duty it is to report on the case."

(PRO WO 71/280)

As this was being communicated to his counsel the Colonel unaware at this stage of the ramifications his suggestion would entail, was making his way out of Reeves Hotel with his two remaining companions at nearly an hour past his normal bedtime. He met his gardener waiting outside in the gig ready to drive him home, before turning to say a melancholy goodbye to his two friends, he climbed in, sinking wearily into the seat and looking seemingly at some lost object far away in the distance. With a slap of the reins, the gig pulled away from the hotel and rattled off into the darkness leaving the two men standing watching it disappear with a sad foreboding.

It was later reported that Colonel Brereton was made aware of the response to his proposal after he arrived home, and it was this response that was to fix his mind and seal his fate. The Colonel was now a worried man and so did not greet his young footman the 18-year-old James Wilson as he usually did, instead he looked down and passed by without comment or command, retiring silently to his sitting room. His housekeeper of 16 years Mary Anne Pitchforth attended him during the hours he remained there, and noticed him writing with pen and ink and then throwing papers into the fire. She heard him pacing the floor for some hours and wondered what to do. For since the Colonel's wife had died she had slept in the nursery with his two young girls, and so did not go to bed until he had kissed them goodnight, which he religiously did every evening, but ominously not on this occasion. It was not until after 2 o'clock that the Colonel retired to his bedroom, with Mrs Pitchforth lighting his way and leaving a candle on the mantelpiece to light the room before leaving. A short time after she was called back and the Colonel gave her some papers addressed to his uncle Lt Colonel Andrew Coghlan in Bath, and asked her to arrange delivery, and soon afterwards, she retired to bed.

Since the Court Martial had begun, the Colonel had become more and more depressed as he saw witness after witness come and drag his good name through the mud. He had expressed from the start that the small body of troops at his disposal were not enough to quell the limitless number of protesters, and with little, or no help from the Mayor or Magistrates he was left to try to contain the rioting until his request for reinforcements had been fulfilled. These same magistrates however who had little energy or proposals during the riots, suddenly became industrious and conscientious when it came to blighting his character and reputation. Worse though was that the Military itself, who were also taking part in the assassination of his character and reputation as a proud military officer, this must have been even more galling. He felt betrayed, for he had given his whole life to the army since leaving home with his uncles as a fresh faced fifteen-year-old in 1798. He had served and fought in the most inhospitable climates and not only survived against the odds, but also prospered. He had diligently laboured for his King and country and worked his way up to his present rank all through hard work, always receiving praise and recommendation from both his superior officers and subordinates right down to the humble soldiers who served under his command. However, no longer in command of his own regular troops, he had during the riots tried to protect and care for the soldiers placed under him by not putting them into any compromising situations or unnecessary dangers. Yet some of these same soldiers were now turning up in court with little regard for his position and the damage their testimonials were bringing down on him. Cornet Kelson's was the last straw, for what he had sworn to, was not only untrue, but most damaging to his reputation as an officer, and made him look like a complete fool.

But by now he also realised what a mistake it had been to make his proposal to Captain Thompson the Judge Advocate, for by agreeing to plead guilty, in a vain attempt to stop the relentless torture of the trial he had achieved no good whatsoever, in fact he had ruined his case. The trial would still go on without remission but by his admission to plead guilty, he had completely ruined his defence. An outcome of guilty was now assured whatever his evidence to the contrary. So what course was now left for him to take? His whole life had been in the army, as had his families for centuries past and so without the army he was nothing, and would face absolute ruin. It was now also ominously close to the anniversary of his wife's recent death and disturbingly in the early hours of Friday the 13th.

The Colonel had spent most of his life in control, in control of his troops, his life and the situations he found himself in. However, now he had no control at all and others were controlling events, so he needed to reinforce his will and regain control in the only way now left open to him.

For here I lie, amid the ruins of my life's esteems
While the cold black wind rattles rain against my window pane
and seeps into my room to dance its devouring dance of death
with the flickering candle flame.

The darkness pervades me, while hostile voices
whisper and conspire in the howling wind
their tongues steeped in lies they stab me
with their mocking ridicule
I am being consumed by the darkness and the
relentless derision of my heartless foes
What end is there in this for me, and their
ceaseless malevolent blows?

'Twas then in my despair I heard a familiar
voice so soft and full of love
Come! Come to me!
So I took a soldiers way and denied the
taunting voices their game of malignity
and blew away my soul, to rejoin my love
in far away eternity.

Mary Pitchforth the Colonel's housekeeper, no doubt thought she could at last get some sleep as she returned to her room and readied herself for bed. However, a loud report broke the stillness of the chilly winter's night, which rooted her to the spot in stark contemplation of its source. Frightened and hesitantly, she once more trod the boards up to her master's room and fearfully peeked in before running downstairs in horror to alert the staff in the kitchen where young James lay sleeping; it was now 3am. She quickly urged him to investigate the report and confirm her fears. James rose startled from his warm bed and raced up the stairs with his heart in his mouth. As he reached the landing, he hesitantly pushed open his master's door calling out and asking if all was well. However, in the dark stillness there was no reply, so he cautiously entered the room. As he entered, the unmistakable acrid smell of sulphur filled his nostrils and a ghostly web of smoke hung in the air illuminated by the pale flickering candlelight still burning on the mantelpiece. As his eyes adjusted he parted the drawn curtains around his master's bed and there to his horror, he could just make out the gruesome visage of the Colonel lying on his back exposing a gaping wound in his chest with the candlelight dancing on the fresh rivulets of blood staining the front of his white shirt. His mouth was wide open, silently frozen in his last act of protestation in this world, while his eyes, fixed onto some far off eternity, perhaps searching for his dear wife and hoping to be reunited, in another, kinder world than this.

The shocked housekeeper who had raised the alarm, now sent a servant the 13 miles to Bath arriving at 5am to inform the Colonel's uncle, Colonel Andrew Coghlan of the fate of his nephew. Raised from his bed, he quickly readied himself and returned to Redfield House before dawn, and was given the papers that she had received for him only hours previously. These papers contained two letters, the first reads:

"My Ever Dearest Uncle,

My unfortunate mind is not now in a state to enter into particulars and can therefore only hope yourself and my dearest aunt will not forsake my innocent and helpless babes who will be but little sensible when they awake tomorrow of the injustices done to their unfortunate father and which deprives them for ever of his protection. Let me request that you will immediately write to Mr Ross who will not fail to give them his protection and let him know the injustice I have been done. Do not let poor Pitchforth want, she has been a faithful creature to me.

I cannot say more, God in heaven bless you both.

T.B.

He continued in a more practical vein by saying;

Captain Phillips will have in his hands upwards of five hundred pounds which includes two stock receipts for about four hundred given to him this morning in order to sell them out for me. There is one more stock receipt in my desk of upwards I believe of six hundred – I scarcely owe anything but half a year's rent to March £50, for the newspapers about £5.10s, Messrs Moss of London about £5.10. Mr Evans and Mr Earl their charges respecting my unfortunate business. Pitchforth will give you all the receipts for the last year or you can find them in my writing desk. If not expensive, let my unfortunate remains be placed beside poor Olivia's. I request that no expense will be incurred that is possible to avoid for my funeral as in my opinion that is a waste of money.*

Every allowance must be made for my present state of mind and which must account for the incorrectness of this last address. T. B.

*(Captain Philips was the Army paymaster
for the Bristol District.)

As the dawn broke, the recently arrived Uncle must have been stunned to read this letter. Colonel Coghlan and his wife Mary had never had children and it seems his young nephew Thomas Brereton only 10 years younger was very close to them both. Therefore, it must have been a terrible shock to read this anguished final letter and to realise that his beloved nephew had been driven to take his own life.

Col Coghlan, who had woken from his bed and rode through the darkness to view his nephews horrific remains must have found it hard to contemplate the speed at which this catastrophe had unfolded. For by 11pm the inquest was swiftly assembled at the late Colonel Brereton's house under the Coroner W. Joyner, and a jury quickly sworn in before proceedings commenced. Their first duty was to view the body still lying in the position it had assumed after death. A more harrowing sight can scarcely be imagined but at least it was in daylight and not by the flickering candlelight and the unsettling quite of early morning, but still, it was a most horrific scene. After retiring downstairs the first witness was called, Mrs Anne Pitchforth the house keeper of some 16 years, who was much moved during her testimony, collapsing as she left the room and had to be attended to by the late Colonel's surgeon Dr Augustus Loinsworth. Next was young James Wilson who had worked for the Colonel for seven years, he too broke down during his testimony but recovered to recount the events of the night. Adding that when he had returned to the room in daylight the shutters had been opened, and it was then he found the discharged pistol lying on the floor where it had fallen after use. He recounted that his master regularly loaded his pistols with balls and slugs to prepare against robbers as there *was, "much talk in the neighbourhood which was a remarkably bad one"*. He also noticed his master had left his watch, comb and spectacles on the mantlepiece and not by his bed as was usual. Dr Loinsworth the forces surgeon was next up and confirmed he had met Colonel Brereton 20 years ago in the West Indies but during the last 13 months he had known him more intimately as the Colonel was his Commanding Officer in the district. He confirmed he had last seen the Colonel on Thursday night at Reeves Hotel and had noticed his behaviour had changed since the riots. He had noticed this change more particular on the Thursday evening, in fact when he parted with him, he was convinced something unpleasant would occur before morning, but felt that as the Colonel was home with his children on whom he doted; this might prevent him doing anything against himself. Apart from his mental state the Doctor also stated that the Colonel's physical health had not been good as he was suffering from a *liver complaint that he had been treating him for. In fact, at the time of the riots he had been suffering from a severe attack and was unfit for making active exertions though he refused to reported ill as he insisted he was still able to perform his duties. He further stated that the Colonel was an exceedingly fond father, and a most kind, benevolent, and humane man; and as to his principals of honour, if anything, he had almost too high a sense of it. He concluded by saying that from the position of the body death must have been instantaneous.

*(This liver complaint was most likely Hepatitis picked up in The West Indies or Africa.)

The jury immediately passed a verdict of;

"Died from pistol wounds, inflicted on himself, while under a fit of temporary derangement."

The jury who had used the late Colonels family Bible to swear in, then noticed inside on the fly leaf, the hand written memoranda of his marriage in Marylebone church to Miss Olivia Ross, and also the birth of his two daughters which concluded;

"14th of January, 1829, 3 o'clock in the morning my beloved wife, Olivia, died at my house, in Clifton Wood."

This drew the attention of those present to the remarkable coincidence that they were enquiring into the Colonels death on the very anniversary of hers. Others wondered if he had intended to take his life on this anniversary but in his confusion had mistaken the date.

The Colonel and his wife had also curiously died at the same time too, 3am. So did the Colonel plan to take his own life on the same date and time of the year in the hope that if he did so he would be reunited with his beloved wife in the afterlife?

During the proceedings the shocked uncle had remained in another room with the two orphaned girls who could be seen peering through the window curiously watching the comings and goings of the inquest, but thankfully due to their young age (three and six, had not yet quite grasped the significant of their father's untimely demise. As the news spread around the neighbourhood, a crowd of women and children gathered at his threshold to mourn their loss as he was well known to all as a kind-hearted benefactor.

"His liberality was the more estimable, as with respect to fortune, he possessed but a small private independence."

(*The court Martial of Colonel Brereton*. Page 39.)

The Colonel's commission was worth around £6,000 but at his death, this was lost, though at the time it was hoped his two children would be eligible for an officer's pension of around £20 to £30 per annum but there is no record they ever received this either.

Later in the day, whispers of the fate of Colonel Brereton started to spread around Bristol too, but no one was sure if it was just a rumour or not. However, when the Court reassembled at 2 o'clock and there was no sign of him even though the Court was particularly crowded with locals anxious to hear what had happened. The President rose and referring to the rumour and the fact that the Colonel had not attended, was afraid there might be some substance in the claim so had sent Major Mackworth to ascertain the facts. Shortly after this announcement, Major Mackworth arrived covered in mud and was addressed by the President, who asked him if he had been to the house of Colonel Brereton. To which the Major replied, *yes he had*. The President then asked, *"Was he alive or dead?" "He was dead,"* came the reply. After this was entered into the court minutes a stunned prosecutor Major General Sir Charles Dalbiac rose and asked the president of the court if he might speak saying;

"if the tragic event which has just been communicated shall have caused pain to the court, how much deeper must that pain be to individual who has had the task assigned to him of conducting the prosecution." He went on to say how distressed he was and that he knew not the Colonel before the Court of Inquiry but even if he had been "his sworn friend and brother officer" he would not have conducted himself any differently."

He seemed greatly affected by what had happened and delivered this short statement with much feeling whilst trying to distance himself from any accusations of impropriety that had arisen, after which he sat down obviously chastised by events. The President, Sir Henry Fane then spoke on behalf of the Court and reassured Sir Charles he had conducted himself most properly and without prejudice to the late prisoner. Sir Henry then went through the formal proceedings before clearing the court he then sent a brief message to Fitzroy-Somerset informing him of the tragic termination of the case and then waited for orders from the Commander-in-Chief.

After the court was adjourned Sir Henry sent a more detailed letter outlining Colonel Brereton's last moments, and noting that it was after he had received the reply from the Judge Advocate about changing his plea late on Thursday night, that Brereton seemed to have decided his case was lost. Sir Henry continued saying;

"It is a melancholy termination of our proceedings, but I am inclined to think from what I hear of the individual that it would have saved him from utter destitution and ruin."

He went on to say that the court had already been able to prove to the public that there was no fault on the part of the military except on the part of Lt Colonel Brereton, before continuing to say that;

"The civil authority will have had the satisfaction of having been able to show that they were neither backward, nor inactive, in the discharge of their duties."

(PRO HO 40/28)

So there we have it, the military and the civil authority were both conveniently off the hook and proved to be blameless; it was all the fault of the Colonel.

Nevertheless, that was not the way the public of Bristol saw it, and they had actually been there and witnessed both the Colonel's actions and the Magistrate's lack of action during the riots.

There was a nasty stench in the streets of Bristol, and it wasn't just the smell of burnt out buildings or the festering corpses rotting within, it was the smell of hypocrisy and the overpowering odour of a Government cover-up.

Once the news of Colonel Brereton death spread around the town there was much sympathy, and some considerable anger, some claiming he had been made a scapegoat for the real culprits, the Magistrates. Renewed and strengthened calls were now being made for them to be also scrutinised as the Colonel had been, and brought to justice.

The Press put these widely held views into print;

The Morning Herald;

"It is lamentable to think that a generous aversion to take the lives of others should have placed him in circumstances which drove him to lift his hand against his own. But why has Colonel Brereton, of all the persons, whose duty it was to protect the peace of Bristol, been made the scapegoat to bear the sins of so many who were recreants to their trust?"

The Bristol Mercury;

"There are some men who would spill human blood like water, though it were only for the protection of a hen coop. We reverence Colonel Brereton for his aversion to this, and however culpable the soldier might be, we think much better of the man. At the same time, we admit that there may be a season in which the employment of military force is not only excusable, but absolutely essential – a time, indeed, it would argue not only a highly culpable neglect of duty, but even inhumanity, in an officer to shrink from his task of dispersing a mob, however repugnant such a task might be to his feelings. Speaking however, to what we saw – and, throughout the whole of this melancholy affair, our opinion has been grounded solely on our personal observations – speaking to what we saw, we are decidedly of opinion that the conduct of Colonel Brereton was not only most honourable to his feeling as a man, but most praiseworthy to him as a soldier."

After a weekend when the only topic of conversation was the tragic events of Friday, there were many discussions amongst the population of Bristol as to who was, or who was not responsible. However, the Court at least felt it had identified the only culprit and so when it reassembled on Monday the 16th. Sir Henry Fane rose and read out a letter he had received from Lord Hill stating:

"Having communicated your letter to the Commander-in-Chief, I have been instructed by his Lordship to request that you

will forthwith dissolve the Court Martial appointed on the late Colonel Brereton."

(PRO HO 40/28)

In compliance with the letter Sir Henry declared the Court dissolved, after which he instructed the Officers present to reassemble the next morning in the same hall, this time to try Captain Warrington of the Third Dragoon Guards who also had some charges against him to answer to.

Although Captain Warrington had been under arrest since the end of the riots, he still did not know exactly what charges were being brought against him. Once the charges were read to him, he asked the Court's permission for an adjournment so he could prepare a proper defence, a defence that would be all the more difficult because his main witness Colonel Brereton, was no longer around to speak in his favour. The Court granted his request and gave him over a week to prepare, and so proceedings were adjourned until later the next week.

Laid to Rest

Two days later at 7am on Thursday 19 January 1832 just a week after Colonel Brereton's fateful day in court, and the events that finally set his suicide into motion, a small private group of mourners arrived at Redfield House to accompany the funeral cortege, scarcely believing that the last time they had seen him alive was after they had dined at Reeves Hotel on that fateful night. His close friend Major Ellard who had been his constant companion at the Court Martial was first to arrive. He was soon followed by Lieutenant Francis, the District Adjutant who he had worked alongside, and Dr Loinsworth, the District Military Surgeon. The only two none military men present Mr T.M. Evans Esq, the Colonel's Solicitor who had conducted his defence, and finally George Lunell Esq. As the hearse arrived and the late Colonel's body was placed within, the mourners lead by yet another Military man, his grieving uncle Lt Colonel Andrew Coghlan, all took there places in the two mourning coaches and the sad procession took its slow clattering passage through the quiet streets of Bristol travelling the few miles to St Andrew's Church, Clifton.

Normally someone of the Colonel's rank with so many years of service would have expected at least some sort of official military representation at the funeral, but due to the circumstances of his death, one suspects this was neither solicited nor welcomed. It is true to say that the Colonel himself felt rather let down by the way he had been treated by the military. Nevertheless, many of the good people of Bristol still smarting from his unjust treatment were not going to let him slip away without a show of solidarity and paying their respects. So despite the early hour, many lined the streets and doffed their hats as the cortege passed, while others walked silently beside the cortege in the very streets his fate was sealed. The procession passed over The Drawbridge at the bottom of Clare Street on its way to St Andrew's at Clifton. There followed a very sad and mournful service where the Colonel was laid to rest as a private gentleman with no military honours beside his dear wife Olivia.

Many were so moved they wrote their feelings in verse such as this below, written by a 16-year-old boy, who was so affected by the Colonel's fate that he wrote this spontaneously and just signed it W.G.H.

ON THE LAMENTED DEATH OF THE LATE COLONEL BRERETON

And he, the gentle, and the brave

Has sunk to an untimely grave;

His noble heart by anguish riv'n

No hope on earth – he flew to heav'n.

I do not praise the desperate deed,

That him from shame and sorrow freed;

But think, so gentle and so kind.

What madness must have wrung his mind.

And urge his soul to fly from pain;

When thoughts of shame burnt through his brain.

What anguish must have torn his breast

When he no more his babes caressed

That dreadful night he did not smile

Nor court his children's custom'd wile-

He did not then with love, how deep!

Watch over the infant's gentle sleep,

But wild, and deep, and dreadful despair,

Forbade the father to go there.

It was a wish no blood to shed that

Brought destruction on his head;

For oh! So gentle was his heart
No bitter feelings seemed a part.
The very servants as they spoke,
And told how that kind heart was broke.
Wept as though ties most close and dear
Joined them to him upon the bier.
And Oh, 'twas mournful then to see
His children sport on infant glee:
Little knew they that grievous moan
Was due to him so lately gone;
To him, the merciful, the brave,
The gallant soldier in the grave.
If ever the beams of mercies light
Have chased the gloom of horror's night.
If ever excuse for crime was made,
If ever compassion lent her aal.
Since madness caused the dreadful deed.
Let pity now for mercy plead –
Mercy the first, but glorious cause
Of all this misery – let none pause'
But from each mouth be these sounds given,
Peace to his soul and rest in heaven.

(Published in the *Worcester Herald*. 20 January 1832)

Less than a week later on Wednesday the 25th Captain Warrington returned to face the four charges that had been brought against him the week before. Later, on Monday 30th January, he commenced his own defence. After telling the Court of his, and his family's, long history in service to his majesty in the British Army for centuries past he took a moment to reflect on the loss of Colonel Brereton nobly saying;

"I would sooner suffer any degradation, or bear all the odium of these charges, than I would place one blot on his escutcheon."

A noble sentiment from a man who had served side by side with the Colonel over the three days of rioting and had obviously developed a loyalty and respect for his late commanding officer. However, he must have felt the loss in more than one way, as the Colonel would have been his main witness.

Nevertheless, in the end Captain Warrington was still found guilty and even though the King declared his clemency. Captain William Henry Warrington was cashiered from his regiment, with the only concession being that he was allowed to sell his commission, yet another casualty of the Bristol riots. On 15 March Captain Warrington is recorded in the 3rd Dragoon Guards muster rolls as *"retired"* and it was at this time that Cornet Kelson purchased the rank of lieutenant, a position created by Warrington's departure.

A week later on 22 March another matter was also nearing its conclusion; it was the affairs of the Late Colonel Brereton. Col Coghlan his uncle had been searching in a vain effort to locate Col Brereton's Will but had been unsuccessful, so the Court decided to use the Colonel's letter written just before his death as his Will. However, of course this needed to be verified, and so the Colonel's brother-in-law Francis Drew of Mocollop Castle in Waterford Ireland arrived, together with Sergeant Major William MacLeod from the Recruiting Office in Bristol. Both made a declaration confirming that the letter was indeed written in the hand of Colonel Brereton. So less than two weeks later the administration of his goods and chattels passed into the hands of Colonel Coghlan who would also be the guardian of his two orphaned children until they reached their majority at the age of 21.

However, what about those others, who were held by many to be the real culprits, the Mayor, the Magistrates the civil authority?

Though swift, if not fair justice had been handed out to others, strangely justice was slow in coming to those who many considered the real miscreants.

The Committee of Inquiry set up by a cross section of Bristolians had collected together much evidence and urged The Home Secretary Lord Melbourne to go ahead with investigating and prosecuting the very men most held responsible, and so with such demand he could hardly refuse, especially as so many others had been dealt with swiftly and severely.

So on 25 February 1832 the *Sheffield Independent* reported that;

Lord Melbourne sent a letter dated 14 February to the Bristol MP Mr Baillie, informing him that a Court of Justice will be inquiring into the conduct of the magistrates during the recent riots.

"This is a redeeming point in the conduct of the Ministers, whose apparent reluctance to proceed against the magistrates was beginning to affect their popularity here, particularly after the fatal results of the Court Martial on Lt Colonel Brereton whose private character was held in universal respect."

Unfortunately the rich and powerful have ways of slowing down the wheels of justice and as time past and no trial materialised, the spring flowers had time to grow and die on the graves of the executed men. While far, far, away on the other side of the world the 27 of their fellow compatriots, whose punishment had been transportation, were also dying, as they toiled relentlessly under the burning antipodean sun.

It was a full year before Mayor Pinney finally received his summons to appear before the Kings Bench in London and by that time, he had completed his tenure as Mayor. Therefore, he was now just plain Charles Pinney. The *Bristol Mercury* had expressed what many were thinking and expecting;

"Hitherto, the trials, whether civil or military, connected with the late riots, have been conducted with peculiar severity; we are prepared to expect that, in the case now pending, the same stern justice will be administered. After what has passed, we believe the country will scarcely be satisfied if the prosecutor be found to lack the vigour of Sir Charles Dalbiac."

(The Bristol Mercury)

Therefore, it was not just Colonel Brereton who had felt that Sir Charles Dalbiac had pursued his *"cruelly unjust"* convictions with relentless vigour.

Perhaps the authorities were waiting for Pinney's Mayoralty to end, so as there would be no ignominy of an acting Mayor being dragged before the courts. But Charles Pinney had already during his tenure as Mayor brought the Mayoralty into disrepute in many peoples eyes as this comment confirms;

"No man entered the mayoralty with brighter prospects than Mr Pinney;" But *"His mayoralty has been vacillation from beginning to end, he leaves it unregretted by any, but spoken of by all as being deficient in the policy and judgement so necessary to the Magisterial character."*

(A Free Reporter)

In the end, however it was all an anti-climax. All the well known details of the riots were once more trotted out, the Mayor's constant vacillation, never giving clear orders to Colonel Brereton or the military, or indeed having a plan at all to give to the anxious citizens when they responded to his request for help. Also never accompanying either of them properly in pursuit of any instructions that were given, which put a great weight on the Colonel shoulders and also the fact that he had chosen to hide from those who had tried to seek his whereabouts and had no plan of action when they did.

But despite all of this, and after a trial lasting less than a week Charles Pinney left the court a free man after being declared *"Not Guilty"* after only 20 minutes deliberation by the jury, who after giving their verdict declared;

"The late Mayor of Bristol acted to the best of his judgement with the highest zeal and courage."

(The Trial of Charles Pinney)

Not every one was impressed with either the verdict or the declaration;

"We were prepared to expect (the acquittal) but when the presiding judge and the jury, for the most part composed of Berkshire Tory justices, talk of His Worship's presence of mind and personal courage, then we are tempted to laugh outright."

(The News)

No other magistrates or civil officials were brought to answer for the dereliction of their duty during the Bristol riots. Despite there being plenty of evidence to prove that they had. Nevertheless, the establishment had had their pound of flesh and had made an example of a few citizens and two Officers to show that justice had at least been seen to be done, even if in reality, it was all just smoke and mirrors.

Dreadful Falsehoods

So there we have it, the official conclusion of the Bristol riots. The Mayor and Magistrates of Bristol, who were by law responsible for the peace of their city were completely innocent? It was all Colonel Brereton's fault as he was a coward and a traitor who temporised with the mob. In fact, according to the Court and despite all the evidence to the contrary the Mayor had somehow acted with the;
"highest zeal and courage".

The Colonels opinion along with all the facts to the contrary were just ignored, but amongst the documents that he had left for his Uncle Colonel Andrew Coghlan, was a certain letter; one might say a suicide note. This was not released at the time, even at the inquest, though Colonel Brereton had requested that;
"it be published to the world at large".

This letter subsequently disappeared and though the military historian J.M. Brereton tracked it down to a descendent of the Colonel's, Group Captain Hamilton Ross of the RAF who had inherited it, he in turn had lent it to a relative in London and it had then disappeared for some time. Later when it resurfaced only edited extracts were ever published and those not until 1979.
In this letter Brereton set out the principle causes of his death to;

"The gross neglect of the Government in sending an inadequate force to Bristol and now wishing to screen themselves employed Major General Dalbiac to conduct the infamous and cruelly unjust prosecution against me in order to show to the world that Eighty Dragoons was sufficient to protect this city against the countless thousands of an infuriated mob and without the smallest assistance from the Magistrates or civil authorities. He further accused Dalbiac of prosecuting with the most malignant and heartless perseverance and hope he would meet his reward for being the chief cause of depriving my innocent and helpless babes of their only protection in this world – supported by the most

gross perjury it is possible to imagine – Brereton alleged that the Mayor, the town Clerk, Alderman Abraham Hillhouse and others had sworn to the most dreadful falsehoods in order to screen themselves and brother Magistrates and further declared that Cornet Kelson's evidence this day as to the orders he stated to have received from me going to the new jail is false in the extreme, but which I have no doubt he gave with a view to screen himself from the blame he highly deserved for not having as far as possible performed his duty upon that occasion. I leave this hasty and badly expressed statement as some proof of the cruelly unjust manner I have been used throughout the entire of the proceedings and which I wish to be published to the world at large as the only satisfaction my friends can have of my untimely end."

However, was there any truth in these four serious allegations?

Lets examine these four points in turn

Point 1

I will examine the Colonel's first point of insufficient force in some detail, as there are so many comparable facts to support it. Colonel Brereton had 80 effective troops in Bristol yet we have already seen that just across the Bristol estuary at Merthyr Tydfil; when they had suffered disturbances earlier in June 1831; they were supplied with 463 Troops there *plus* the regular cavalry, which arrived just as the Magistrates had defused the situation. Obviously, the Magistrates in Merthyr were also much more courageous and active than the ones in Bristol in doing their duty. In addition, they did have many more troops, even without including the regular cavalry and yet the population of Merthyr at the time was only 22,083. Also at the nearby Forest of Dean where from 50 to 400 men were involved in the non-violent disturbances, a troop of 50 lead by Major Mackworth were turned away by the Magistrates as insufficient. Order was only restored when 120 men of the 3rd Dragoon Guards arrived later joined by 180 men of the 11th Foot Regiment. When Major Mackworth arrived again with his man-power now increased to 70 he was again told he was not needed.

The Forest Of Dean rioters showed no inclination to violence, yet 370 troops were sent to suppress them.

Yet in Bristol, Brereton was supplied with around 93 and with injuries; this was reduced to 80 in a city with a population of 104,000. Judging with these two contemporary yet separate comparison it seems Brereton was indeed right.

However, the Rioting that bares the most similarities to those in Bristol took place in Nottingham, just a few weeks before Bristol on Sunday 9 October during the annual Goose Fair. News of the latest defeat of the Reform Bill in the House of Lords reached the inhabitants and caused rioting which as in Bristol also lasted three days, ending on Tuesday 11th. Therefore, it is interesting to compare how they were dealt with, and the numbers of troops involved. Nottingham at this time had a population of around 50,000, less than half the population of Bristol's 104,000. Yet they were initially supplied with about the same number of troops. Colonel Brereton in Bristol was supplied initially with around 93 Dragoons but with injuries was only left with 80 but on the second day of rioting and after the controversial removal of the 14th Dragoons he had less than 30.

In Nottingham, the troops were commanded by Colonel Joseph Thackwell of the 15th Hussars. Colonel Thackwell was one of the officers who had charged the crowd at St Peter's Field, Manchester on 16 August 1819. This peaceful rally attended by 60,000–80,000 men, women, and children who were also demanding political reform were mercilessly cut down. So Thackwell can hardly be accused of being cowardly and temporising as Brereton was.

This must have weighed heavily on the shoulders of Colonel Thackwell as he now decided his modus operandi in controlling an actual riot only twelve years later in Nottingham.

However, Colonel Thackwell was fully supported by the Mayor of Nottingham who knew his duty and so was present during *all* manoeuvres ready to give direction and authorisation to Thackwell and the[1] 75 men and horses he had at his disposal (slightly less than the initial number available to Colonel Brereton). However, after confronting crowds estimated at 1,000 strong on the first day of rioting and losing control, even he declared he had insufficient troops. This lead to Nottingham Castle being attacked and burnt to the ground, while the troops stood by and could do nothing to stop it. On the second day of rioting, the Colonel returned from his local barracks where he was stationed with a further 20 Hussars. Thus taking his available regular troops to 95, but he had also called out the South Nottingham Yeomanry Calvary which consisted of[2], 21 officers and 275 men making a total of 391 men under his command, Over four times the numbers available to Lt Colonel Brereton. And that doesn't include the[3] several hundred Special Constables who had been sworn in by the Mayor, and also unlike in Bristol, *the full co-operation and involvement of the Mayor and Magistrates* . Nevertheless, despite such numbers, it still took him from the Sunday until Tuesday to regain control and he too instructed his men to use the flats of their sword not the extremities, just as Brereton did in Bristol to much criticism, but they were both following the official instructions in dealing with civil Insurrections of the day.

"The Commander in Bristol, though a gallant officer in the field, conceived himself bound to adopt, in civil dissentions, the new system so strongly recommended from headquarters;

(*Blackwoods Quarterly*; February 1832.)

So if both officers were only following the official procedures why was only Brereton criticised for it and yet in Bristol Beckwith who did not follow these procedures at all, praised?

([1]*Military Memoirs of Lt-General Sir Joseph Thackwell.* page 97.)

([2]*Historical Records of the South Nottinghamshire Hussars Yeomanry*)

(British Empire (online) *The South Nottingham Hussars Yeomanry, The Reform Bill Riots 1831*)

([3]*Nottingham Rising*. Chapter 6 "To the Castle". Page 93.)

Also unlike in Bristol, several hundred Special Constables were also sworn in by the dutiful Mayor of Nottingham after the first days rioting when Colonel Thackwell and the Magistrates admitted they had lost control. In Bristol on the first day of rioting Brereton (who let's not forget, faced much larger numbers, with estimates of some 20,000. Yet he defeated the rioters and returned the city to peace despite having far fewer troops and no assistance from the Mayor or the unruly Special Constables.

Major Mackworth wasn't alone when he said; *"I really thought the worst of the riot was over"*.

Indeed it might well have been right, had not the controversial killing of a man by the 14th Dragoons occurred during the night.

On the third and final day of rioting in Nottingham, an increasingly confident mob of 2,000–3,000 attacked Beeston Silk Mill and burned it to the ground in broad daylight. Yet on the third day (Monday) of rioting in Bristol Brereton defeated the remaining rioters with only his remaining 30 men of the 3rd Dragoon Guards. So surely, he deserved praise not condemnation!

Interestingly, in Nottingham even more troops were employed after the rioters marched to Wollaton Hall, which was defended by yet further troops under the command of a Colonel Hancock and the 70 strong Wollaton Yeomanry, plus several cannon and a "strong body" of colliers. So compared to Colonel Brereton's forces, even at their height, Nottingham was much better served with a total number of troops including officers of 362 men supplemented with several hundred Special Constables and a "strong body" of colliers not to mention several cannon. All to defend a town with fewer than half the population of Bristol, so again it seems that Colonel Brereton did indeed have a point when he said he didn't have enough troops.

This fact can be further strengthened when one examines the different reactions to the troop's use of firearms.

In Nottingham, the rioting was brought to an end when Colonel Thackwell's Hussars came to the rescue of the Wollaton Yeomanry who were escorting prisoners captured after a failed attempt to storm Wollaton Hall. During this engagement, an officer of the Hussars shot one of the rioters (an incident that Colonel Thackwell tried to cover up). The shot man was a local tailor Thomas Aukland a former soldier and Waterloo veteran who was badly wounded and probably died of his wounds. The use of firearms in Bristol and in Nottingham both proved to be a turning point, but in totally different ways.

For in Nottingham this act chastened the rioters who from this moment on began to melt away terrified that they could also be shot. In Bristol however the opposite happened, the mob was enraged by the shooting of Stephen Bush late Saturday night and actually attacked the 14th Dragoons responsible when they assembled in Queen Square the next morning. It was this escalation of violence that compelled Brereton to remove them from the square and back to their stables for their own protection. However, unsatisfied the enraged mob continually attacked them on route, pelting them with missiles and trying to un-horse any they came in contact with. It was during one such incident that the 14th Dragoons fired another shot at their tormentors killing another man. But again, unlike in Nottingham, this only infuriated the mob further ,who followed them to their stables, and were now threatening to burn them down with the soldier's inside. This is the point where Brereton decided it would be prudent to remove them temporarily from the City for their own protection and to calm the situation until reinforcements arrived.

These completely opposite reactions to the use of firearms in the two cities, prompts the question, why?

In Bristol, it was claimed it was because Brereton refused to attack the rioters in the first instance with enough severity and only using the flat of the swords. However, as we have seen this is exactly how Colonel Thackwell dealt with the rioters in Nottingham too, as this was standard army practise.

So could the answer be the very same one as put forward by Brereton, Insufficient Troops?

In Nottingham, with such a large intimidating force the crowd avoided any confrontation after one of their number was shot. However, in Bristol the crowd were aware that they had the upper hand, as the troops were in such small numbers. So the shootings just inflamed them further as had been shown even *before* the removal of the 14th.What other reason could there be?

The only facts that do are those put forward by Colonel Brereton, *Insufficient numbers!*

So in all three comparable cases it is proved beyond doubt that Colonel Brereton did not have sufficient numbers, and it's worth pointing out also that in the forest of Dean Rioting, the Magistrates turned away Major Mackworth and his 50 troops saying;

"We do not doubt your ability, but bloodshed will be the consequence. Our object is not to murder the peasantry, but to show them such force as will convince all but fools and idiots that resistance will be in vain"

(*Warren James and the Dean Forest Riots.*
By Ralph Astis. Page 103.)

So if 50 troops would only infuriate 50 to 400 non-violent protesters in the Forest Of Dean surely 93 would infuriate even more the 20,000 violent rioters in Bristol, and as the Forest Magistrates predicted, would only cause bloodshed. Moreover, this is exactly what happened in Bristol, and which Brereton was powerless to stop without reinforcements.

If Horseguards were aware of this, and surely they must have been, why did they persecute Brereton? What could possibly be their motives? If it was proved that they had not supplied enough troops? In addition, why didn't Mackworth arrive in uniform with extra troops as he had done twice recently before Bristol?

A retired Army Officer writing in *The Times* from London on 24 November 1831 also questions Horseguards actions before and during the riots and questions on who's authority Major Mackworth was in Bristol issuing advice to the Magistrates and engaged in considerable activity and concludes that he must of been;

"ordered to that spot by the Home Department, no other having authority to order him thither nor could any other be justified in sending an officer of the Army (not already stationed there) to Bristol, unless that order originated from the Home Department."

He further concludes that his presence there could only be as an official observer to spy on the conduct of the reformers but that as;

"he has neither added credit or éclat to his own character, or that of the Commander-in-Chief's, upon whom, at the present

crisis, there prevails rather an unfavourable opinion, in consequence of the line of conduct that nobleman has thought proper to pursue upon the reform question. Men who are actually employed should at all times do their duty, and I hope that Lord Hill can put his hand on his heart and say that he has conscientiously done so since he has been in office at the Horseguard's"

(The writer is of course referring to General, Lord Rowland Hill, 1st Viscount who was Commander-in-Chief of the Army from 1828)

It seems that the writer of this letter was not the only one questioning whether they had done their duty. In another letter from Sir John Singleton Copley, first Baron Lyndhurst, Kemp Town, Brighton, Sussex, to Arthur Wellesley, first Duke of Wellington: dated 11 January 1832. He reported rumours that after the Bristol riots he had heard that Lord Grey was about to sack both Hill and Somerset and;

"Sir James Kempt is to succeed Lord Hill and Napier, Fitzroy Somerset;"

And that also

"the activity of Digby Mackworth to be made in some shape the subject of complaint."

(*The Wellington papers* 1/1213/13)

Therefore, it seems that there were questions being asked even at the time about the motives and measure being taken in Bristol by the Military Commander-in- Chief at Horseguards, General Lord Rowland Hill, who let's not forget was himself a Tory and vehemently opposed to reform, as well as being a close friend and confidant of Wellington, who had recently lost his office as Prime Minister over his refusal to allow reform. However, in fact Lord Grey did not sack Lord Hill as C-in-C he continued in this position until not long before his death in 1842 and there was no inquiry into the conduct of Major Mackworth. Instead, Mackworth was rewarded for his activities in Bristol and appointed Knight, Hanoverian Order (K.H.) in 1832. The very same year that Brereton had been Court Martialed and driven to suicide. So why was

Mackworth rewarded with such a high order, his action in Bristol were minimal and some what controversial? One can only assume that his role was greater than the one we are aware of and he was indeed acting as a spy on the reformers just as he had been accused of, why else would he have been honoured ?

Point 2

Brereton's second accusation regarding Major-General Sir Charles Dalbiac of being sent to pursue a conviction by, *"prosecuting with the most malignant and heartless perseverance"* as Colonel Brereton accused. This claim has added weight when one learns of the advice the Colonel had received from an expert in Military Law who told him it was actually *against Military Law to appoint as the prosecutor in a Court Martial the same man who had presided over the Court of Inquiry.**

* Juris Militaris, Letter dated 19 January and published in *The Spectator.* Page 12. 28 January 1832.

Yet contrary to this, Dalbiac was indeed appointed to both, but why if it was illegal? Was it as Brereton accused, in order to convict him? It would have been both advantageous to the anti-reformers both in and out of Government and also the military itself, anxious to relieve itself of any blame or infamy. The 14th Dragoons behaviour in killing an innocent man in the early hours of Sunday morning was a turning point, further acerbated by the killing of yet another later in the day by the church door.

In addition, after they returned on the Monday and were joined by their comrades with Major Beckwith they seemed determined to take their revenge on the people of Bristol. Yet they were actually praised for their brutality rather than being admonished. But is it any wonder when Sir Charles Dalbiac, who was not only the militaries prosecutor against Brereton, but also in fact Inspector General of Calvary, so all the troops that were under Colonel Brereton during the riots, were under the immediate command of Dalbiac. Surely, this too shows a conflict of interests that would also make him ineligible. His priorities can be judged later when looking to the officers gathered at the Court Martial of

Captain Warrington only a few days after Brereton's death, many who were also Calvary officers. Dalbiac declared with much passion that they were all brothers in arms, and being such did they not all feel;

"the magic of that sympathy which binds those Corps which have fought and conquered together, as it were, in the bond of sacred brotherhood?"

Before continuing;

"I have said that the honour of this Corps is dear and valuable to me! But in saying this, do I not bind myself to the most solemn form, to preserve that honour, and to bring down the weighty arm of justice on all those whose conduct may have fixed a stain upon it?"

(The Court Marshall of Captain Warrington. Page 49.)

Nevertheless, how far would he go to expunge the dark stain of dishonour that he felt had befallen them? Brereton, had already been marked out for blame by the Mayor and Magistrates and the evidence shows he was also set up from the start as a ready-made scapegoat by the authorities both civil and military. Therefore, by ignoring all the evidence in Brereton's favour, and placing the blame clearly on his shoulders, Dalbiac could allow the cavalry to rise phoenix like, and blameless above the disaster, free of any guilt or shame just as they had after Peterloo and despite the behaviour of the 14th. So yet again, it seems Brereton had indeed justification in his deathbed accusations. Why else would Dalbiac be appointed to prosecute Brereton illegally at both courts and when he had such blatant conflict of interest if not to achieve Brereton's conviction. This would further explain why Dialbiac was so upset when he heard of Brereton suicide, a suicide he had been instrumental in driving him to. Though he seemed to have recovered his composure the next day when he ruthlessly persecuted Captain Warrington.

Point 3

This brings us to Brereton's third accusation of perjury;

"supported by the most gross perjury it is possible to imagine – Brereton alleged that the Mayor, the Town Clerk, Alderman

Abraham Hillhouse and others had sworn to the most dreadful falsehoods in order to screen themselves and brother Magistrates."

This is a shocking accusation against those entrusted with maintaining the very law and order they were accused of betraying. Yet again, there is much evidence to support this accusation too. First and not known at the time was the Mayor's letter where he had admitted *he* had ordered the troops not to fire, not Brereton as he later accused. Therefore, he did commit perjury when he would not admit this even under oath in any of the court cases and claimed it was Brereton who would not allow it. Another letter not available at the time talks of a *"secret plan"* to incriminate Brereton. This is without even considering the second letter that the Mayor claimed to have sent to Brereton late Sunday night regarding his whereabouts that have question marks regarding its very existence.

As I said earlier, why were any secret plans necessary if Brereton was guilty? Sir Thomas Denman the chief justice at the Mayors trial stated that Pinney had neglected his responsibilities, and;

"withdrew from being found by those who wished to discover him".

He had also not given Colonel Brereton any firm orders, and what vague orders he had issued, he had not gone with him to see them executed as was his duty and which he was required to do. This lack of action was contrary to what had been the case in Merthyr Tydfil, the Forest of Dean and Nottingham, where the Magistrates had all done their duty. Yet the Mayor and Magistrates of Bristol despite neglecting their duty escaped any punishment whatsoever.

For as *The Times* reported on the 14 January 1832;

"It ought to be recollected, that in his last military acts, he was surrounded by difficulties such as never before, we believe, surrounded any officer; and it is equally necessary to recollect, that all the civilians, who gave evidence against him, had a direct interest in his condemnation, as the only event which in public or private estimation could prevent their own."

Alderman Hillhouse who had portrayed himself as the one barking out orders and making demands to the military, which even at the Court Martial raised eye brows and prompted the Court to ask under whose authority he was making these demands?

Alderman Hillhouse also claimed, as the Mayor and Magistrates had, that Colonel Brereton was a coward and a traitor, but a year later rescinded these remarks, now saying that;

"he felt the Colonel was just keeping the mob in temper until reinforcements arrived".

Sergeant Ludlow also repeated a similar statement at the London trial of Charles Pinney on Tuesday 30 October 1832, when he related that Colonel Brereton had told him; *"I am ready to risk my own life, if I can do any good, but I cannot, unnecessarily, risk the lives of those under my command".*

Ludlow then told the Court;

"I now firmly believe that he was perfectly sincere; and I am also bound to declare, that I judged very erroneously in supposing that he was not at the time. Many declared him to be a "traitor" and a "coward". And I participated in the unworthy suspicions. I now believe him to be a brave and honest man, who, if he did err, erred from motives of humanity."

Perhaps their consciences were troubled by the perjury Colonel Brereton had accused them of committing because again as can be seen there is much evidence to support it.

Point 4

As to Brereton's last accusation regarding Cornet Kelson, there is also some evidence that shows he could well have been right about this as well. For after the trial and the departure of Captain Warrington from the 3rd Dragoon Guards there became a vacancy, so all the officers moved up a rank, allowing Kelson to purchase the rank immediately above him of Lieutenant. However, strangely he did not remain in this highly desirable position for very long, for he retired out of the Army altogether after only a few weeks. Why after paying out a considerable sum of money to achieve this desirable promotion, did he leave the unit and the army altogether so soon after? Did the remaining Dragoons who knew the truth resent him prospering from Brereton and Warrington's misfortune? I doubt if we will ever know, but it does make you wonder, was Brereton again correct, in what he had said regarding Kelson's testimony?

The Times again writing in an article dated 18 January 1832 had no doubt who the real culprits were;

"It has become an almost universal impression, that the Magistrates of Bristol, by their criminal neglect of all rational and legal means for averting the outrages which they ought to have foreseen in that great city, – and foreseeing, were bound by every tie of duty to provide against, – have been the immediate and undoubted authors of the worst results of the October tumults; included amongst them the much lamented fate of the amiable officer whose remains lie still unburied."

So these death bed claims of Brereton were not without evidence to support them even at the time and further evidence that has surfaced since his death are all in his favour. In addition, Brereton was regarded as a man of honour, would a man of honour make such claims, particularly just before he was about to receive the judgement of his maker? A serious issue to our 19th century ancestors, who still believed whole-heartedly in God's Judgment and the resurrection. In addition, these claims would offer no advantage to him whatsoever after death, so why did he feel he had to make them? He would be beyond all such accusations, unless of course, he felt that they were undeniable facts that needed to be said, and as they were facts, they would not affect his final judgement before God.

This unquestionable faith in God and his judgement after resurrection was to be shattered later when Charles Darwin published his; *On the Origin of Species*. Darwin hadn't formed his opinions though at the time of Colonel Brereton's death as he was busy on his famous voyage of discover on board *HMS Beagle*, gathering the research that would eventually lead to it. He was aware of the Colonel's story though, as his sister E. Catherine Darwin had written to him on 19 January 1832 after reading about the Colonel's death saying;

"You must read the melancholy account of poor Colonel Brereton putting an end to the Court Martial on him, by shooting

himself through the heart. It is certain he would certainly have been broke, if he had lived."

(The Darwin Archive DAR 204.6.1 I 'the Syndics of Cambridge University Library'.)

Though the Colonel was not aware of the blows to his faith that Darwin's later book would deliver, he was fully aware that he; *"would certainly have been broke"* and indeed ruined socially, *"if he had lived"*. Therefore, he had in effect been shamefully driven to an early death by others in an effort to save their own skins at his expense.

Conclusion

I set out in this book to write the complete story of Colonel Brereton's life before Bristol and then show the true story of the riots and prove conclusively that he was innocent.

In fact, with the limited troops he had and the complete abdication of their duty by the Magistrates he did remarkably well only losing control for one day, the Sunday. This book is called Readeption, which means to restore or regain what was lost and it works on many levels in this book. First, I wanted to restore Thomas to his family and ancestors by showing my years of family research starting at the foundation of the Brereton family in Cheshire England and their rise to power during the Tudor and Elizabethan reigns. Then the establishment of the Irish branch and the birth of Thomas Brereton and restore his connection to them and then regain my own family connection to him, which had also been lost. Then finally and most importantly, to regain the Colonel's lost reputation that had been besmirched and destroyed by years of lies and misinformation that had become regarded and quoted as facts. Colonel Brereton just like his ancestor William Brereton of Malpas was innocent of the charges brought against him and both were sacrificed for political expediency

This wrongful portrayal of Thomas was necessitated by the desire to make him fit the role assigned for him by those trying to escape proper scrutiny of their own failings. The Colonel was not a coward as accused by the disgraceful Magistrates, *they were*! As perfectly demonstrated by their own behaviour.

Colonel Brereton's record of service testifies to this fact, as anyone who could command so successfully the most difficult and dangerous troops in the British Army was by example no coward and would not be cowed by a mere rabble of drunken rioters. This is further reinforced when you see the impressive list of testimonials that he provided at his Court Martial. All from very distinguished officers that he had impressed while serving under, such as;

General Sir Thomas Triggs, General Sir George Beckwith, General Sir Charles Wale, General Sir John Keen, and General Sir Herbert Taylor as well as Major General Sir Henry Torrens K.C.B., who was the former Adjutant-General to the forces whom he acted under in the penal Royal Africa Corps. Together with a letter of recommendation from the Commander-in-Chief himself, His Royal Highness the Duke of York, you can't get much higher appraisals than that. Unfortunately, though, because of his long years of service most of these eminent army officers and the Duke of York himself were all now dead. Therefore, they could no longer speak on his behalf or influence the proceedings.

After his shocking death, the Colonel's two young daughters went to live with his beloved Uncle and Aunt in Bath. Unfortunately, only five years later on 31 March 1837 after a long and painful illness Andrew Coghlan then in his sixties breathed his last breath and went to meet his maker. At the end of April Colonel Brereton's two daughters sailed to South Africa to start a new life with their grandfather Hamilton Ross, amongst their possessions was their father's precious sword that had been presented to him by the Royal African Corps.

Bristol Mercury Saturday 8 April 1837

"The two infant female orphans of the late Colonel Brereton are about to sail at the latter end of this month for the Cape of Good Hope. These Children will carry with them the sword presented to their father by the 49th Regiment." Sic,

Unfortunately during the arduous voyage, the elder child Catherine Leticia, (like her namesake before her) passed away on the very day of her 11th birthday, 2 May.

Fortunately, Mary 1828–93 was luckier than her sister, managing to grow into adulthood and was later to marry her cousin Charles Hunter Hodgson. They went on to have two children of their own and after returning to England left descendants. Mary died on 27 April 1893 (age 65 years) at the famous *Burford Bridge Hotel*, Mickleham, Surrey, England. This famous Hotel had an enviable list of notable clientele, including Queen Victoria who as a young princess had met Mary's father Thomas in Bristol in 1830. Thomas's eldest child, his natural son also called Thomas

1815–87, lived for a while with his younger half-brother William in Mayfair West London, not far from Hyde Park, Thomas junior never married. The two boy's only connection being their father, it leads you to believe that Lt Colonel Brereton must have had contact with both and perhaps played an active part in their lives, otherwise how would they have known about each other, let alone lived together? Thomas junior was a clerk in a brewery but later took up hairdressing and died aged 71 at the Union Workhouse in St Albans Hertfordshire in 1887 without any known issue. At this time there was of course no National Health Service so the workhouse increasingly became a refuge for the elderly, infirm and sick. The younger of the two half brothers William Pellett Brereton 1817–49 was only 14 when his father died and though there is no mention of either of them in the letter used as the Colonel's Will, perhaps there was amongst the other papers that we know were kept private. It's possible Andrew Coghlan chose to only publish the letter the two boys were not mentioned in, to avoid embarrassment and avoid them making any claim against the late Colonel's estate. Also by the standards of the time they were pretty much grown up, so instead only his two vulnerable young daughters were mentioned. I wonder if William however travelled to Bristol to visit his father's grave. For on 27 February 1839 at St Luke's, Chelsea (Now called Chelsea Old Church) he married Jane Tanner of Bristol, the daughter of John Tanner a Bristol Silversmith. It seems more than just mere coincidence that his bride was a Bristolian. Also proudly written in the column of their marriage certificate marked father is "Lt Colonel Thomas Brereton", so William was fully aware who his father was, and so it seems likely that they had some sort of relationship especially as all the reports describe the Colonel as a kind and honourable man. When William grew up he became a Tailor in Mayfair with his wife acting as a cutter, they had five children together. Moreover, they lived just off Piccadilly, only half a mile away from where his father had his first marriage at St James Church Piccadilly. Unfortunately William died sometime around the later part of 1849 tragically just before his last child John Tanner Brereton was born in January 1850. He was just 33 years old and probably died due to the cholera outbreak that spread through London in 1849 killing over 14,137 people. His wife Jane left the city to seek a safer place for herself and their children in Gloucestershire, staying with relatives in the countryside just outside Bristol, where they stayed until the danger had passed. It is from William's third child Thomas Henry Brereton that I am descended, and who was perhaps named in honour of his grandfather. Thomas Henry 1846–1900 had eight children the youngest was my grandfather Percy Edgar Brereton 1888–1960 who like many of his ancestors chose the Army as a career joining the First Battalion the Middlesex Regiment nicknamed *The Die Hards* in 1907. He served in India for several years and was present at the Imperial Delhi Durbar in 1911 which was the only one attended by the sovereign, King George V. At the outbreak of World War One he was transferred back to Europe to fight and was awarded the *Military Medal* with the "under fire clasp" (11.10.16 *London Gazette*) awarded for resupplying the front line with ammunition while under fire and enrolled a *"Comrade of The Great War"*. He was later enrolled on 28 February 1919 in the "*Old Contemptibles Association*". Less than twenty years later his eldest son Percy Edgar John, (Jack) my father, also joined the Army "The Royal Engineers" and fought at Dunkirk and then later through North Africa under the famous General Montgomery (yet another of Norman decent). After the defeat of Rommel, he crossed the Mediterranean Sea and fought in Sicily and all through Italy including the famous battle of Monte Casino, pushing the retreating Germans all the way up to Austria. It was while he was busy fighting abroad that the Germans actually bombed St Andrew's Church at Clifton sadly destroying Colonel Brereton and his wife Olivia's last resting place. Today only a small rectangle wall remains of the church with the original steps leading into what was once the interior, but now clothed in grass. My family had no idea of our illustrious forebears until on a damp foggy London day in the late 1940's, when a certain Patrick Montague-Smith came to call at my grandfather's house in Chiswick West London. Thereafter, if it had not been for my dear father, who just happened to mention it to me, no one would have been any the wiser.

www.ingramcontent.com/pod-product-compliance
Lightning Source LLC
LaVergne TN
LVHW051937100826
845154LV00002B/12

* 9 7 8 1 7 8 6 2 3 1 8 5 7 *